문법과 내신을 동시에 잡는

시험지에서 가져온~ 중학영문법

Level 1

랭기지플러스

구성과 특징

시험을 위해, 시험을 통해 익히는 Grammar

기본적인 문법의 핵심은 물론 놓치기 쉬운 부분까지 정리하여 영어의 문법을 확실히 숙달할 수 있습니다. 약 3,000여개의 학교 시험지를 분석하여 시험에 좋은 점수를 받기 위해 반드시 풀어봐야 할 문제들을 변형하여 구성하였습니다. 다양한 유형의 문제를 풀어보며 자신이 학습한 문법의 어느 부분이 시험에 출제되는지 익힐 수 있고 시험에 대한 자신감을 기를 수 있는 것은 물론, 신유형 문제와 높은 배점을 가지고 있는 서술형 문제도 대비할 수 있습니다.

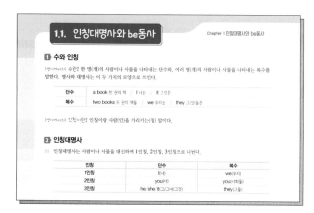

1 개념학습

영문법의 핵심 내용을 한 눈에 쏘옥~!
복잡한 설명보다는 간단 명료하게 내용을 정리하여 보다 확실히 내용을 이해하고 한 눈에 학습할 수 있도록 하였습니다.

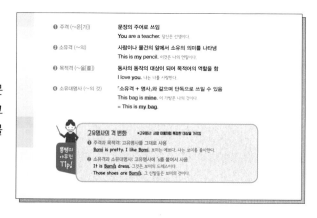

2 뽐쌤의 야무진 tip!

시험에서 잘 나오기 때문에 반드시 알아야 하는 관련 문법을 살펴볼 수 있는 코너입니다. 현장에서 강의를 하고 있는 김보미 선생님만의 시험 만점 Know-how를 살펴볼 수 있습니다.

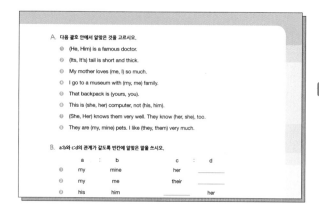

3 연습문제

문법에 대해 얼마나 이해를 했는지 확인할 수 있는 연습문제입니다. 이해도를 돕기 위해 난이도는 쉽지만 핵심을 간단 명료하게 파악할 수 있는 다양한 문제들로 구성하였습니다. 문제를 풀어보면서 학습한 문법 내용 확인은 물론 작문 실력도 향상시킬 수 있습니다.

4 단원평가 3단계

출제된 모든 문제들은 실제 기출문제들을 변형하여 구성하였기 때문에 내신 시험을 완벽하게 대비할 수 있습니다.

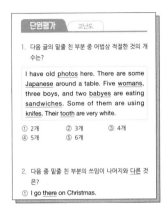

① 단원평가 – 몸풀기

쉬운 문제를 통해 배웠던 문법의 이해 확인 및 영어 문제 풀기의 자신감을 주는 단계

② 단원평가 – 실전대비

좀 더 수준 높은 문제들을 통해 시험에 대한 감각을 기르고 실전에 대비할 수 있는 단계

③ 단원평가 – 고난도

까다로운 문제들을 통해 다양한 유형을 접하고 고득점을 준비할 수 있는 단계

5 서술형 대비학습

시험에서 비중이 높아지고 있는 서술형 평가를 대비할 수 있게 준비된 코너입니다. 시험에서 높은 배점을 가진 문제인 만큼 실수하지 않도록 다양한 문제 유형으로 충분히 연습할 수 있도록 구성하였습니다.

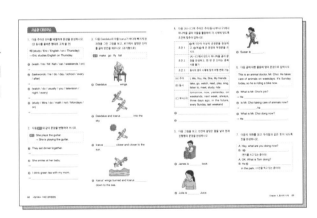

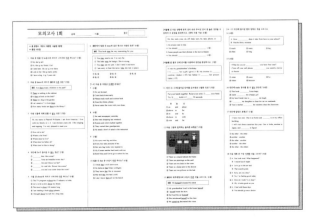

6 실전 모의고사

내신 시험에 완벽하게 대비할 수 있도록 출제 확률이 높았던 문제들을 모아 실전 모의고사 4회를 수록하였습니다.

시작하기 전에

1. 문장성분

문장성분이란? 문장을 이루는 구성요소를 말한다. 영어는 주어, 보어, 동사, 목적어, 수식어로 나누어 진다.

❶ **주어(Subject)**: 문장에서 동작을 행하는 주체로, '∼은(는), ∼이(가)'로 해석한다.

- **I** study hard. 나는 공부를 열심히 한다.
- **She** stayed in New York. 그녀는 뉴욕에 머물렀다.

❷ **동사(Verb)**: 주어의 상태나 동작을 나타내는 말로 '∼이다, ∼하다'로 해석한다.

- I **drive**. (주어와 동사만으로도 문장을 만들 수 있다.) 나는 운전한다.
- He **goes** to school. 그는 학교에 간다.

❸ **목적어(Object)**: 주어가 하는 동작의 대상이 되는 말로 '∼을(를), ∼에게'라고 해석한다.

- I love **you**. 나는 너를 사랑한다.
- He can speak **Japanese**. 그는 일본어를 할 수 있다.

❹ **보어(Complement)**: 주어와 목적어를 보충 설명해주는 말로, 주어를 설명해 주는 것을 주격보어, 목적어를 설명해주는 것을 목적격보어라고 한다. 'A는 B이다'에서 B에 해당하며, 동사나 목적어 뒤에 온다.

- My cat is **lovely**. 나의 고양이는 사랑스럽다.
- I found English **difficult**. 나는 영어가 어렵다는 것을 알았다.

❺ **수식어(Modifier)**: 다른 말을 꾸며주어 뜻을 더 풍부하게 만들어주는 말이다. 수식어는 문장에 꼭 있어야 하는 요소는 아니므로 생략해도 된다.

- She likes coffee. 그녀는 커피를 좋아한다.
  - ➔ She likes **iced** coffee. 그녀는 차가운 커피를 좋아한다.
- I go **to school by subway at 8 in the morning**. 나는 (학교에) (지하철을 타고) (아침) (8시에) 간다.

2. 8품사

품사란? 영어 단어를 뜻과 역할에 따라 동사, 명사, 대명사, 형용사, 부사, 전치사, 접속사, 감탄사로 나눈 것

❶ **동사**: 사람, 동물, 사물의 동작이나 상태를 나타내는 말

  be, have, eat, sleep, play, buy …

- He **buys** some apples. <동작> 그는 약간의 사과를 산다.
- I **am** a student. <상태> 나는 학생이다.

❷ **명사**: 사람, 동물, 사물, 장소의 이름을 나타내는 말이며 문장에서 주어, 목적어, 보어로 쓰인다.

  Bomi, cat, dog, pen, movie, school, love, information …

- **Bomi** likes **dogs**. 보미는 개를 좋아한다.
- That is my **pen**. 저것은 나의 펜이다.

❸ **대명사:** 명사를 대신하는 말이며 명사와 마찬가지로 주어, 목적어, 보어로 쓰인다.

　　She, I, He, You, They, This, That, Those, One, them …

- Jim has many aunts. **He** loves **them**. 짐은 이모들이 많이 있다. 그는 그들을 사랑한다.
- **It** is a beautiful bag. 그것은 아름다운 가방이다.

❹ **형용사:** 명사 또는 대명사의 성질이나 상태를 나타내는 말이며 문장에서 보어, 수식어로 쓰인다.

　　cute, beautiful, happy, sad, long, short …

- My sister is **cute**. <보어> 내 여동생은 귀엽다.
- I have a **cute** sister. <수식어> 나는 귀여운 여동생이 있다.

❺ **부사:** 형용사, 동사, 다른 부사나 문장 전체를 꾸며주는 말이며 문장에서 수식어로 쓰인다.

　　very, really, hard, here, often, well, luckily …

- I studied **hard**. <동사수식> 나는 열심히 공부했다.
- She is **very** pretty. <형용사수식> 그녀는 아주 예쁘다.
- I love you **so** much. <부사 수식> 나는 너를 아주 많이 사랑한다.

❻ **전치사:** 명사 또는 대명사 앞에 놓여 시간, 장소, 방향, 목적 등을 나타내는 말이다.

　　　at, on, in, from, to, for, after, before …

- I get up **at** 7 a.m. 나는 7시에 일어난다.
- She lives **in** Japan. 그녀는 일본에 산다.

❼ **접속사:** 단어와 단어, 구와 구, 절과 절을 이어주는 말이다.

　　and, but, or, so, because, when, if, although …

- I will have a dog **and** two cats. 나는 개 한 마리와 두 마리의 고양이를 기를 것이다.
- She is sad **because** her mom is sick. 그녀는 그녀의 엄마가 아파서 슬프다.

❽ **감탄사:** 감정을 표현하는 말이다.

　　　　Oh, Wow, Oops, Oh my god …

- **Wow**, she looks gorgeous! 와우! 그녀는 정말 멋져!

3. 문장 규칙

❶ 문장은 '주어 + 동사'로 이루어진다.

- I　eat. 나는 먹는다.
  주어　동사

  cf.　eat　an egg 계란을 먹는다 ➡ 주어가 없이 동사와 목적어로만 구성되었으므로 문장이 아니다.
  　　동사　목적어

❷ 문장의 첫 글자는 반드시 대문자로 시작하며 문장의 끝에는 문장부호(마침표 또는 물음표)를 찍는다.

- **T**hey are honest**.** 그들은 정직하다.
  대문자　　　　　문장부호

목차

Chapter 1
인칭대명사와 be동사

1.1. 인칭대명사와 be동사

1 수와 인칭

(영어에서의) 수란? 한 명(개)의 사람이나 사물을 나타내는 단수와, 여러 명(개)의 사람이나 사물을 나타내는 복수를 말한다. 명사와 대명사는 이 두 가지의 모양으로 쓰인다.

단수	a book 한 권의 책 / I 나 / it 그것
복수	two books 두 권의 책들 / we 우리 / they 그(것)들

(영어에서의) 인칭이란? 인칭이랑 사람(인)을 가리키는(칭) 말이다.

2 인칭대명사

》》》 인칭대명사는 사람이나 사물을 대신하며 1인칭, 2인칭, 3인칭으로 나뉜다.

인칭	단수	복수
1인칭	I(나)	we(우리)
2인칭	you(너)	you(너희들)
3인칭	he/she/it(그/그녀/그것)	they(그들)

》》》 명사 주어는 인칭과 수에 따라 알맞은 인칭대명사로 바꿔 쓸 수 있다.

the boy/Brian ➡ he   the girl/Cindy ➡ she   the chair/the elephant ➡ it

my brother and I ➡ we   you and my mother ➡ you   Brian and Suji ➡ they

3 be동사

》》》 be동사는 '~이다', '~(에) 있다'라는 뜻으로 주어의 인칭과 수에 따라 모양이 바뀐다.

주어	be동사	축약형
I	am	I'm
You/We/They	are	You're/We're/They're
He/She/It	is	He's/She's/It's

They **are** firefighters. <~이다> 그들은 소방관이다.

He **is** in the room. <~(에) 있다> 그는 방 안에 있다.

A. 다음 보기와 같이 밑줄 친 부분을 인칭대명사로 바꿔 문장을 완성하시오.

> 보기 <u>Jack and Brian</u> are my classmates. ➡ <u>They</u> are my classmates.

1. <u>My sister</u> is 2 years old. ➡ _____ is 2 years old.

2. <u>Eric</u> is a famous actor. ➡ _____ is a famous actor.

3. <u>The bag</u> is very expensive. ➡ _____ is very expensive.

4. <u>Jisu and you</u> are in the library. ➡ _____ are in the library.

5. <u>Carol and I</u> are happy to hear the news. ➡ _____ are happy to hear the news.

6. <u>Roy</u> is very handsome. ➡ _____ is very handsome.

7. <u>The weather</u> is hot and humid. ➡ _____ is hot and humid.

8. <u>Mrs. Brown</u> is a great doctor. ➡ _____ is a great doctor.

B. 다음 빈칸에 알맞은 be동사를 쓰시오.

1. I _____ very beautiful.

2. My niece _____ so cute.

3. My parents _____ math teachers.

4. She _____ kind to me.

5. Kate and Helen _____ very sleepy.

6. They _____ from Sydney.

7. Your cat _____ too big.

8. Ms. Han _____ our new history teacher.

C. 다음 빈칸에 be동사 am, are, is 중 알맞은 것을 쓰고, 그 의미가 어떤 것인지 고르시오.

1. Mike _____ in the kitchen.　　☐ ~이다　☐ ~(에) 있다

2. You _____ a good cook.　　☐ ~이다　☐ ~(에) 있다

3. Her name _____ Anne Frank.　　☐ ~이다　☐ ~(에) 있다

4. The bag _____ at the door.　　☐ ~이다　☐ ~(에) 있다

5. Children _____ our future.　　☐ ~이다　☐ ~(에) 있다

1.2. be동사의 부정문과 의문문

1 be동사의 부정문

》》 be동사 바로 뒤에 not을 붙이며 '~이 아니다'라고 해석한다.

주어	부정형	축약형
I	am not	-
You/We/They	are not	aren't
He/She/It	is not	isn't

긍정문》 She **is** pretty. 그녀는 예쁘다.

부정문》 She **is not** pretty. 그녀는 예쁘지 않다.

축약형》 She **isn't** pretty.

2 be동사의 의문문

》》 주어와 be동사의 순서가 바뀐다.

> 의문문》 **Be동사 + 주어 ~?**
>
> 대답》 **Yes, 주어 + be동사. / No, 주어 + be동사 not.**
>
> (부정형 대답은 be동사와 not의 축약형으로 사용하는 게 좋다.)

긍정문》 Sam **is** hungry. Sam은 배가 고프다.

의문문》 **Is Sam** hungry? Sam은 배가 고프니?

대답》 **Yes, he is.** 응, 그래. / **No, he isn't.** 아니, 그렇지 않아.

* be동사의 과거형은 주어가 단수일 때 was, 주어가 복수일 때 were를 쓰며 '~였다'라고 해석한다.

주어	be동사의 과거	부정문	의문문
I/He/She/It	was	주어 + was not[wasn't] ~	Was + 주어 ~?
You/We/They	were	주어 + were not[weren't] ~	Were + 주어 ~?

긍정문》 Jane **was** a swimmer. Jane은 수영선수였다.

부정문》 Jane **was not[wasn't]** a swimmer. Jane은 수영선수가 아니었다.

의문문》 **Was Jane** a swimmer? Jane은 수영선수였니? –**Yes, she was.** / **No, she wasn't.**

A. 다음 주어진 문장을 지시대로 바꿔 빈칸을 채우시오.

❶ He is kind to me. 부정문으로〉 He ＿＿＿＿＿＿＿＿＿＿ kind to me.

❷ My brother is intelligent. 부정문으로〉 My brother ＿＿＿＿＿＿＿＿＿＿ intelligent.

❸ It is a new desk. 부정문으로〉 It ＿＿＿＿＿＿＿＿＿＿ a new desk.

❹ I am wrong. 의문문으로〉 ＿＿＿＿＿＿＿＿＿＿ wrong?

❺ They are lazy. 의문문으로〉 ＿＿＿＿＿＿＿＿＿＿ lazy?

❻ You are late for school. 의문문으로〉 ＿＿＿＿＿＿＿＿＿＿ late for school?

❼ I am still in the bathroom. 부정문으로〉 I ＿＿＿＿＿＿＿＿＿＿ still in the bathroom.

B. 다음 문장을 의문문과 부정문으로 만드시오.

❶ Mrs. Kim is a science teacher.

의문문〉 ＿＿＿＿＿＿＿＿＿＿＿＿＿＿＿＿＿＿＿＿＿＿＿＿＿＿＿＿

부정문〉 ＿＿＿＿＿＿＿＿＿＿＿＿＿＿＿＿＿＿＿＿＿＿＿＿＿＿＿＿

❷ She is from Brazil.

의문문〉 ＿＿＿＿＿＿＿＿＿＿＿＿＿＿＿＿＿＿＿＿＿＿＿＿＿＿＿＿

부정문〉 ＿＿＿＿＿＿＿＿＿＿＿＿＿＿＿＿＿＿＿＿＿＿＿＿＿＿＿＿

❸ They are diligent.

의문문〉 ＿＿＿＿＿＿＿＿＿＿＿＿＿＿＿＿＿＿＿＿＿＿＿＿＿＿＿＿

부정문〉 ＿＿＿＿＿＿＿＿＿＿＿＿＿＿＿＿＿＿＿＿＿＿＿＿＿＿＿＿

C. 다음 대화의 빈칸에 알맞은 말을 쓰시오.

❶ A: Are you from Hawaii?

B: No, I'm ＿＿＿＿＿＿.

❷ A: ＿＿＿＿＿＿ ＿＿＿＿＿＿ your uncle?

B: Yes, he is.

❸ A: Is your brother a high school student?

B: Yes, ＿＿＿＿＿＿ ＿＿＿＿＿＿.

1.3. 인칭대명사의 격 변화

》》 인칭대명사는 문장에서의 역할에 따라 형태가 바뀐다.

주격 (~은[가])	소유격 (~의)	목적격 (~을[를])	소유대명사 (~의 것)
I	my	me	mine
you	your	you	yours
he	his	him	his
she	her	her	hers
it	its	it	-
we	our	us	ours
they	their	them	theirs

❶ 주격 (~은[가])

문장의 주어로 쓰임
You are a teacher. 당신은 선생이다.

❷ 소유격 (~의)

사람이나 물건의 앞에서 소유의 의미를 나타냄
This is **my** pencil. 이것은 나의 연필이다.

❸ 목적격 (~을[를])

동사의 동작의 대상이 되어 목적어의 역할을 함
I love **you**. 나는 너를 사랑한다.

❹ 소유대명사 (~의 것)

「소유격 + 명사」와 같으며 단독으로 쓰일 수 있음
This bag is **mine**. 이 가방은 나의 것이다.
= This is **my bag**.

뽐쌤의
야무진
Tip!

고유명사의 격 변화 ＊고유명사: 사람 이름처럼 특정한 대상을 가리킴

❶ **주격과 목적격:** 고유명사를 그대로 사용
<u>Bomi</u> is pretty. I like <u>Bomi</u>. 보미는 예쁘다. 나는 보미를 좋아한다.

❷ **소유격과 소유대명사:** 고유명사에 's를 붙여서 사용
It is <u>Bomi's</u> dress. 그것은 보미의 드레스이다.
Those shoes are <u>Bomi's</u>. 그 신발들은 보미의 것이다.

A. 다음 괄호 안에서 알맞은 것을 고르시오.

❶ (He, Him) is a famous doctor.

❷ (Its, It's) tail is short and thick.

❸ My mother loves (me, I) so much.

❹ I go to a museum with (my, me) family.

❺ That backpack is (yours, you).

❻ This is (she, her) computer, not (his, him).

❼ (She, Her) knows them very well. They know (her, she), too.

❽ They are (my, mine) pets. I like (they, them) very much.

B. a:b와 c:d의 관계가 같도록 빈칸에 알맞은 말을 쓰시오.

	a	:	b	c	:	d
❶	my		mine	her		_____
❷	my		me	their		_____
❸	his		him	_____		her
❹	your		yours	_____		his
❺	we		our	_____		its
❻	Sam		_____	Mary		Mary's

C. 다음 밑줄 친 인칭대명사의 격을 쓰시오.

❶ We are very upset now.   (   )

❷ You are my teacher.   (   )

❸ The chairs are theirs.   (   )

❹ I miss them so much.   (   )

❺ They are my nephews.   (   )

❻ These pencils are mine.   (   )

❼ You like them very much.   (   )

1. 다음 중 밑줄 친 부분과 바꿔 쓸 수 있는 말로 알맞은 것은?

> Amy and I are best friends.

① It   ② He   ③ We
④ You   ⑤ They

2. 다음 중 명사를 대명사로 바꿀 때 <u>잘못된</u> 것은?

① Ms. Yun ⇒ she
② the boy ⇒ he
③ Seho and I ⇒ you
④ the book ⇒ it
⑤ Tom and Jerry ⇒ they

3. 다음 대화의 빈칸에 알맞은 것은?

> A: Are you a student?
> B: _____ I go to Hankook Middle
>   School.

① Yes, I do.
② Yes, I am.
③ No, I'm not.
④ Yes, you are.
⑤ No, you aren't.

4. 다음 문장을 부정문으로 바꿀 때 not이 들어갈 곳은?

> ① They ② are ③ middle ④ school students
> ⑤.

5. 다음 중 축약형이 <u>잘못된</u> 것은?

① You are a teacher.
   ⇒ You're a teacher.
② It is my favorite song.
   ⇒ It's my favorite song.
③ I am not from New York.
   ⇒ I amn't from New York.
④ She is not a nurse.
   ⇒ She isn't a nurse.
⑤ What is your name?
   ⇒ What's your name?

6. 다음 빈칸에 공통으로 알맞은 것은?

> - You _____ a good cook.
> - We _____ very diligent.

① am   ② are   ③ is
④ can   ⑤ has

7. 다음 대화의 빈칸에 알맞은 것은?

> A: Excuse me. Are you Susan?
> B: _____ I'm Susan Brown.

① Yes, she is.
② No, I'm not.
③ Yes, you are.
④ Yes, I am.
⑤ No, you aren't.

8. 다음 문장을 부정문으로 바꿀 때 빈칸에 알맞은 말을 쓰시오.

> They are busy.
> ⇒ They _____ _____ busy.

9. 다음 중 밑줄 친 부분과 바꿔 쓸 수 있는 말로 알맞지 <u>않은</u> 것은?

① <u>John and Jim</u> are good brothers. (=We)
② <u>Your mother</u> is a science teacher. (=She)
③ <u>My brother</u> is seven years old. (=He)
④ <u>You and Jane</u> are in the classroom. (=You)
⑤ <u>The cat</u> is very big. (=It)

10. 다음 문장을 의문문으로 바꿀 때 빈칸에 알맞은 말을 쓰시오.

> ❶ You are tired.
> ⇒ _____ _____ tired?
> ❷ Her father is a director.
> ⇒ _____ _____ _____ a director?

단원평가 실전대비

1. 다음 두 문장을 한 문장으로 바꿀 때 빈칸에 알맞은 것은?

> A: I'm from Busan.
> B: I'm from Busan, too.
> = A+B: _____ are from Busan.

① We ② You ③ Our
④ They ⑤ Their

2. 다음 대화의 빈칸에 알맞은 말을 한 단어로 쓰시오.

> Fairy: Do you like this dress?
> Cinderella: Yes, it's beautiful.
> Fairy: Do you like these shoes, too?
> Cinderella: Yes, I like _____ very much.

3. 다음 보기와 같이 빈칸에 알맞은 말을 쓰시오.

> 보기 This is Ms. Lee. <u>She</u> is my teacher.
> <u>She</u> <u>is</u> beautiful.

❶ This is Adam. _____ is my friend.
_____ _____ very smart.
❷ This is Elizabeth. _____ is my sister.
_____ _____ so kind.

4. 다음 빈칸에 알맞지 <u>않은</u> 것은?

> He is _____.

① kind ② short ③ honest
④ bags ⑤ handsome

5. 다음 중 밑줄 친 부분의 의미가 나머지와 <u>다른</u> 것은?

① <u>Is</u> that a dog?
② Mike <u>is</u> a firefighter.
③ <u>Is</u> she his friend?
④ Jim <u>is</u> at school.
⑤ She <u>is</u> my sister, Rose.

6. 다음 질문에 대한 응답으로 알맞은 것은?

> A: Is he sick?
> B: _____

① Yes, I am.
② No, I amn't.
③ Yes, he is.
④ Yes, she isn't.
⑤ No, he is.

7. 다음 중 밑줄 친 부분의 쓰임이 나머지와 <u>다른</u> 것은?

① What<u>'s</u> this?
② She<u>'s</u> a student.
③ Mary<u>'s</u> dog is cute.
④ He<u>'s</u> my brother.
⑤ That<u>'s</u> a cat.

8. 다음 빈칸에 들어갈 알맞은 말로 짝지어진 것은?

> - My grandma _____ at home.
> - We _____ at school.
> - His cousin _____ in the playground.
> - Her dogs _____ at the park.

① is – are – is – are
② is – are – are – is
③ are – is – are – is
④ is – are – is – is
⑤ are – is – is – are

9. 다음 보기에서 알맞은 말을 골라 빈칸에 쓰시오.

> 보기 I You He She It

❶ _____ are very beautiful!
❷ _____ am hungry now.
❸ Jane is a girl. _____ is smart.
❹ A book is on the desk. _____ is new.
❺ James is a student. _____ is kind.

10. 다음 중 대화가 올바르게 짝지어진 것은?

① A: Are you from New Zealand?
   B: Yes, you are.
② A: Is she your homeroom teacher?
   B: Yes, she is.
③ A: Are Suji's friends angry?
   B: No, she aren't.
④ A: Were you at work?
   B: Yes, I am.
⑤ A: Is this your photo album?
   B: Yes, I am.

11. 다음 중 어법상 옳은 것은? (정답 2개)

① You and I are good friends.
② I have a sister. She eyes are small.
③ Suji and Sejin is 14 years old.
④ It's nickname is interesting.
⑤ My teachers are so kind to me.

12. 다음 중 어법상 옳은 것은?

① These is mine.
② I isn't at home.
③ Are the cats small?
④ Are she busy today?
⑤ Jina and Emily is friendly.

13. 다음 보기에서 어법상 틀린 표현이 포함된 문장의 개수는?

> 보기
> - Jane and her sister is upset.
> - My parents is very tall.
> - The girl's uniform is not big.
> - Is Suji and Sumi sisters?
> - Is you brother a basketball player?

① 1개　　　② 2개　　　③ 3개
④ 4개　　　⑤ 5개

14. 다음 대화에서 어법상 적절하지 않은 것은?

> A: ⓐIs Nara at school?
> B: No, she ⓑisn't. She ⓒis at home.
> A: ⓓAre your cat big?
> B: Yes, it ⓔis.

① ⓐ　　　② ⓑ　　　③ ⓒ
④ ⓓ　　　⑤ ⓔ

15. 다음 중 (A)~(C)에 들어갈 말이 알맞게 짝지어진 것은?

> - I (A) (am not / are not) in my room.
> - They (B) (am / are) tired.
> - Is (C) (the hamster / the hamsters) cute?

　　(A)　　　(B)　　　(C)
① am not – am – the hamster
② am not – are – the hamsters
③ am not – are – the hamster
④ are not – am – the hamsters
⑤ are not – are – the hamster

16. 다음 밑줄 친 부분을 대명사로 바르게 바꾼 것은?

① My cats like playing balls. ⇒ They
② You and I are best friends. ⇒ You
③ Susan is late for game again. ⇒ It
④ Joseph and you walk to school this morning. ⇒ They
⑤ Sara and John are siblings. ⇒ You

17. 다음 글에서 틀린 부분을 바르게 고친 것은?

> English ⓐare my favorite subject. English ⓑnot is easy, but it ⓒare interesting and fun. ⓓMe favorite teacher is my math teacher, Mr. Kim. He ⓔam tall and handsome.

① ⓐ are ⇒ am
② ⓑ not is ⇒ is not
③ ⓒ are ⇒ am
④ ⓓ Me ⇒ I
⑤ ⓔ am ⇒ are

18. 다음 글의 빈칸 ⓐ~ⓔ에 알맞은 것은?

> Jonathan and Suji are brother and sister. ⓐ_____ are from Paris, France. Suji is ten and ⓑ_____ brother Jonathan is twelve. ⓒ_____ friends, Sam and Betty, are from Paris, too. ⓓ_____ school is on King Street. ⓔ_____ name is Elizabeth School.

① ⓐ You　　② ⓑ she　　③ ⓒ They
④ ⓓ Their　　⑤ ⓔ It's

19. 다음 중 대화가 올바르게 짝지어진 것은?

① A: Are you busy?
　 B: Yes, they are.
② A: Is he a doctor?
　 B: No, I'm not.
③ A: Am I right?
　 B: Yes, I am.
④ A: Are they kind?
　 B: Yes, you are.
⑤ A: Is she a doctor?
　 B: No, she isn't.

20. 다음 대화에서 생략 가능한 부분을 찾아 쓰시오.

A: Is Mr. James your uncle?
B: Yes, he is my uncle.

단원평가 　　고난도

1. 다음 중 빈칸에 들어갈 be동사가 나머지와 <u>다른</u> 것은?

① Why _____ you angry?
② Jisu's sister _____ a member of the club.
③ She and I _____ not ready yet.
④ _____ those boys your nephews?
⑤ Mr. and Mrs. Parker _____ nice to me.

2. 다음 중 빈칸에 같은 말이 들어가는 것으로 짝지 어진 것은?

① My sister and I _____ lazy in the morning.
　 Your hamster _____ very cute.
② He and I _____ at school.
　 They _____ sleepy during the class.
③ Everyone _____ special.
　 My students _____ smart.
④ I _____ good at swimming in the sea.
　 She _____ a good swimmer.
⑤ The bank _____ far from here.
　 My brothers _____ 12 years old.

3. 다음 글의 ⓐ~ⓔ에 들어갈 말로 알맞은 것은?

Hi, my name ⓐ Mina. I ⓑ from Singapore. I ⓒ a middle school student. ⓓ you a middle school student, too? I live with my parents, my brother and Happy. Happy ⓔ my sister. It is my dog. We play together every day.

① ⓐ – be　　② ⓑ – are　　③ ⓒ – is
④ ⓓ – Are　　⑤ ⓔ – am

4. 다음 중 밑줄 친 be동사의 의미가 나머지와 <u>다른</u> 하나는?

① My best friend, Susan <u>is</u> tall.
② Hi, this <u>is</u> my friend, Miran.
③ Come here. My car <u>is</u> here.
④ I bought a dog. It <u>is</u> 5 years old.
⑤ Look at him. He <u>is</u> really handsome.

5. 다음 빈칸에 알맞지 <u>않은</u> 것은?

> Jane is _____.

① a nurse
② lovely
③ beautifully
④ kind to everyone
⑤ a very smart student

6. 다음 대화의 ⓐ~ⓒ에 순서대로 알맞은 것은?

> Nara: Mom, I can't find my umbrella.
> Mom: Jisu took your umbrella this morning.
> Nara: Jisu? Why does he always use ⓐ?
>   Where's ⓑ?
> Mom: He couldn't find his umbrella.
> Nara: Then may I use ⓒ?
> Mom: Yes, you may.

	ⓐ	ⓑ	ⓒ
①	mine	his	yours
②	his	mine	yours
③	yours	mine	hers
④	mine	hers	yours
⑤	yours	mine	his

7. 다음 빈칸에 알맞지 <u>않은</u> 것은?

> _____ were already in the classroom.

① Nadia and I
② They
③ Our teacher
④ Some classmates
⑤ The boys

8. 다음 중 밑줄 친 부분의 쓰임이 보기 와 <u>다른</u> 것은?

> 보기 This is <u>her</u> book.

① It is <u>her</u> homework.
② Jude is <u>her</u> little brother.
③ They doesn't know <u>her</u> well.
④ I don't know <u>her</u> age.
⑤ <u>Her</u> name is Sophie.

9. What are the right expressions for ⓐ, ⓑ and ⓒ?

> A: Look. Your bike ⓐ next to the tree.
> B: Really? Where is it?
> A: Over there. I think it is ⓑ.
> B: You're right. It's ⓒ.

	ⓐ	ⓑ	ⓒ
①	is	his	hers
②	is	mine	his
③	is	yours	mine
④	are	mine	yours
⑤	are	yours	mine

10. 다음 중 어법상 옳은 것은?

① I amn't a history teacher.
② Suji isn't sick today.
③ Cindy and I am good friends.
④ Her aunts is very generous.
⑤ Ivan and Tom isn't good at soccer.

1. 다음 Emma에 대한 소개를 보고 틀린 문장의 기호를 쓰고 고쳐 쓰시오.

> Name: Emma
> Country: Mexico
> Job: hair designer
> Hobby: taking a walk with her dogs

> ⓐ Her name is Emma. ⓑ She is from Mexico. ⓒ She is a hair designer. ⓓ She likes dogs. ⓔ Her dogs is cute and smart. ⓕ She often takes a walk with them.

⇒ (   ) _____

2. 다음 우리말과 뜻이 같도록 괄호 안에 주어진 어구를 활용하여 빈칸에 알맞은 말을 쓰시오. (필요하면 형태를 바꾸시오.)

> 그의 아이들은 집에 있지 않다. 그들은 학교에 있다.

> His children _____.
> (be, at home)
> They _____. (be, at school)

3. 다음 문장을 부정문으로 만드시오.

❶ He is my brother.

⇒ _____

❷ This is a cat.

⇒ _____

❸ I am a student.

⇒ _____

❹ She is a teacher.

⇒ _____

4. 보기와 같이 괄호 안에 주어진 주어를 사용하여 의문문을 완성하시오.

> 보기 I'm hungry. (you) ⇒ Are you hungry?

❶ You're short and thin. (your brother)

⇒ _____ ?

❷ I'm busy today. (Chris)

⇒ _____ ?

❸ Mr. Choi is a dentist. (Mrs. Choi)

⇒ _____ ?

❹ We're at the zoo. (they)

⇒ _____ ?

5. 주어진 정보를 사용하여 Danny의 자기소개 문장을 완성하시오.

> ❶ Name: Danny
> ❷ Age: 13
> ❸ From: England
> ❹ Favorite color: Blue
> ❺ Hobby: Listening to music

❶ My name is Danny.

❷ I _____ .

❸ I _____ .

❹ My favorite color _____ .

❺ My hobby _____ .

Chapter 2
일반동사

1 동사의 종류

be동사	~이다, 있다	am, are, is
일반동사	사람이나 사물의 움직임이나 상태를 나타내는 말로 be동사와 조동사를 제외한 동사	love, like, play, sleep, eat, study, have 등
조동사	be동사와 일반동사를 도와주는 동사	will, can, may, should 등

2 일반동사의 현재형

》》 현재의 상태, 반복적인 일상 또는 일반적인 사실을 나타낼 때 현재형을 사용한다. (chapter 5 참조)

❶ 주어가 1인칭: 동사원형 사용

I **like** a dog. 나는 개를 좋아한다.

We **like** a dog. 우리는 개를 좋아한다.

❷ 주어가 2인칭: 동사원형 사용

You **like** a cat. 너는 고양이를 좋아한다.

❸ 주어가 3인칭: 복수일 때는 동사원형, 단수일 때는 동사원형의 끝에 −s/−es를 붙임

They like dogs and cats. 그들은 개와 고양이를 좋아한다.

He likes dogs and cats. 그는 개와 고양이를 좋아한다.

3 3인칭 단수 현재형 만들기

대부분의 동사	+ -s	play → play**s**, sing → sing**s**, want → want**s**
o, -s, -ch, -sh, -x로 끝나는 동사	+ -es	go → go**es**, teach → teach**es**, wash → wash**es**
「자음 + y」로 끝나는 동사	y → i + -es	cry → cr**ies**, study → stud**ies**
「모음 + y」로 끝나는 동사	+ -s	play → play**s**, say → say**s**

* 불규칙 동사: have → has, do → does

4 3인칭 단수 현재형의 −(e)s의 발음

발음	용법
[s]	무성음 (p, k, t, f 등) 뒤에서 ▶stops, forgets, cooks
[z]	유성음 (b, d, g, v, 모음 등) 뒤에서 ▶arrives, finds, sings, tells
[iz]	-s, -sh,- ch, -x, -ge로 끝나는 동사 뒤에서 ▶mixes, touches, changes

A. 다음 동사의 3인칭 현재 단수형을 쓰시오.

① impress   ② read   ③ go

④ fly   ⑤ show   ⑥ cheer

⑦ touch   ⑧ close   ⑨ catch

⑩ sit   ⑪ miss   ⑫ reach

⑬ believe   ⑭ lay   ⑮ pass

⑯ mix   ⑰ ride   ⑱ wash

⑲ cross   ⑳ throw   ㉑ say

B. 다음 보기 와 같이 주어진 문장의 주어를 바꾸어 빈칸을 완성하시오.

보기 They have a nice backyard and they are very happy.
➡ She has a nice backyard and she is very happy.

❶ They go to school and study very hard.

➡ Suji _____.

❷ Koreans enjoy eating Kimchi.

➡ Minho _____.

❸ Jimmy and Barbie drink a lot of water every day.

➡ Inho _____.

❹ My wife worries about her health.

➡ My grandparents _____.

C. 다음 괄호 안에 알맞은 말을 고르시오.

❶ A baby (cry, cries).

❷ Susan (speak, speaks) four languages.

❸ I always (close, closes) the window at night.

❹ They never (drink, drinks) coffee in the morning.

❺ The earth (go, goes) round the sun.

2.2. 일반동사의 과거형

1 일반동사의 과거형

>>> 과거에 일어난 일을 나타낼 때 동사의 과거형을 사용한다. 일반동사의 과거형은 주어의 인칭과 수에 따라 형태가 변하지 않는다.

2 과거형 규칙변화

대부분의 동사	+ -ed	visit → visit**ed**, want → want**ed**
-e로 끝나는 동사	+ -d	live → live**d**, like → like**d**
「자음 + y」로 끝나는 동사	y → i + -ed	study → stud**ied**, try → tr**ied**
「모음 + y」로 끝나는 동사	+ -ed	play → play**ed**, stay → stay**ed**
「단모음 + 단자음」으로 끝나는 동사	마지막 자음 한번 더 쓰고 + -ed	stop → stop**ped**, drop → drop**ped**, plan → plan**ned**

3 과거형 규칙변화 동사의 발음 (부록 참조)

[t]	[t]를 제외한 무성음 ▶looked, watched
[d]	[d]를 제외한 유성음 ▶played, lived
[id]	[d]나 [t]로 끝날 때 ▶wanted, needed

4 과거형 불규칙 변화

❶ 현재형과 과거형이 다른 동사

have → had	go → went	give → gave	get → got	see → saw
eat → ate	meet → met	buy → bought	teach → taught	do → did
write → wrote	come → came	think → thought	take → took	make → made
draw → drew	lose → lost	forget → forgot	run → ran	sing → sang
leave → left	bring → brought	swim → swam	know → knew	wear → wore

❷ 현재형과 과거형이 같은 동사

put → put   cut → cut   hit → hit   set → set   read[ri:d] → read[red]

A. 다음 동사의 과거형을 쓰시오.

① shop   ② wish   ③ love

④ jump   ⑤ arrive   ⑥ hurry

⑦ swallow   ⑧ practice   ⑨ play

⑩ answer   ⑪ carry   ⑫ drop

⑬ learn   ⑭ spell   ⑮ kick

⑯ miss   ⑰ want   ⑱ raise

⑲ plan   ⑳ cry   ㉑ obey

B. 다음 문장의 밑줄 친 부분을 바르게 고쳐 쓰시오.

① She has a party last weekend.

② I do well on the match yesterday.

③ Bob buy a car in 2003.

④ They meet my girlfriend three years ago.

⑤ Peter draw the picture last night.

⑥ She pass the exam two months ago.

C. 다음 괄호 안에 알맞은 말을 고르시오.

① She (helps, helped) her mother every day.

② He (works, worked) hard last year.

③ The train (stops, stoped, stopped) at the station last night.

④ They (have, has, had) a good time last week.

⑤ Jim (study, studies, studied) science last night.

⑥ My dad always (read, reads) a newspaper in the morning.

⑦ Bob (lose, loses, lost) his cell phone last month.

⑧ I (forget, forgets, forgot) to bring my umbrella yesterday.

2.3. 일반동사의 부정문과 의문문

1 일반동사의 부정문

》》》 일반동사의 부정문은 현재시제일 때 「do[does] not + 동사원형」, 과거시제일 때 「did not + 동사원형」으로 쓴다.

주어	부정형	축약형	주어	부정형	축약형
I You	do not + 동사원형	don't	We You They	do not + 동사원형	don't
	did not + 동사원형	didn't			
He She It	does not + 동사원형	doesn't		did not + 동사원형	didn't
	did not + 동사원형	didn't			

I **do not[don't] like** him. 나는 그를 좋아하지 않는다.

She **does not[doesn't] look** good today. 그녀는 오늘 좋아 보이지 않는다.

He **did not[didn't] go** to work yesterday. 그는 어제 일하러 가지 않았다.

2 일반동사의 의문문

》》》 일반동사의 의문문은 「Do/Does/Did + 주어 + 동사원형 ~?」으로 쓴다.

시제	주어	의문문	대답
현재	I/You/We/They	Do + 주어 + 동사원형 ~?	Yes, 주어 + do. / No, 주어 + do not[don't].
	He/She/It	Does + 주어 + 동사원형 ~?	Yes, 주어 + does. / No, 주어 + does not[doesn't].
과거	모든 주어	Did + 주어 + 동사원형 ~?	Yes, 주어 + did. / No, 주어 + did not[didn't].

Do you know my phone number? 너는 내 전화번호를 아니?

–Yes, I do. / No, I don't. 응, 알아. / 아니, 몰라.

Does she get up early in the morning? 그녀는 아침에 일찍 일어나니?

–Yes, she does. / No, she doesn't. 응, 일찍 일어나. / 아니, 그렇지 않아.

Did you check your e-mail? 너는 네 이메일을 확인했니?

–Yes, I did. / No, I didn't. 응, 했어. / 아니, 안 했어.

A. 다음 문장을 부정문으로 바꿔 쓰시오.

➊ We sing Christmas carols. ➡ _____

➋ You rode a bike yesterday. ➡ _____

➌ Her brother eats curry and rice. ➡ _____

➍ He knew my name. ➡ _____

➎ Minho invited her to his birthday party. ➡ _____

➏ Suji goes to school by bus. ➡ _____

➐ Jim read comic books last week. ➡ _____

➑ My father went fishing a year ago. ➡ _____

➒ Minho and Suji like skating. ➡ _____

➓ I lost my pet dog in the street. ➡ _____

⑪ My washing machine works well. ➡ _____

⑫ We believed the story. ➡ _____

B. 다음을 주어진 문장을 의문문으로 바꾸어 쓰고, 대답을 완성하시오.

➊ She watched TV last night.

➡ _____ Yes, _____.

➋ Suji left a message yesterday.

➡ _____ No, _____.

➌ Charlie jogs with his friend every morning.

➡ _____ Yes, _____.

➍ They always wash their car on Sundays.

➡ _____ Yes, _____.

➎ She passed the exam.

➡ _____ No, _____.

1. 다음 괄호 안에 동사를 알맞은 형태로 바꾸시오.

> A: What did you do yesterday?
> B: I (take) a walk in the park.

2. 다음 괄호 안에서 알맞은 것을 고르시오.

❶ I (am, was) tired last night.
❷ I (visit, visited) my grandparents' last summer vacation.
❸ We (didn't, wasn't) do our homework.
❹ Suji doesn't (practice, practices) the piano.
❺ Mr. and Mrs. Smith (teach, teaches) English.

3. 다음 우리말을 영어로 바르게 옮긴 것은?

① 너 TV 보았니?
  ⇒ Did you watched TV?
② 너 수학 공부했니?
  ⇒ Did you studyed math?
③ 너 네 방을 청소했니?
  ⇒ Did you cleaned your room?
④ 너 음악을 들었니?
  ⇒ Did you listen to music?
⑤ 너 엄마를 도와 드렸니?
  ⇒ Did you helping your mon?

4. 다음 중 동사의 원형과 과거형의 연결이 바르지 <u>못한</u> 것은?

① work – worked
② like – liked
③ go – went
④ make – maked
⑤ come – came

5. 다음 질문에 대한 대답으로 알맞은 것은?

> What did you do last Friday?

① I played basketball.
② I go shopping.
③ I am going to school.
④ I swim in the river.
⑤ I play ping-pong with my friend.

6. 다음 대화의 빈칸에 알맞은 것은?

> A: Did you watch TV yesterday?
> B: _____ I listened to music.

① Yes, I am.   ② No, I'm not.
③ Yes, I was.   ④ No, I didn't.
⑤ Yes, I did.

7. 다음 괄호 안에 동사를 알맞은 형태로 바꾸시오.

> She (go) jogging every day.

8. 다음 대화의 빈칸에 공통으로 알맞은 것은?

> A: How _____ the weather yesterday?
> B: It _____ cloudy.

① is   ② are   ③ was
④ were   ⑤ does

9. 다음 대화의 빈칸에 알맞은 말을 한 단어로 쓰시오.

> A: I had a good time yesterday.
>   I enjoyed swimming in the river.
> B: You enjoyed what?
> A: I _____ in the river. It was very
>   exciting.

10. 다음 밑줄 친 부분을 알맞은 형태로 고쳐 쓰시오.

❶ She <u>go</u> to the library yesterday.

❷ I <u>meet</u> my cousin last week.

❸ She <u>read</u> a story book every night.

단원평가   실전대비

1. 다음 중 어법상 옳지 <u>않은</u> 것은?

① I don't like a cat.
② He doesn't likes music.
③ I am not a doctor.
④ I have a TV set in my room.
⑤ You don't play the piano.

---

2. 다음 대화의 빈칸에 순서대로 알맞은 것은?

> A: Where _____ you yesterday?
> B: I _____ at the park near my house.

① were – was   ② were – am
③ was – was   ④ is – am
⑤ was – were

[3-4] 다음은 수지가 일주일 동안 한 일을 적어 놓은 것
이다. 표를 보고 질문에 알맞은 답을 고르시오.

Mon	do homework
Tue	play soccer
Wed	ride a bike
Thu	clean the room
Fri	go swimming
Sat	go to a movie
Sun	go to church

3. When did Suji go to a movie?

① Monday   ② Tuesday
③ Friday   ④ Saturday
⑤ Sunday

4. What did Suji do last Tuesday?

① She cleaned her room.
② She played soccer.
③ She did her homework.
④ She went to see a movie.
⑤ She rode a bike.

5. 다음 빈칸에 알맞지 <u>않은</u> 것은?

> He went to New York _____.

① in 1998   ② yesterday
③ last year   ④ now
⑤ this morning

[6–8] 다음 글을 읽고 물음에 답하시오.

> Last Sunday ⓐ_____ a terrible day. Some of our players ⓑ_____ sick. We tried hard, but we did not win. We ⓒ_____ the game. My coach said, "Cheer up! You ⓓ_____ your best. Winning is not everything." We will play again next week. I hope we will play better.

6. 윗글의 빈칸 ⓐ와 ⓑ에 차례로 알맞은 것은?

① is – are   ② was – was
③ was – were   ④ were – was
⑤ were – were

7. 윗글의 빈칸 ⓒ에 알맞은 것은?

① play   ② played   ③ lose
④ lost   ⑤ tried

8. 윗글의 빈칸 ⓓ에 알맞은 동사를 쓰시오.

9. 다음 중 어법상 옳은 것은?

① Did he liked her?
② Was it rain last night?
③ She didn't wrote a letter.
④ Did you do your homework?
⑤ Does she get up early yesterday?

10. 다음 대화에서 <u>틀린</u> 두 군데를 찾아 고쳐 쓰시오.

> A: I played basketball yesterday. Did you play basketball, too?
> B: No, I don't. I watch a movie yesterday.

11. 다음 중 부정문으로 바꿀 때 <u>잘못된</u> 것은?

① She picked up a teapot.
   ⇒ She didn't pick up a teapot.
② He played the piano.
   ⇒ He didn't play the piano.
③ He is a doctor.
   ⇒ He isn't a doctor.
④ She has a dog.
   ⇒ She doesn't have a dog.
⑤ You ate a hamburger.
   ⇒ You don't eat a hamburger.

12. 다음 중 밑줄 친 부분의 현재형이 알맞지 <u>않은</u> 것은?

① She <u>came</u> to my house today. ⇒ comes
② He <u>went</u> to bed early last night. ⇒ goes
③ I <u>had</u> lunch with Mrs. Park. ⇒ have
④ I <u>saw</u> a very wise woman at the party. ⇒ see
⑤ There <u>were</u> a lot of students in the classroom. ⇒ is

13. 다음 중 대화의 괄호 안에 들어갈 말이 알맞게 짝 지어진 것은?

A: What did you do yesterday?
B: I _____ math. (study)
A: Did you go to bed early?
B: No, I didn't. I _____ to bed at 11:30.
(go)

① study – go
② studying – going
③ studyed – goed
④ studies – goes
⑤ studied – went

14. 다음 빈칸에 알맞지 <u>않은</u> 것은?

I _____ last Sunday.

① went shopping
② had a great time
③ did a lot of things
④ study all day long
⑤ made some food

15. 다음 문장을 의문문으로 알맞게 바꾼 것은?

He studied English yesterday.

① Does he study English yesterday?
② Did he study English yesterday?
③ Did he studied English yesterday?
④ Do he studied English yesterday?
⑤ Does he studied English yesterday?

16. 다음 글의 밑줄 친 부분 중 바르지 <u>못한</u> 것은?

Mrs. Brown ① <u>work</u> ② <u>in</u> a flower shop.
③ <u>In</u> spring, she ④ <u>sells</u> ⑤ <u>many</u> flowers.

17. 다음 중 짝지어진 대화가 <u>어색한</u> 것은?

① A: What did you do last weekend?
   B: I went to Everland with my family.
② A: How was the party?
   B: I enjoyed myself.
③ A: When did you get the letter?
   B: I got your letter two weeks ago.
④ A: What do you want to do on the
      weekend?
   B: I wanted to go to a concert.
⑤ A: What do you do after school?
   B: I usually play soccer with my friends for
      an hour.

18. 다음 중 어법상 옳은 것은?

① She work hard at the cafeteria.
② I likes ice cream.
③ Miss Lee sell fruits in a market.
④ He doesn't like TV.
⑤ I go to school 3 days ago.

19. 다음 대화의 빈칸에 차례대로 알맞은 것은?

A: _____ your mother like dramas?
B: No, she doesn't. She _____ sports.

① Does – does
② Does – do
③ Do – like
④ Does – likes
⑤ Do – likes

20. 다음 중 어법상 옳은 것은?

① Did you met Tom yesterday?
② She didn't pass me the picture.
③ I don't played the violin every day.
④ What do you do last Sunday?
⑤ They didn't got up early yesterday.

단원평가 　 고난도

1. 다음 문장들을 시간 순으로 바르게 배열한 것은?

> ⓐ After lunch, I went shopping with my mother.
> ⓑ In the evening, I helped my sister with her homework.
> ⓒ Today, I was very busy.
> ⓓ I did the dishes after breakfast.

① ⓐ-ⓑ-ⓒ-ⓓ　　② ⓒ-ⓓ-ⓐ-ⓑ
③ ⓒ-ⓐ-ⓓ-ⓑ　　④ ⓓ-ⓒ-ⓐ-ⓑ
⑤ ⓐ-ⓓ-ⓑ-ⓒ

2. 다음 빈칸에 공통으로 알맞은 것을 쓰시오.

> - She _____ books last night.
> - My brother _____ a novel yesterday.

3. 다음 중 괄호 안에 단어들을 알맞게 배열한 것은?

> A: Did (ⓐhave, ⓑsome pizza, ⓒyesterday, ⓓyou)?
> B: Yes, I did.

① ⓐ-ⓑ-ⓒ-ⓓ　　　② ⓑ-ⓒ-ⓐ-ⓓ
③ ⓒ-ⓑ-ⓐ-ⓓ　　　④ ⓓ-ⓐ-ⓑ-ⓒ
⑤ ⓓ-ⓑ-ⓒ-ⓐ

4. 다음 글에서 어법상 틀린 표현이 포함된 문장의 개수는?

> Yesterday Sam goes to a dinner party at his friend's house. It was great. There was a lot of people. There were a lot of foods, too. He has a good time there.

① 1개　　　② 2개　　　③ 3개
④ 4개　　　⑤ 5개

5. 다음 보기의 빈칸에 들어갈 수 없는 것은?

> **보기**
> - _____ they your sisters?
> - Your brother _____ handsome.
> - _____ your grandparent live in Seoul?
> - _____ Jim wear glasses?
> - _____ Minji and James watch TV?

① is　　　② are　　　③ do
④ does　　⑤ doesn't

6. 다음 주어진 **보기**의 단어만을 이용하여 문장을 완성하려고 할 때 완전한 문장을 만들 수 <u>없는</u> 것은?

보기 am   are   doesn't   don't   do

My name is Sora. ① I (   ) outgoing. I dance very well, but ② I (   ) sing well. My close friend is Minho. He is smart. He is not good at sports. ③ He (   ) like basketball. ④ He always (   ) his homework hard. ⑤ We (   ) good friends.

7. 다음 글에서 틀린 곳 6개에 밑줄을 치고 수정하시오.

 Jina has a little brother, Junsu. Her brother is an elementary school student. He likes to read books, but don't like sports. Jina likes sports, so she often says to him. "Are you see the boys outside? Going out and play with them. There is lots of exciting sports." But he doesn't listens to her and just read books at home all the time. Jina is not happy about it.

8. 다음 중 동사가 옳지 <u>않은</u> 것은?

① They built the house last year.
② He wore the shorts last time.
③ She spent all her money yesterday.
④ The policeman caught the thief last night.
⑤ He spoken in English at the meeting this morning.

9. 다음 표를 보고 글의 밑줄 친 말이 무엇을 의미하는지 구체적인 영어 문장으로 적으시오.

Wed	O	O	X	O	X
Thu	O	O	O	O	X
Fri	O	O	X	O	O

On Wednesdays, Bella cleans the living room. She washes the dishes and feeds the dog, too. But she doesn't clean the bathroom. Also she doesn't water the plants. <u>She only does it on Fridays.</u>

10. 다음 **보기**에서 어법상 <u>틀린</u> 문장끼리 묶인 것은?

보기
a. She didn't do her homework.
b. He ates lunch.
c. She doesn't like music.
d. She swim very well.
e. He didn't likes math.

① b, d   ② a, b   ③ b, c, e
④ a, c   ⑤ b, d, e

1. 다음 그림을 보고 문장을 완성하시오.

	Maria does	Maria does not
❶		
	watch	listen
❷		
	play	sing

❶ _____, but

_____.

❷ _____, but

_____.

2. 다음 괄호 안에 단어를 이용하여 빈칸을 완성하시오.

It was my mom's birthday. I ❶ _____ her a gift.(give) My sister ❷ _____ cookies.(make) My father ❸ _____ her picture.(take)

3. 다음 주어진 단어들을 이용하여 우리말에 맞게 알맞은 문장을 만드시오. (현재시제를 사용)

❶ John은 부산에 살고 있다. (live in)

⇒ _____

❷ 그들은 공포영화를 좋아하니?

(like, horror movies)

⇒ _____

❸ 그녀는 매일 영어를 연습하지 않는다.

(practice, every day)

⇒ _____

[4–5] 다음 박스 안에 A, B, C에서 단어를 하나씩 골라 현재시제와 과거시제의 긍정문, 부정문, 의문문을 만드시오.

A(주어)	B(동사)	C(시간표현)
He	play	yesterday
My girlfriend	go	every other day
Sumi and I	write	last night
Tom	cook	a week ago
They	make	usually
	go	on weekends

조건
1. 한번 선택한 단어는 다시 사용 불가
2. 5단어 이상의 문장으로 쓸 것

4. 현재시제

❶ _____ (긍정문)

❷ _____ (부정문)

❸ _____ (의문문)

5. 과거시제

❶ _____ (긍정문)

❷ _____ (부정문)

❸ _____ (의문문)

6. 다음 Eric의 체크리스트를 보고 보기처럼 아래 문장을 완성하시오.

What did Eric do last Saturday?	
read a comic book	√
visit his aunts	
❶ clean his house	√
❷ send an e-mail to Suji	
❸ play soccer with his friends	√
❹ go shopping	√
❺ study English	

> 보기 He <u>read a comic book</u> last Saturday.
> He <u>didn't visit his aunts</u> last Saturday.

❶ He _____ last Saturday.

❷ He _____ last Saturday.

❸ He _____ last Saturday.

❹ He _____ last Saturday.

❺ He _____ last Saturday.

7. 다음 문장을 지시대로 바꾸어 쓰시오.

❶ They closed the door last night. (의문문으로)

⇒ _____

❷ Jonathan had breakfast. (현재시제 부정문으로)

⇒ _____

8. 다음 표를 보고, 수지네 가족이 일요일에 하는 일을 써 보시오.

What Suji's family does on Sundays		
Mother	Brother	I
cleaning the house	watching soccer games	playing with our dog, Dongki

My mother _____,
my brother _____,
and I _____ on
Sundays.

9. 어제 민호가 한 일을 참고하여 글을 완성하시오.

2시	콘서트에 감	9시	숙제
8시	저녁식사	10시	잠자기

Yesterday Minho _____ _____ _____
_____ at 2. At 8, he _____ _____. At 9,
he _____ _____ _____ and _____
_____ _____ at 10.

10. 다음 질문에 자신의 경우에 맞게 완전한 문장으로 답변을 쓰시오.

❶ Your birthday is coming up. What do you want to do?

⇒ _____

❷ What did you do last Saturday?

⇒ _____

memo

Chapter 3
조동사

》》 조동사란? 본동사(main verb)와 함께 쓰여 능력, 허가, 미래, 의무, 요청, 추측 등의 의미를 더해준다.

I speak English. + can(능력의 조동사) = I **can** speak English.

나는 영어를 말한다 + 할 수 있다 = 나는 영어를 말할 수 있다.

I drink coffee. + will(미래의 조동사) = I **will** drink coffee.

나는 커피를 마신다 + 할 것이다 = 나는 커피를 마실 것이다.

* 조동사의 종류: will, can, may, must, should 등

1 조동사의 특징

》》 주어와 인칭의 수에 따라 절대 모양이 바뀌지 않는다.

He **cans** do it. (x)   He **can** do it. (o)

》》 주어의 인칭과 수에 상관없이 언제나 「조동사 + 동사원형」의 형태로 쓰인다.

She should **is** quiet. (x)   She should **be** quiet. (o)

》》 두 개의 조동사는 연속으로 함께 쓰일 수 없으므로 뒤에 있는 조동사를 비슷한 표현으로 바꿔 써야 한다.

We **will can** get there on time. (x)

➡ We **will be able to** get there on time. (o)

2 조동사의 부정형

》》 「조동사 + not + 동사원형」

You **should not[shouldn't] park** here. 너는 이곳에 주차를 하면 안 된다.

We **will not[won't] open** the door. 우리는 문을 열지 않을 것이다.

3 조동사의 의문문

》》 「조동사 + 주어 + 동사원형 ～?」

May I close the window? 제가 문을 닫아도 될까요?

긍정 대답 》 Yes, you may. 네, 됩니다.

부정 대답 》 No, you may not. 아니요, 안됩니다.

A. 다음 밑줄 친 부분을 바르게 고치시오.

① Susan <u>may be not</u> late.

② We will <u>can</u> play tennis tomorrow.

③ She <u>mays</u> go to the movies.

④ May I <u>takes</u> your order?

⑤ <u>Cans</u> he explain the game rules for us?

⑥ A: Can he speak Japanese fluently?   B: Yes, he <u>must</u>.

⑦ A: May I turn the volume down?   B: No, you <u>doesn't</u>.

⑧ They <u>not will</u> eat junk food.

⑨ <u>Mays</u> I use your dictionary?

⑩ Will you <u>lent</u> me your house?

⑪ Mr. Choi <u>musts</u> stop smoking.

⑫ She <u>read will</u> a book tonight.

⑬ You may <u>caught</u> a cold in this cold weather.

⑭ My bird <u>fly can</u> in the sky.

⑮ You <u>don't must</u> enter this room.

B. 다음 괄호 안에서 알맞은 것을 고르시오.

① She will (be able to, can) go with us.

② Yuna may (has, have) a lot of money.

③ He can (ran, run) 15 km.

④ Minju (must not, doesn't must) take pictures in the museum.

⑤ (Will, Wills) she learn how to play the flute?

⑥ Should we (being, be) quiet here?

⑦ You (may no, may not) park at the corner.

⑧ Will she (is, be) able to bake cookies at school?

3.2. will, be going to

1 will

》》 의미

❶ 미래의 일 또는 주어의 의지 (~할 것이다, ~하겠다)

It **will** snow tomorrow. (미래) 내일 눈이 내릴 것이다.

I **will** get up early in the morning. (의지) 나는 아침에 일찍 일어날 것이다.

❷ 요청 「will[would] you ~?」 (~해주겠니?, ~해 주시겠어요?)

Would you open the window? 창문 좀 열어주시겠어요?

》》 형태

❶ 부정문: 「will not[won't] + 동사원형」

I **will not[won't] borrow** money from her. 나는 그녀에게 돈을 빌리지 않을 것이다.

❷ 의문문: 「Will + 주어 + 동사원형 ~?」

Will you join the movie club? –Yes, I will. / No, I won't.

너는 영화 동아리에 가입할 거니? -응, 할거야. / 아니, 안 할거야.

2 be going to

》》 가까운 미래 또는 이미 계획된 미래를 나타내며 '~할 것이다', '~할 예정이다'라고 해석한다.

※ will과 비슷한 표현으로 바꿔 쓰기도 한다.

We **are going to** leave soon. (미래) 우리는 곧 떠날 것이다.

The meeting **is going to** start. (계획된 미래) 그 회의는 시작할 것이다.

❶ 부정문: 「be동사 + not + going to + 동사원형」

He **is not[isn't] going to stay** up all night. 그는 밤을 새지 않을 것이다.

❷ 의문문: 「be동사 + 주어 + going to + 동사원형 ~?」

Is Yuna going to help me with the work? –Yes, she is. / No, she isn't.

유나는 내 일을 도와줄 거니? -응, 도와줄 거야. / 아니, 안 도와줄 거야.

A. 다음 문장을 괄호 안에 지시대로 바꿔 쓰시오.

① He is going to do his homework after dinner. (의문문으로)

➡ _____

② She takes a computer lesson. (will을 이용한 미래시제)

➡ _____

③ My parents will arrive in Busan tomorrow. (be going to를 이용한 미래시제)

➡ _____

④ The train will leave on time. (부정문으로)

➡ _____

B. Eva와 Tim의 겨울 방학 계획표를 보고, 내용과 일치하도록 will 또는 be going to를 사용하여 빈칸을 채우시오.

	Monday	Tuesday	Wednesday	Thursday	Friday
Eva	study English	take yoga classes	read a book	take piano lessons	watch movies
Tim	walk a dog	play computer games	wash the dishes	go swimming	watch movies

① Tim _____ _____ _____ on Thursday.

② Eva _____ _____ _____ _____ _____ on Monday.

③ Tim _____ _____ _____ _____ _____ on Wednesday.

④ Eva and Tim _____ _____ _____ _____ _____ on Friday.

C. 다음 괄호 안에 알맞은 것을 고르시오.

① Are you going to meet him (last evening, this evening)?

② She is not going to (take, taking) a tennis lesson next month.

③ I'm going to play soccer (tomorrow, yesterday).

④ I won't go to Paris (this, last) summer vacation.

⑤ Will you (drop, to drop) by my house?

3.3. can, may

1 can

))) 의미

❶ 능력 · 가능 (~할 수 있다) ※ be able to와 바꿔 쓸 수 있다.

He **can** speak Italian. (=He **is able to** speak Italian.) 그는 이탈리아어를 말할 수 있다.

❷ 허가 · 허락 (~해도 된다, ~해도 좋다)

You **can** go to the restroom now. 너는 지금 화장실에 가도 된다.

❸ 요청 「Can[Could] you ~?」 (~해 주겠니?, ~해 주시겠어요?)

Can[Could] you turn on the radio? 라디오를 켜 주시겠어요?

※ Could you ~?는 Can you ~?보다 더 정중한 요청의 표현이다. could는 can의 과거형의 모습이지만 과거를 의미하는 것이 아니며, Will you ~? 또는 Would you ~?로 바꿔 쓸 수 있다.

))) 형태

❶ 부정문: 「cannot[can't] + 동사원형」

I **cannot[can't] climb** the tree. (불가능) 나는 나무에 오를 수 없다.

You **cannot[can't] eat** fast food. (금지) 너는 패스트푸드를 먹어선 안 된다.

❷ 의문문: 「Can + 주어 + 동사원형 ~?」

Can I go now? –Yes, you can. / No, you can't. 지금 가도 될까요? -네, 돼요. / 아니요, 안됩니다.

2 may

))) 의미

❶ 허락 (~해도 좋다) ※ can과 바꿔 쓸 수 있지만, can보다 좀 더 정중한 표현이다.

You **may** invite your friend. 너의 친구를 초대해도 좋다.

❷ (약한) 추측 (~일지도 모른다)

The guests **may** arrive soon. 손님들이 곧 도착할지도 모른다.

))) 형태

❶ 부정문: 「may not + 동사원형」

He **may not be** honest. (추측) 그는 정직하지 않을 수도 있다.

You **may not go** home now. (금지) 너는 지금 집에 가면 안 된다.

❷ 의문문: 「May I + 동사원형 ~?」 ※ May I ~?는 허락을 구하는 표현이다.

May I have go now? –Yes, you may. / No, you may not. 지금 가도 되나요? -네, 됩니다. / 아니요,안 됩니다.

A. 다음 문장을 [보기]와 같이 바꾸어 쓸 때 빈칸을 완성하시오.

> [보기] I can drive a car. ➡ I am able to drive a car.

① They could find the answers.

➡ They _____ the answers.

② Can you fix this car?

➡ _____ you _____ this car?

③ Susan couldn't remember my name.

➡ Susan _____ my name.

④ Can she make it at seven?

➡ _____ she _____ it at seven?

⑤ This washing machine can dry clothes.

➡ This washing machine _____ clothes.

⑥ Tommy can bake a cake at home.

➡ Tommy _____ a cake at home.

B. 다음 문장의 밑줄 친 부분이 추측과 허가 중 어떤 의미를 지니는지 구분하여 쓰시오.

① <u>May</u> I borrow your book? _____

② You <u>may</u> use my pen. _____

③ He <u>may</u> be 17 years old. _____

④ You <u>may</u> not want to see us again. _____

⑤ <u>May</u> I try on this shirt? _____

⑥ You <u>may</u> not take pictures here. _____

3.4. must, have to, should

1 must

❶ (강한) 의무 (~해야 한다)

You **must** finish your homework. 너는 너의 숙제를 끝내야 한다.

❷ (강한) 추측 (~임에 틀림없다)

The boy **must** be sleepy. 그 소년은 졸린 것임에 틀림없다.

> ※ '~일 리가 없다'라는 강한 부정의 추측은 can't [cannot]를 쓴다. He cannot be a liar. 그는 거짓말쟁이일 리가 없다.

❸ (강한) 금지 (~해서는 안 된다)

You **must not** tell a lie. 너는 거짓말을 해서는 안 된다.

2 have to

❶ (강한) 의무 (~해야 한다)   ※ must와 바꿔 쓸 수 있다.

We **have to** respect our parents. = We **must** respect our parents. 우리는 부모님을 존경해야 한다.

❷ 불필요 (~할 필요가 없다)

I **don't have to** get up early on Sundays. 나는 일요일마다 일찍 일어날 필요가 없다.

뿜쌤의 야무진 Tip!

❶ have to와 must

have to와 must는 긍정문에 쓰이면 뜻이 같지만 부정문으로 쓰이면 뜻이 달라진다.

You <u>must</u> change the rule. = You <u>have to</u> change the rule.
너는 규칙을 변경해야 한다. = 너는 규칙을 변경해야 한다.

I <u>must not</u> run in the hallway. ≠ I <u>don't have to</u> run in the hallway.
나는 복도에서 뛰어선 안 된다. ≠ 나는 복도에서 뛸 필요가 없다.

❷ must의 시제 표현

must의 과거형은 had to, 미래형은 will have to로 쓴다.

We <u>had to</u> leave then. 우리는 그때 떠났어야 했다.
We <u>will have to</u> leave. 우리는 떠나야 할 것이다.

3 should

>>> 의무, 충고 제안을 나타내며 '~해야 한다'라고 해석한다.   ※ ought to와 바꿔 쓸 수 있다.

You **should** believe me. = You **ought to** believe me. (의무) 너는 나를 믿어야 한다.

You **should** practice harder. (조언) 너는 더 열심히 연습해야 한다.

A. 주어진 동사와 must 또는 must not을 사용하여 [보기] 처럼 각 표지의 의미를 말하시오.

park, wear, use, take, cross, smoke, be quiet

[보기] You <u>must not park</u> here.

① You _____ the street here.

② You _____ here.

③ You _____ the seat belt.

④ You _____ your cellphone here.

⑤ You _____ pictures.

B. 다음 빈칸에 have[has] to 또는 had to를 넣어 문장을 완성하시오.

① We missed the last bus. We _____ take a taxi.

② Tomorrow is Teacher's Day. I _____ buy a present for my teacher.

③ Jack is starving. He _____ eat some food.

④ I will go on a trip tomorrow morning. I _____ pack my things.

⑤ It's very cold outside. You _____ wear a thick coat.

C. 다음 우리말과 뜻이 같도록 주어진 말을 알맞게 배열하시오.

① 그녀가 또다시 거짓말을 하고 있음에 틀림없다. (be, telling a lie, must, she, again)

➡ _____

② 아이들은 불량식품을 먹으면 안 된다. (junk food, not, should, eat, children)

➡ _____

③ 그들은 신발을 벗어야 한다. (ought, to, take off, their shoes, they)

➡ _____

1. 다음 빈칸에 알맞은 것은?

> Can he _____ well?

① dancing
② dance
③ dances
④ danceing
⑤ danced

2. 다음 괄호 안에서 알맞은 단어를 고르시오.

> A: Can you play the violin?
> B: Yes, I (do, can, don't, can't).

3. 다음 중 어법상 옳은 것은?

① Can this bird fly?
② Can you helping me, please?
③ He cans not play the piano.
④ I will am a mother next year.
⑤ It will rains tomorrow.

4. 다음 대화의 빈칸에 알맞은 것은?

> A: Will cars run on the street?
> B: _____ They will fly in the sky.

① Yes, it will.
② Yes, it won't.
③ No, it won't.
④ No, they will.
⑤ No, they won't.

5. 다음 빈칸에 알맞은 것은?

> Julia can speak Italian.
> = Julia _____ speak Italian.

① does
② are able to
③ is able to
④ is
⑤ do

6. 다음 우리말과 일치하도록 빈칸에 알맞은 말을 쓰시오.

❶ I _____ meet Jerry tomorrow.
　(나는 내일 Jerry를 만날 것이다.)

❷ She _____ ride a bike.
　(그녀는 자전거를 탈 수 있다.)

[7-8] 다음 빈칸에 알맞지 <u>않은</u> 것은?

7.

> He _____ basketball.

① will play
② can play
③ want to play
④ plays
⑤ likes

8.

> She can _____.

① meet him
② see her friends
③ will swim
④ help me
⑤ eat something

9. 다음은 어느 장소에서 지켜야 할 규칙인가?

- You must turn off your cellphone.
- You must put books in the right places.

① Street　　② Library　　③ Hospital
④ Museum　　⑤ Train Station

10. 다음 중 밑줄 친 부분과 의미가 같은 것은?

You <u>must</u> clean your desk.

① can　　② do　　③ will
④ have to　　⑤ need to

단원평가 　실전대비

1. 다음 빈칸에 순서대로 알맞은 것은?

- My eyes are not good. I _____ see very well.
- I have an English exam next Wednesday. I _____ study hard during the weekend.

① can – will　　② can't – will
③ can't – won't　　④ will – can
⑤ won't – can't

2. 다음 대화의 빈칸에 알맞은 것은?

A: Can you wash the dishes for me?
B: _____ I'm late for school now.

① Sure, why not?　　② Yes, I can.
③ No problem.　　④ Of course.
⑤ Sorry, but I can't.

3. 다음 질문에 대한 대답으로 알맞은 것은?

A: Taeho doesn't answer the phone.
B: _____

① He doesn't be at home.
② He doesn't may at home.
③ He may be not at home.
④ He may not be at home.
⑤ He does may not be at home.

4. 다음 중 짝지어진 대화가 <u>어색한</u> 것은?

① A: Can you fly, Susan?
　 B: No, I can't.
② A: Can your pet swim or fly?
　 B: No, it can.
③ A: Is there a soccer ball in the box?
　 B: Yes, there is.
④ A: Will you keep a pet?
　 B: No, I won't. I don't like an animal.
⑤ A: Can you think of happy things now?
　 B: Of course, I can.

5. 다음 중 어법상 옳은 것은?

① Edison have to wear glasses.
② You don't must be late for school again.
③ Everyone has to be quiet in the gallery.
④ May I to ask a personal question?
⑤ I must finishing this report today.

6. 다음 빈칸에 가장 알맞은 것은?

It's sunny. You _____ take your umbrella.

① can　　② must　　③ have to
④ can not　　⑤ don't have to

7. 다음 괄호 안에 들어갈 알맞은 말로 짝지어진 것은?

- He can't [A](speak, speaks) Japanese.
- Can she [B](make, makes) cookies?
- I can [C](teach, teaches) different songs.

    [A]   [B]   [C]
① speak – makes – teaches
② speak – make – teaches
③ speak – make – teach
④ speaks – make – teach
⑤ speaks – makes – teach

8. 다음 대화의 빈칸에 순서대로 알맞은 것은?

A: Is it cold today, Mom?
B: Yes, it is. You _____ go out.
A: OK. I'll stay home and read some comic books.
B: You _____ do your homework first.

① must – will
② should – will
③ should – must
④ should not – will
⑤ should not – should

9. 다음 중 일반적인 도서관 규칙에 적합하지 <u>않은</u> 것은?

Rules in the Library
① You should not talk loud.
② You should turn off your cell phone.
③ You should return your book in two weeks.
④ You should not bring pets into the library.
⑤ You should not put trash in the trash can.

10. 다음 중 거짓말을 많이 해서 코가 길어지는 피노키오에게 할아버지가 할 수 있는 가장 알맞은 조언은?

① You must be quiet.
② You must tell the truth.
③ You have to be on time.
④ You have to stand in line.
⑤ You must brush your teeth every day.

11. 다음 주어진 문장과 의미가 같은 것은?

She is very good at swimming.

① She can swim very well.
② She will swim very well.
③ She must swim very well.
④ She needs to swim very well.
⑤ She wants to swim very well.

12. 다음 중 밑줄 친 부분의 의미가 나머지와 <u>다른</u> 것은?

① Erica <u>can</u> play the violin.
② <u>Can</u> Minho write the alphabet?
③ <u>Can</u> you read this book?
④ <u>Can</u> I leave now?
⑤ She <u>cannot</u> swim fast like you.

13. 다음 사항을 지켜야 할 장소로 알맞은 곳은?

- You must listen to the teacher carefully.
- Always be on time.
- You must not talk with a friend in class.
- Clean the classroom every day.

① Park   ② School   ③ Hospital
④ Library   ⑤ Restaurant

14. 다음 빈칸에 알맞은 것은?

> You should _____.

① sees a dentist
② are back tomorrow
③ gave up smoking
④ driving more carefully
⑤ wear a car seat belt

15. 다음 중 부정문으로 바꿀 때 잘못된 것은?

① You can use my computer.
⇒ You can't use my computer.
② I will watch the sports game tonight.
⇒ I won't watch the sports game tonight.
③ She is going to go abroad.
⇒ She is not going to go abroad.
④ You must get home before nine.
⇒ You not must get home before nine.
⑤ She has to clean her room.
⇒ She doesn't have to clean her room.

16. 다음 빈칸에 알맞은 것은?

> He doesn't look good. He must _____.

① be sick   ② be rich
③ be happy   ④ be a doctor
⑤ have many friends

17. 다음 중 어법상 옳지 않은 것은?

① He won't come back soon.
② I will swim across the river.
③ Sumi will wake up early yesterday.
④ Will Kelly write a letter after school?
⑤ They won't go to school in the future.

18. 다음 중 어법상 옳은 것은?

① James have to wear glasses.
② You don't must turn on your cell phone.
③ Everyone has to be in the class on time.
④ May I to go to the toilet?
⑤ I must meeting her today.

19. 다음 두 문장의 의미가 같도록 빈칸에 알맞은 것은?

> We _____ to plant the trees tomorrow.
> = We _____ plant the trees tomorrow.

① will – can   ② may – will
③ are going – can   ④ are going – will
⑤ are going – may

20. 다음 중 밑줄 친 부분의 쓰임이 나머지와 다른 것은?

① She <u>may</u> be Canadian.
② He <u>may</u> be a doctor.
③ The news <u>may</u> be true.
④ It <u>may</u> be fine tomorrow.
⑤ You <u>may</u> go out with your friends.

21. 다음 빈칸에 순서대로 알맞은 것은?

> - The door was dirty. I _____ clean it.
> - Jina _____ play the violin a few years ago.

① must – can   ② must – could
③ have to – could   ④ had to – can
⑤ had to – could

1. 다음 표를 설명한 문장 중 적절하지 <u>않은</u> 것은?
(I can: ○ I can't: ×)

	Eric	Minho	Susan	Jin
speak Japanese	○	×	×	×
sing	○	○	×	○
make a cake	×	○	○	×
do yoga	○	×	○	○

① Eric can speak Japanese, but he can't make a cake.
② Jin can sing and do yoga, but he can't speak Japanese.
③ Minho and Susan can make a cake.
④ Eric and Jin can do yoga, but they can't make a cake.
⑤ Susan can speak Japanese but she can't sing.

2. What is the correct etiquette(manners) in a movie theater?

① You should talk or eat loudly.
② You should turn on your cell phone.
③ You should throw away trash in the trash can.
④ You should kick the chair in front of you with your foot.
⑤ You should go inside after starting the movie.

3. 다음 중 밑줄 친 부분의 쓰임이 나머지와 <u>다른</u> 것은?

① I'm not sure about his style. He <u>may</u> like skinny jeans.
② He <u>may</u> be a good father but he's a terrible husband.
③ I <u>may</u> not have any special talent.
④ You passed the exam. Now you <u>may</u> go to the movies.
⑤ You <u>may</u> be late for school. Hurry up!

4. 다음 대화의 밑줄 친 sign에 해당하는 것은?

A: Is there any place to park?
B: Over there.
A: But there is a <u>sign</u>. It says, "You must not park here."

①　　②　　③　

④　　⑤　

5. 다음 중 밑줄 친 부분의 쓰임이 보기 와 <u>다른</u> 것은?
(정답 2개)

보기 I <u>can</u> make spaghetti and pizza.

① It <u>cannot</u> be wrong.
② Kate <u>can</u> ride a bike.
③ <u>Can</u> I go to the bathroom?
④ Cats <u>can</u> see well at night.
⑤ Jane <u>can</u> speak French very well.

6. 다음 중 빈칸에 들어갈 말이 나머지와 <u>다른</u> 것은?

① Minho _____ study hard for a better grade.
② You _____ turn off your cell phone in the concert.
③ People _____ be cruel to animals.
④ You _____ return the books to the library.
⑤ We _____ put trash in the trash can.

7. 다음 중 짝지어진 문장의 관계가 나머지와 <u>다른</u> 것은?

① A – You should listen to me.
  B – You ought not to listen to me.
② A – He must wash his face.
  B – He doesn't wash his face.
③ A – Let's go out for dinner.
  B – Let's not go out for dinner.
④ A – Be careful.
  B – Don't be careful.
⑤ A – She has to do her homework.
  B – She need not do her homework.

8. 다음 중 짝지어진 대화가 <u>어색한</u> 것은?

① A: I have a headache.
  B: You should take the medicine.
② A: I lied to my parents.
  B: You should tell them the truth.
③ A: My shoes have holes in the bottom.
  B: You should buy new shoes.
④ A: I am going to ride a motorcycle.
  B: OK, but you should wear a helmet.
⑤ A: I got a poor grade in math.
  B: I should call the manager.

9. 다음 중 밑줄 친 부분의 쓰임이 보기와 같은 것은?

보기 In each city, the skaters <u>must</u> collect a stamp.

① She was not in class today. She <u>must</u> be sick.
② To be a top model, I <u>must</u> learn to pose.
③ She won first prize in the math contest. She <u>must</u> be smart.
④ You were too rude to the teacher. He <u>must</u> be angry with you.
⑤ Coming to school every day <u>must</u> be difficult for her, but she always smiles.

10. 다음 우리말을 영어로 옮긴 것이 <u>어색한</u> 것은?

① 우리는 교통법규를 지켜야 한다.
  We must obey the traffic rules.
② 나는 내일 Jenny를 만날 것이다.
  I'm going to meet Jenny tomorrow.
③ 나는 그의 이야기를 이해할 수 없었다.
  I couldn't understand his story.
④ 너는 학교에 늦으면 안 된다.
  You shouldn't be late for school.
⑤ 너는 돈을 가지고 갈 필요가 없다.
  You must not bring money.

1. 다음 도표의 내용을 보고 Andy와 Eric이 할 수 있는 것과 할 수 없는 것을 can과 can't를 이용하여 문장을 완성하시오.

	Andy	Eric
play the piano	○	×
ride a bike	○	○
make pizza	×	○

할 수 있는 것

❶ Eric _____ .

❷ Andy _____ .

할 수 없는 것

❸ Eric _____ .

❹ Andy _____ .

2. 다음 문장에서 어법상 틀린 부분을 찾아 바르게 고치고, 바르게 고친 문장의 부정문을 만드시오.

> Jack wills be okay.

❶ 틀린 부분을 찾아 바르게 고치시오.
  (완전한 문장을 쓸 것)

  ⇒

❷ 바르게 고친 문장의 부정문을 만드시오.
  (반드시 축약형을 사용할 것)

  ⇒

3. 다음 문장을 주어진 지시대로 바꾸어 빈칸을 채우시오.

❶ I have to wash the dishes. (주어를 She로)

⇒ _____ wash the dishes.

❷ We have to wake up early. (부정문으로)

⇒ _____ wake up early.

4. 다음 주어진 상황에 이어질 문장을 have to와 괄호 안에 주어진 단어를 모두 활용하여 완성하시오.(단, have to는 시제나 주어 등에 따라 형태가 바뀔 수 있음.)

❶ Bob's room is very dirty. He can't find anything easily in his room. He _____ his room right now. (clean)

❷ I wear my school uniform on weekdays. But I don't go to school on weekends, so I _____ it on weekends. (wear)

❸ I usually wake up at six in the morning. But yesterday I went fishing with my family, so I _____ at five yesterday. (wake up)

5. 다음 표지판을 보고, 빈칸에 알맞은 말을 쓰시오.

❶ You must _____ _____ here.

❷ You _____ _____ _____ here.

6. 다음 우리말에 맞게 빈칸에 알맞은 말을 쓰시오.

❶ 나는 어머니를 도와드릴 거야.

⇒ I _____ help my mother.

❷ 우리 집에 올래?

⇒ _____ you come to my house?

❸ 그는 부자임에 틀림없다.

⇒ He _____ be rich.

7. 다음 두 문장의 의미가 같도록 빈칸에 알맞은 말을 쓰시오.

❶ When will Suji arrive?

= When _____ Suji _____ _____ arrive?

❷ You must go to school.

= You _____ _____ go to school.

8. 다음 보기 에서 단어를 골라 우리말과 의미가 같도록 조건에 맞게 문장을 완성하시오.

보기
English, high school students, will, speak, can, well

조건
1. 보기 의 단어들을 모두 사용할 것
2. 필요한 경우 어휘 형태를 변형, 추가할 것

❶ 우리는 2019년에 고등학생이 될 것이다.

We _____ in 2019.

❷ 너는 영어를 잘 말할 수 있다.

You _____.

9. 대화를 읽고 문장 빈칸에 알맞은 단어를 순서대로 쓰시오.

G: Listen! Brian wrote this song.
B: Wow, it is so beautiful! Can he sing well, too?
G: Well, no. He can't sing well.

Brian is very good at _____ songs, but he is not a good _____.

10. 다음 괄호 안에 설명에 해당하는 조동사를 쓰시오.

❶ She _____ speak English very well. (능력)

❷ He _____ remember my name. (약한 추측)

❸ You _____ have anything here. (허가)

❹ He _____ clean his room before breakfast. (의무)

❺ The boy _____ be very kind. (강한 추측)

한 눈에 파악하는 조동사

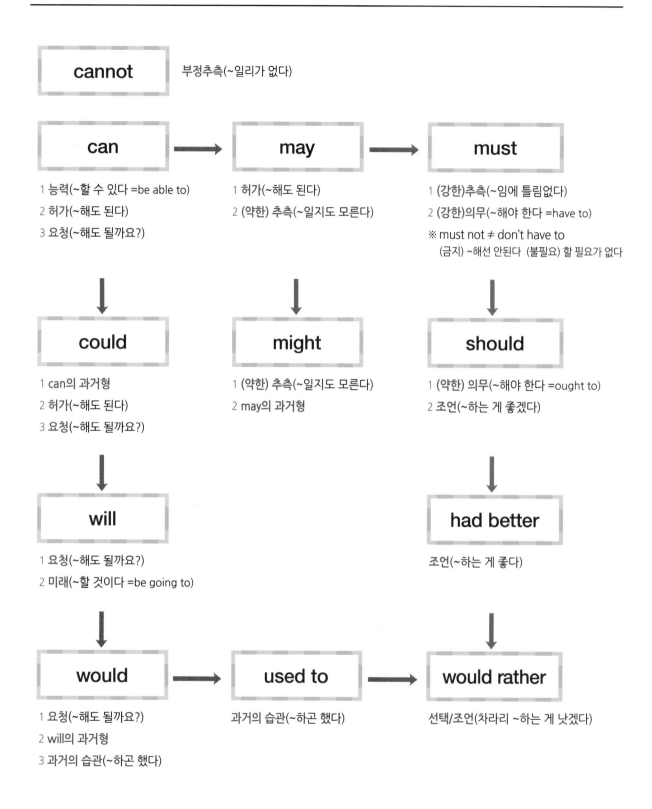

cannot   부정추측(~일리가 없다)

can

1 능력(~할 수 있다 =be able to)
2 허가(~해도 된다)
3 요청(~해도 될까요?)

may

1 허가(~해도 된다)
2 (약한) 추측(~일지도 모른다)

must

1 (강한)추측(~임에 틀림없다)
2 (강한)의무(~해야 한다 =have to)
※ must not ≠ don't have to
  (금지) ~해선 안된다 (불필요) 할 필요가 없다

could

1 can의 과거형
2 허가(~해도 된다)
3 요청(~해도 될까요?)

might

1 (약한) 추측(~일지도 모른다)
2 may의 과거형

should

1 (약한) 의무(~해야 한다 =ought to)
2 조언(~하는 게 좋겠다)

will

1 요청(~해도 될까요?)
2 미래(~할 것이다 =be going to)

had better

조언(~하는 게 좋다)

would

1 요청(~해도 될까요?)
2 will의 과거형
3 과거의 습관(~하곤 했다)

used to

과거의 습관(~하곤 했다)

would rather

선택/조언(차라리 ~하는 게 낫겠다)

Chapter 4
동사의 시제

4.1. 현재시제와 과거시제

1 현재시제

⟩⟩⟩ 현재의 상태, 반복적인 일상, 현재의 습관 등을 나타낸다.

I **feel** sad. (현재 상태) 나는 슬프다.

She **goes** to school on foot. (반복적 일상) 그녀는 걸어서 학교에 간다.

My sister **has** two meals a day. (현재 습관) 나의 언니는 하루에 두 끼를 먹는다.

⟩⟩⟩ 일반적 사실, 과학적인 진리, 속담 및 격언 등은 항상 현재시제를 사용한다.

Paris **is** the capital of France. (일반적 사실) 파리는 프랑스의 수도이다.

Three plus two **is** five. (불변의 진리) 3 더하기 2는 5이다.

An early bird **catches** the worm. (속담) 일찍 일어나는 새가 벌레를 잡는다.

⟩⟩⟩ 현재시제와 자주 쓰이는 시간 표현: now, today, every day, 빈도부사(always, usually 등)

I **am** busy **today**. 나는 오늘 바쁘다.

She **always goes** to bed at **10 p.m.** 그녀는 항상 10시에 잠자리에 든다.

2 과거시제

⟩⟩⟩ 이미 끝난 과거의 동작·상태를 나타낸다.

I **had** a good time with Tom **last weekend**. (과거의 동작) 나는 지난 주말에 탐과 좋은 시간을 보냈다.

She **was** in hospital **yesterday**. (과거의 상태) 그녀는 어제 병원에 있었다.

⟩⟩⟩ 역사적인 사실은 항상 과거시제를 사용한다.

The Korean War **broke** out **in 1950**. 한국 전쟁은 1950년에 발발했다.

⟩⟩⟩ 과거시제와 자주 쓰이는 시간 표현: yesterday, last night[week, year, Monday], ~ ago 등

I **got up** late **yesterday**. 나는 어제 늦게 일어났다.

They **moved** to Hawaii **three years ago**. 그들은 3년 전에 하와이로 이사했다.

A. 다음 괄호 안에서 알맞은 말을 고르시오.

① John (watches, watched) movies last night.

② The sun (gives, gave) us light every day.

③ Water (boiled, boils) at 100 °C.

④ Practice (makes, made) perfect.

⑤ Mina (flies, flew) to Paris a month ago.

B. 다음 괄호 안에 동사를 시제에 맞게 변형하여 쓰시오.

① Mr. Smith (go) to Japan every year.

② My younger sister (ride) a bicycle yesterday.

③ Minho (put) the box on his desk an hour ago.

④ The plane usually (arrive) at 12:30.

⑤ World War II (end) in 1945.

⑥ My best friend, Tom never (talk) about people behind their backs.

⑦ He (go) to bed early last night.

⑧ The weather (be) terrible this morning.

⑨ Susan always (play) basketball after school.

⑩ Seoul (be) the capital of Korea.

C. 다음 문장을 don't, doesn't 또는 didn't를 넣어 완성하시오.

① She _____ visit England last year.

② My grandparents _____ go hiking on weekends.

③ I _____ eat breakfast every morning.

④ My sister and I _____ get up late last Sunday.

⑤ She _____ go skiing every winter.

⑥ Sam _____ go to the gym yesterday.

4.2. 진행시제 (현재진행, 과거진행)

>>> 진행시제란? 어느 특정 시점에서 진행 중인 일을 묘사할 때 사용한다.

1 현재진행

>>> be동사[am/are/is] + 동사원형 ~ing: '~하고 있다'

I **am listening** to music. 나는 음악을 듣고 있다.

2 과거진행

>>> be동사의 과거[was/were] + 동사원형 ~ing: '~하고 있었다'

My parents **were sitting** on the sofa. 나의 부모님은 소파에 앉아 계셨다.

3 진행시제의 부정문과 의문문

부정문	be동사 + not + 동사원형 ~ing	She is not having sandwiches. 그녀는 샌드위치를 먹고 있지 않다.
의문문	Be동사 + 주어 + 동사원형 ~ing?	Was he walking down the street? 그는 거리를 걷고 있었니? -Yes, he was. / No, he wasn't. 응, 그랬어. / 아니, 안 그랬어.

4 동사원형(v-ing) 만들기

대부분 동사	동사원형 ing	walk → walk**ing**
-e로 끝나는 동사	e를 빼고 ing	take → tak**ing**
-ie로 끝나는 동사	ie를 y로 고치고 ing	lie → ly**ing**
「단모음 + 단자음」으로 끝나고 그 단모음에 강세가 있는 동사	자음을 한 번 더 쓰고 ing	begin → begin**ning**
1음절 동사 중 「단모음 + 단자음」으로 끝나는 동사		get → get**ting**

뽐쌤의
야무진
Tip!

진행형으로 만들 수 없는 동사

소유, 감정, 인식, 지각의 동사(have, belong, like, love, know, see, hear, want)

I am liking English. (x)   I like English. (o)

단, have가 '가지고 있다'란 의미가 아닌 '먹다'의 의미로 쓰인 경우는 가능하다.

I am having a bag. (x)   I am having dinner. (o)

A. 다음 동사의 ~ing형을 쓰시오.

① arrive   ② begin   ③ come

④ cut   ⑤ cry   ⑥ dance

⑦ die   ⑧ drive   ⑨ get

⑩ go   ⑪ hit   ⑫ jog

⑬ live   ⑭ swim   ⑮ wake

⑯ write   ⑰ run   ⑱ ring

B. 다음 주어진 문장을 지시대로 고치시오. (의문문의 대답은 빈칸을 채우시오.)

① He takes a walk in the forest.

현재진행형:

현재진행형의 부정문:

현재진행형의 의문문: / Yes, _____ _____.

② Suji runs after her dog.

과거진행형:

과거진행형의 부정문:

과거진행형의 의문문: / Yes, _____ _____.

C. 다음 괄호 안에 알맞은 말을 고르시오.

① I (am, was) doing my homework at that time.

② You were (clean, cleaning) the living room.

③ Jack and Yuna (are, were) watching TV yesterday.

④ I (am, was) helping my mother in the kitchen now.

⑤ He was (listen, listening) to the radio at that time.

1. 다음 대화에서 어법상 적절하지 <u>않은</u> 것은?

A: What did you (a)<u>did</u> yesterday?
B: I (b)<u>saw</u> a movie.
A: (c)<u>Did</u> you enjoy it?
B: Yes, I (d)<u>did</u>. It (e)<u>was</u> interesting.

① (a) ② (b) ③ (c)
④ (d) ⑤ (e)

2. 다음 중 진행형이 올바른 것 두 개는?

① eat – eating ② ride – riding
③ stop – stoping ④ swim – swiming
⑤ lie – lieing

3. 다음 주어진 문장을 진행형으로 알맞게 바꾼 것은?

Jisu doesn't clean his room.

① Jisu doesn't cleaning his room.
② Jisu is cleaning his room.
③ Jisu is cleaning not his room.
④ Jisu isn't cleaning his room.
⑤ Jisu does cleaning not his room.

4. 다음 대화의 빈칸에 알맞지 않은 것은?

A: What did you do _____?
B: I studied science.

① this morning ② after lunch
③ last weekend ④ tomorrow
⑤ yesterday

5. 다음 중 밑줄 친 동사의 형태가 알맞은 것은?

① She is <u>writeing</u> a card.
② I'm not <u>cleaning</u> my desk.
③ She is <u>listenning</u> to music.
④ My dad is <u>siting</u> on the chair.
⑤ Are David and Charles <u>eatting</u> cookies?

6. 다음 빈칸에 알맞지 <u>않은</u> 것은?

They _____ last night.

① had a great time
② were at the park
③ played tennis
④ didn't go out
⑤ study math

7. 다음 대화의 빈칸에 순서대로 알맞은 것은?

A: What _____ you do last Sunday?
B: I _____ English.

① do – study ② do – studied
③ did – study ④ are – studied
⑤ did – studied

8. 다음 빈칸에 알맞지 <u>않은</u> 것은?

Tom's sister is _____.

① singing a song
② very kind
③ a good teacher
④ plays the piano
⑤ taking a walk in the park

[9-10] 다음 빈칸에 알맞은 것은?

9.

_____ she reading a book?

① Does ② Do ③ Is
④ Am ⑤ Are

10.

_____ she read a book?

① Does ② Do ③ Is
④ Am ⑤ Are

단원평가 / 실전대비

1. 다음 빈칸에 순서대로 알맞은 것은?

- Suji _____ tennis every Tuesday.
- Look at her! She _____ the piano now.

① is playing, plays
② is playing, is playing
③ play, is playing
④ plays, play
⑤ plays, is playing

2. 다음 중 어법상 옳은 것은?

① Did he dances yesterday?
② These cookies look sweet.
③ She goes to Kimhae last weekend.
④ Who did sent the picture?
⑤ Suji didn't the dishes after dinner.

3. 다음 보기에서 단어를 골라 빈칸에 알맞게 고쳐 써 넣으시오.

보기 play rain are bring don't

Yesterday I ❶_____ soccer with Henry. Bob ❷_____ play with us. He just watched us. It ❸_____ on us. We ❹_____ wet and hungry. Bob ❺_____ some umbrellas to us.

4. 다음 표에 관한 설명 중 어색한 것은?

	Mon	Tue	Wed
Alex	listen to music	swim	exercise
Angela	study English	swim	read a book

① Alex listens to music on Monday.
② Angela studies English on Tuesday.
③ Alex exercises on Wednesday.
④ Angela reads a book on Wednesday.
⑤ Alex and Angela swim on Tuesday.

[5-6] 다음 중 어법상 어색한 것은?

5.

① Suji isn't kind at all.
② The sun rose in the east.
③ I go to the park every day.
④ Was she at home this morning?
⑤ We took a trip to Sydney last summer.

6.

① Did you jump rope yesterday?
② I don't go to bed early.
③ Paris was the capital of France.
④ She is winning the game.
⑤ My dad cooks dinner.

7. 다음 보기에서 어법상 옳은 문장끼리 묶인 것은?

보기
ⓐ Hanbin is studying English.
ⓑ Bomin is siting on the floor.
ⓒ Sihyun is dancing to the music.
ⓓ Teahoon is runing in the park.
ⓔ Bobae is eatting an ice cream.

① ⓐ, ⓑ   ② ⓐ, ⓒ
③ ⓑ, ⓒ, ⓔ   ④ ⓓ, ⓔ
⑤ ⓒ, ⓓ

8. 다음 그림의 설명이 잘못된 것은?

① A man is buying some shoes.
② A man is cleaning the window of a bookstore.
③ A boy is riding a bicycle.
④ A girl is coming out of a bookstore.
⑤ Two boys are playing with a basketball.

9. 다음 중 밑줄 친 부분이 잘못된 것은?

① James loves <u>taking</u> pictures.
② Hojin likes <u>playing</u> the guitar.
③ Tom is <u>swiming</u> in the pool.
④ Mina is <u>running</u> on the playground.
⑤ What do you like <u>doing</u> on Sunday?

10. 다음 대화의 빈칸 ⓐ, ⓑ에 순서대로 알맞은 것은?

A: Are Kate and Anna listening to music?
B: ⓐ_____ They are studying English.
A: Is Sam riding a bike?
B: ⓑ_____ He is writing a letter.

	ⓐ	ⓑ
①	Yes, they are.	Yes, he is.
②	Yes, they are.	No, he isn't.
③	No, they aren't.	Yes, he is.
④	No, they aren't.	No, I'm not.
⑤	No, they aren't.	No, he isn't.

11. 다음 대화의 빈칸에 들어갈 do의 형태가 순서대로 알맞은 것은?

A: What _____ she do every day?
B: She goes to school.
A: What _____ she do last Sunday?
B: She went camping.

① does – does   ② did – did
③ did – does   ④ does – did
⑤ did – do

12. 다음 중 밑줄 친 부분이 잘못된 것은?

① He read newspaper yesterday.
② I went shopping last weekend.
③ Romeo and Juliet studied together.
④ They visited their grandparents.
⑤ We eated pizza in the restaurant.

13. 다음 중 빈칸에 was[Was]가 들어갈 수 없는 것은?

① Why _____ he laughing?
② My sister _____ calling her friend.
③ _____ she wearing a blue shirt?
④ Susan _____ going to the bus stop.
⑤ _____ he send a letter last night?

14. 다음 중 어법상 옳지 않은 것은?

① They are sitting on the floor.
② I am not playing computer games.
③ She is having very big hamburgers.
④ The teacher is knowing the answer.
⑤ She is wearing a red cap and has long hair.

15. 다음 글에서 어법상 적절하지 않은 것은?

Jonathan didn't go to school. He ①had a bad cold. He ②went to see a doctor. He ③took some medicine and ④slept all day. But now he ⑤felt great.

[16–17] 다음 빈칸에 알맞은 것은?

16.

It _____ heavily last summer.

① rained   ② raining   ③ rains
④ will rain   ⑤ rain

17.

This washing machine is making loud noise _____.

① now   ② yesterday
③ tomorrow   ④ this evening
⑤ last Sunday

18. 다음 중 어법상 옳은 것은?

① Jimmy read a novel now.
② This morning, I fell off the bike.
③ Where did you went last weekend?
④ He has his birthday party yesterday.
⑤ A man was listen to music in the room.

19. Choose the correct word for the blank.

M: Hey, where is Justin?
W: He's _____ in bed. He has a runny nose and fever.

① lied   ② lying   ③ lie
④ lies   ⑤ going to lie

20. 다음 글의 빈칸 (A)~(C)에 알맞은 것은?

This is a picture of my dad's birthday. It was yesterday, July 7th. We (A)_____ a birthday party with my grandparents. I (B)_____ a cake for my dad. My brother gave a gift to him. My mother (C)_____ a picture of us. It was a great party.

	(A)	(B)	(C)
①	had	bought	took
②	was	bought	took
③	had	bought	take
④	have	buy	take
⑤	were	buy	taken

단원평가 고난도

1. 다음 중 빈칸에 들어갈 말이 (a)와 <u>다른</u> 것은? (정답 2개)

Today was the first day of middle school. I was happy but also worried. The first class (a) with my homeroom teacher, Mr. Choi. He is a math teacher. I didn't know anyone in my class, but I talked to some of my classmates.

① It _____ lunch time then.
② The room _____ dirty yesterday.
③ Mina _____ at home 2 hours ago.
④ Amy and I _____ in China last month.
⑤ They _____ elementary school students last year.

2. 다음 중 지시대로 알맞게 바꾼 것은?

① Tom watches TV. (과거의문문)
 ⇒ Did Tom watches TV?
② He got up at 6:30 in the morning. (의문문)
 ⇒ Did he got up at 6:30 in the morning?
③ I don't buy a new cell phone. (과거긍정문)
 ⇒ I bought a new cell phone.
④ Ben went to New York by plane. (부정문)
 ⇒ Ben did not went to New York by plane.
⑤ My sister ate lunch at 12. (현재진행형)
 ⇒ My sister eat lunch at 12.

3. 다음 중 밑줄 친 부분이 <u>잘못된</u> 것은?

① The girl is <u>looking</u> at the boy.
② I'm <u>knowing</u> your little brother.
③ Kristin <u>washes</u> her hair every other day or so.
④ Tony usually <u>sits</u> in the front row during class.
⑤ After six days of rain, I'm glad that the sun <u>is shining</u> today.

4. 다음 중 짝지어진 대화가 <u>어색한</u> 것은?

① A: What are you doing?
 B: I'm writing a card to my grandmother.
② A: When is it?
 B: It's this Saturday.
③ A: What are you looking at?
 B: My family pictures.
④ A: Are you studying?
 B: Yes, I was studying.
⑤ A: Where is it?
 B: It's at Tom's Pizza House.

5. 다음 중 어법상 옳은 것은?

① He is dancing last night.
② He can plays the guitar.
③ They are sitting on the sofa.
④ We can't did anything to help him.
⑤ Are you read a book?

6. 다음 질문에 대한 대답으로 알맞은 것은?

Q: What did your sister do last weekend?
A: _____

① He didn't study at all for the test.
② He practices singing for the school festival.
③ She is busy doing science homework.
④ She went to the library and read books.
⑤ She usually visits my grandparents.

[7–8] 다음 중 밑줄 친 부분의 쓰임이 나머지와 <u>다른</u> 것은?

7.

① Are you <u>sleeping</u> on the floor?
② What are you <u>going</u> to eat for dinner?
③ We are <u>going</u> to the zoo together.
④ Mary is <u>baking</u> some cookies for her brother.
⑤ I am <u>drinking</u> water now.

8.

① Minho is <u>jumping</u> high.
② Are you <u>washing</u> your hands?
③ The birds are <u>flying</u> very fast.
④ The movie was very <u>interesting</u>.
⑤ Was Mike <u>calling</u> me?

9. 다음 보기에서 어법상 올바른 문장을 적은 학생의 수는?

보기
민아: I stoped the car.
정우: Was Kate at home yesterday?
지원: Did you passed the exam last year?
현진: She wents to school by bus yesterday.
혜민: They were nervous before the speech.
수지: Jane and I played tennis and she won easily.

① 1명   ② 2명   ③ 3명
④ 4명   ⑤ 5명

10. 다음 중 어법상 틀린 것을 모두 골라 고치시오.

It is Saturday afternoon now. Mr. Jang taught English to his students. But they are not study hard. They want a break.

11. 다음 중 빈칸에 was가 들어갈 수 <u>없는</u> 것은?

① Why _____ Mina crying?
② My brother _____ calling his friend.
③ _____ she write a postcard last night?
④ She _____ wearing blue pants?
⑤ Ken _____ going to the subway station.

1. 다음 주어진 단어를 배열하여 문장을 완성하시오. (단 동사를 올바른 형태로 고쳐 쓸 것)

예) (study / Eric / English / on / Thursday)
⇒ Eric studies English on Thursday.

❶ (wash / his / Mr. Nah / car / weekends / on)

⇒ _____

❷ (taekwondo / he / do / day / school / every / after)

⇒ _____

❸ (watch / do / usually / you / television / night / every)

⇒ _____

❹ (study / Mira / do / math / not / Mondays / on)

⇒ _____

2. 다음 보기와 같이 문장을 변형하여 쓰시오.

보기 She plays the guitar.
    ⇒ She is playing the guitar.

❶ They eat dinner together.

⇒ _____

❷ She smiles at her baby.

⇒ _____

❸ I drink green tea with my mom.

⇒ _____

3. 다음 Daedalus의 아들 Icarus가 바다에 빠지게 된 과정을 그린 그림을 보고, 보기에서 알맞은 단어를 골라 빈칸을 채우시오. (과거형으로)

보기 make go fly fall

❶ Daedalus _____ wings.

❷ Daedalus and Icarus _____ into the sky.

❸ Icarus _____ closer and closer to the sun.

❹ Icarus' wings burned and Icarus _____ down to the sea.

4. 다음 (A)~(C)에 주어진 주어/동사/부사(구)에서 하나씩을 골라 이들을 활용하여 각 시제에 맞도록 조건에 맞추어 답하시오.

조건 1	❶에 5단어 이상의 긍정문을 완성하고, ❷에 ❶에 쓴 문장의 부정문을 쓰시오.
조건 2	(A)~(C)에서 반드시 하나씩을 골라 문장을 완성하고, 한 번 쓴 단어는 중복 사용 불가
조건 3	동사의 경우 시제에 맞게 어형 변화 가능

(A) 주어	I, We, You, He, She, My friends
(B) 동사	take, go, watch, read, play, sing, listen to, meet, study, ride
(C) 부사(구)	tomorrow, now, yesterday, on weekends, next week, always, three days ago, in the future, every Sunday, last weekend

❶ _____

❷ _____

5. 다음 그림을 보고, 빈칸에 알맞은 말을 넣어 현재진행형의 문장을 완성하시오.

❶ James is _____ book.

❷ Julia is _____ Juice.

❸ Susan is _____.

6. 다음 글에 대한 물음에 영어 문장으로 답하시오.

This is an animal doctor, Mr. Choi. He takes care of animals on weekdays. It's Sunday today, so he is riding a bike now.

❶ What is Mr. Choi's job?

⇒ He _____.

❷ Is Mr. Choi taking care of animals now?

⇒ _____, he _____.

❸ What is Mr. Choi dong now?

⇒ He _____.

7. 다음의 대화를 읽고 우리말과 같은 뜻이 되도록 칸을 완성하시오.

A: Hey, what are you doing now?
B: I ❶ _____ _____ _____ _____.
　　(편지를 쓰고 있는 중이야)
A: OK. What is Tom doing?
B: He ❷ _____ _____ _____ _____
　　in the park. (사진을 찍고 있는 중이야)

8. 다음은 수지의 하루 일과이다. 보기와 같이 문장을 완성하시오.

> 보기 It's 4:00 a.m. <u>She is sleeping.</u>

6:00 a.m. ~ 7:00 a.m.	Take a shower
7:00 a.m. ~ 7:30 a.m.	Have breakfast
7:30 a.m. ~ 8:00 a.m.	Go to school
8:00 a.m. ~ 4:00 p.m.	Study at school
4:00 p.m. ~ 6:00 p.m.	Play with friends
6:00 p.m. ~ 7:00 p.m.	Have dinner
7:00 p.m. ~ 9:00 p.m.	Do homework
9:00 p.m. ~ 10:00 p.m.	Watch TV
10:00 p.m. ~ 6:00 a.m.	Sleep

❶ It's 6:50 a.m.

⇒ _____

❷ It's 7:10 a.m

⇒ _____

❸ It's 7:40 a.m.

⇒ _____

❹ It's 10:20 a.m.

⇒ _____

❺ It's 5:00 p.m.

⇒ _____

❻ It's 6:30 p.m.

⇒ _____

❼ It's 7:40 p.m.

⇒ _____

❽ It's 9:15 p.m.

⇒ _____

9. 다음 괄호 안에 주어진 낱말을 활용하여 진행형으로 빈칸을 완성하시오.

> Yesterday, Steve _____ (wear) a blue shirt. He _____ (clean) up the classroom. Today, he _____ (wear) a red shirt. He _____ (talk) with Jim now.

10. 다음 우리말과 뜻이 같도록 괄호 안에 단어들을 바르게 배열하시오.

❶ 밖에 비가 내리고 있니? (raining / is / it / outside)

⇒ _____ ?

❷ 그들은 나의 의사 선생님들이었다. (my doctors / they / were)

⇒ _____ .

❸ 너는 왜 화가 났었니? (were / you / angry / why)

⇒ _____ ?

11. 다음 문장에서 틀린 부분을 두 군데 찾아 전체를 바르게 고쳐 쓰시오.

> My son is cooking something last night. He was bakeing a cake for me.

⇒ _____

_____

Chapter 5
명사와 관사

5.1. 명사의 종류

1 보통명사

》》》 사람, 사물, 동물의 공통적인 이름

ex) a boy, a tree, a teacher, a piano, an hour, a zoo, a dog ...

2 집합명사

》》》 사람, 동물, 사물이 모인 집합체의 이름

ex) cattle(소떼), family, class ...

3 물질명사

》》》 일정한 형태를 갖지 않는 물질에 붙이는 이름

ex) water, milk, air, paper, glass, sugar, meat, butter, oil, gas ...

※ 물질명사는 수를 셀 수 없으므로, ① 관사를 붙일 수 없음, ② 복수형도 없음, ③ 수가 아닌 양을 표시하는 much(많은), some(약간의), little(거의 없는), a little(적은) 등의 형용사와 함께 쓸 수 있음.

4 추상명사

》》》 일정한 형태가 없는 성질 · 상태 · 동작 등 추상적인 것들에 붙이는 이름

ex) love, friendship, beauty, silence, justice, advice, news, information ...

5 고유명사

》》》 사람 · 사물 · 장소 등에 쓰이는 고유한 이름

ex) Bomi, Seoul, Korea, Mt. Everest, Peter ...

※ 고유명사는 ① 관사를 붙일 수 없음, ② 복수형도 없음, ③ 첫 글자는 대문자로 씀

뽐쌤의 야무진 Tip!

명사는 또한 크게 셀 수 있는 명사(가산 명사)와 셀 수 없는 명사(불가산 명사)로 나뉘어지는데, 보통명사는 가산 명사이며, 물질명사, 추상명사, 고유명사는 불가산 명사로 구분된다. 집합명사의 경우는 단어에 따라서 가산도 될 수 있고 불가산이 될 수도 있다.

가산 명사(셀 수 있는 명사) – 보통명사, 집합명사

불가산 명사(셀 수 없는 명사) – 물질명사, 추상명사, 고유명사, 집합명사

A. 다음 중 단어의 성격이 나머지 넷과 다른 것을 고르시오.

① ① nose   ② computer   ③ juice   ④ coin   ⑤ book

② ① animal   ② love   ③ lesson   ④ girl   ⑤ boy

③ ① class   ② snow   ③ truth   ④ gas   ⑤ air

④ ① advice   ② freedom   ③ hope   ④ life   ⑤ paper

⑤ ① France   ② Korea   ③ zoo   ④ Mt. Everest ⑤ Japan

⑥ ① bus   ② village   ③ tree   ④ Mike   ⑤ kite

⑦ ① family   ② audience   ③ band   ④ team   ⑤ sister

⑧ ① information ② hope   ③ rain   ④ kindness   ⑤ beauty

B. 다음 괄호 안에서 알맞은 것을 고르시오.

① (A Korea, Korea) has four seasons.

② We love (peace, peaces).

③ Students want to enjoy (a freedom, freedom).

④ My baby is the reason for my (happiness, happy).

⑤ (A Jessica, Jessica) has a nice bag.

⑥ She drew (a tree, tree) on the paper.

⑦ Karen added (sugars, sugar) to her soup.

⑧ He bakes fresh (bread, breads).

⑨ Her (family, families) is now in Osaka.

⑩ I don't have any (money, moneys).

C. 다음 밑줄 친 부분을 어법에 맞게 고쳐 쓰시오.

① She comes from <u>an Australia</u>.

② Time <u>fly</u> like an arrow.

③ I need to drink a lot of <u>waters</u> every day.

④ People get a lot of <u>informations</u> from the Internet.

⑤ My mom needs <u>cheeses</u> for her food.

5.2. 명사의 복수형

»»» 명사의 수란? 셀 수 있는 명사가 하나이면 단수, 둘 이상이면 복수라고 한다.

1 명사의 규칙 복수형

❶ 일반적인 명사: 단수형 + s

cups, books, cows

❷ 어미가 s, sh, ch, x로 끝나는 명사 + es

buses, dishes, benches, boxes

❸ 「자음 + o」로 끝나는 명사 + es

potatoes, tomatoes, heroes 예외) autos, pianos, photos, radios

❹ 「자음 + y」로 끝나는 명사는 y를 i로 바꾸고 + es

baby → babies, lady → ladies, story → stories

❺ 「모음 + y」로 끝나는 명사 + s

boys, monkeys

❻ −f, −fe로 끝나는 명사는 f 또는 fe를 −ves로 바꿈

leaf → leaves, wife → wives, knife → knives 예외) roofs, safes

2 명사의 불규칙 복수형

❶ 모음이 변하는 형

man → men, woman → women, foot → feet, tooth → teeth, mouse → mice
goose → geese

❷ −en, −ren을 첨가하는 형

ox → oxen, child → children

❸ 단수 · 복수가 동일한 형

deer, sheep, fish, Japanese, Swiss, Chinese

뽐쌤의
야무진
Tip!

짝을 이루는 의류, 도구

❶ 복수형을 써야 하고, ❷ 복수 취급을 받는다.

ex) shoes(구두), glasses(안경), socks(양말), pants(바지) 등

A. 다음 명사의 복수형을 쓰시오.

① party   ② video   ③ roof

④ present   ⑤ bus   ⑥ egg

⑦ self   ⑧ poster   ⑨ headache

⑩ ox   ⑪ tooth   ⑫ habit

⑬ woman   ⑭ deer   ⑮ child

⑯ potato   ⑰ brush   ⑱ map

B. 다음 괄호 안에 복수가 되는 단어를 써 넣으시오.

① one monkey - a few (　　　), one watch - some (　　　), one zebra - several (　　　)

② one tooth - lots of (　　　), one key - two (　　　), one octopus - two (　　　)

③ one apple - two (　　　), one rabbit - many (　　　), one ox - two (　　　)

④ one house - two (　　　), one cat - two (　　　), one family - two (　　　)

C. 다음 문장의 괄호 안에서 알맞은 것을 고르시오.

① Move the (boxs, boxes).

② Mary and Jane are (women, womans).

③ Suji buys many (fish, fishes).

④ Do you have many (watchs, watches)?

⑤ A lot of (leafs, leaves) fall in fall.

⑥ I need some (penes, pens) for my test.

⑦ My mother raised a lot of (goose, geese).

⑧ My (feet, foots) are about eight inches long.

⑨ Five (students, studentes) are walking along the lake.

⑩ Several (photos, photoes) are on the desk.

5.3. 명사의 수량표현

	많은	약간의	거의 없는
셀 수 있는 명사(가산 명사) 앞	many	a few	few
셀 수 없는 명사(불가산 명사) 앞	much	a little	little
셀 수 있는 명사와 셀 수 없는 명사 모두의 앞	a lot of = lots of	some(긍정문) any(부정문, 의문문)	-

My daughter has **many dolls** in her room. 나의 딸은 방에 많은 인형을 가지고 있다.

We don't have **much time** now. 우리는 지금 시간이 많이 없다.

I have **some questions**. / Do you have **any questions**? 저는 질문이 있습니다. / 질문이 있습니까?

》》 셀 수 없는 명사는 양을 측정하기 위해 용기나 단위 명사를 사용한다. 복수형은 단위나 용기를 나타내는 명사에 −s/es를 붙여 쓴다.

잔(찬 음료)	a glass of / two glasses of	water, juice, milk, wine
잔(뜨거운 음료)	a cup of / two cups of	coffee, tea
덩어리(빵류)	a loaf of / two loaves of	bread, meat, soap
덩어리(설탕)	a lump of / two lumps of	sugar
파운드(무게)	a pound of / two pounds of	sugar, meat, flour
조각/점	a piece of / two pieces of	furniture, information, advice, paper, bread, pizza, cheese * 추상명사는 piece와 함께 잘 쓰인다.
얇은 조각	a slice of / two slices of	bread, cheese, pizza, cake, meat
그릇	a bowl of / two bowls of	rice, soup, salad
숟가락	a spoonful of / two spoonfuls of	salt, sugar, vinegar, soy sauce
병	a bottle of / two bottles of	water, wine, beer, juice, milk

I ate **two slices of bread**. 나는 빵 두 조각을 먹었다.

Would you like to drink **a glass of juice**? 주스 한 잔 드시겠습니까?

She added **three spoonfuls of salt**. 그녀는 세 숟가락의 소금을 넣었다.

뽐쌤의
야무진
Tip!

짝을 이루는 명사

socks, shoes, gloves, glasses, scissors, jeans, pants 등과 같이 짝을 이루는 명사는 a pair of를 이용하여 센다.

I have a pair of scissors. 나는 가위를 가지고 있다.

I bought two pairs of shoes. 나는 신발 두 켤레를 샀다.

A. 다음 빈칸에 a few 또는 a little을 쓰시오.

1. I can speak English _____.

2. Jessica made _____ mistakes.

3. We had _____ snow last night.

4. I write _____ letters every week.

5. Please call again in _____ minutes.

6. I have _____ money. Let's have coffee.

B. 다음 괄호 안에서 어법에 맞는 것을 고르시오.

1. Do you want a (glass / loaf) of water?

2. Kelly drinks a (glass / piece) of milk every day.

3. Tim added a (spoonful / piece) of salt to his soup.

4. My mother needs two (piece / pieces) of cheese.

5. We had a (cup / pair) of tea.

6. I need a (lump / sheet) of paper for homework.

7. I will buy a (pair / pairs) of sports shoes.

8. Mr. Smith has four (cup / cups) of coffee.

9. She needs to buy two pairs of (glove / gloves).

10. She bought three (tons of coal / ton of coals).

C. 다음 빈칸을 알맞은 말을 쓰시오.

1. Do you want a _____ of pants?

2. I drink three _____ of cold milk a day.

3. It's a _____ of cake. (식은 죽 먹기-중요속담)

4. Julia bought a _____ of furniture yesterday.

5. Jim put two _____ of sugar to his tea.

5.4. 관사의 종류

1 부정관사 a와 an

》》 막연한 하나를 나타내며 셀 수 있는 명사가 단수일 때 그 앞에 쓰인다.

❶ a + 첫소리가 자음으로 발음되는 명사

a boy, a doll, a radio　* a university, a useful book, a uniform →[j]는 반자음이므로 자음으로 발음된다.

❷ an + 첫소리가 모음으로 발음되는 명사

an apple, an egg, an island, an orange　* an hour, an honest man → h는 묵음이므로 모음으로 발음된다.

〈부정 관사의 의미〉

수량 하나	I have **a banana** and **an apple**. 나는 바나나 한 개와 사과 한 개를 가지고 있다.
~마다(=per)	I call her once **a day**. 나는 그녀에게 하루에 한 번 전화한다.
대표단수(종족 대표)	**A horse** is a useful animal. 말은 유용한 동물이다.
같은(=the same)	We are of **an age**.(= We are of the same age.) 우리는 같은 나이이다.

2 정관사 the

앞에 나온 명사가 다시 반복될 때	I have a dog. **The dog** is brown. 나는 개 한 마리가 있다. 그 개는 갈색이다.
서로 이미 알고 있는 것을 가리킬 때	Open **the window**, please. 창문을 열어주세요.
수식을 받아 대상이 분명할 때	**The book** on the table is mine. 탁자 위에 있는 책은 내 것이다.
세상에서 유일한 것	Look at **the moon** in the sky. 하늘에 달을 보아라. ex) the White House, the Tames, the sun …
악기, 서수, 최상급, same, only 앞	I can't play **the violin**. 나는 바이올린 연주를 못한다. She is **the prettiest** in her class. 그녀는 반에서 가장 예쁘다.
종족 대표	**The horse** is a useful animal. 말은 유용한 동물이다. =A horse is a useful animal. = Horses are useful animals.
정관사를 붙이는 고유명사	❶ language가 뒤에 붙을 때 Korean 또는 the Korean language ❷ 「신문, 서적」 the New York Times, the Bible ❸ 「관공서, 공공건물」 the White House, the British Museum ❹ 「복수형 국가명」 the United States (of America), the Philippines ❺ 「강, 바다, 산맥」 the Han River, the Pacific ocean, the Alps

A. 다음 괄호 안에서 알맞은 것을 고르시오.

❶ I will become (a, an) pilot.

❷ Sue is (a, an) American girl from California.

❸ He may not be (a, an) honest man.

❹ My mother washes her car once (a, the) week.

❺ What time is (a, the) first train to Seoul?

❻ He likes swimming in (a, the) sea.

❼ Pass me (a, the) pepper, please.

❽ (A, The) moon moves around (a, the) earth.

❾ I always exercise in (a, the) evening.

❿ Tim has a dog, and (a, the) dog was sick last week.

⓫ Do you know (a, the) woman with long hair?

⓬ She teaches English at (a, an) university.

B. 다음 밑줄 친 부분을 올바르게 고치시오.

❶ A sun rises in the east.

❷ Joshua is reading book on the sofa.

❸ Nancy ate an apples every morning.

❹ My brother is good at playing cello.

❺ You are a handsome.

❻ Kate painted the wall with a Tim.

❼ Hyori played a piano on the stage.

❽ We will cross the bridge over Han River.

❾ I found a his ball under the chair.

❿ She reads a Bible every night.

⓫ The Jane is my best friend.

⓬ She has to take the medicine twice the day.

5.5. 관사의 생략

1 호격(부르는 말)

Boys, be ambitious. 소년들이여, 야망을 가져라.

2 식사명

We had **breakfast** at seven. 우리는 7시에 아침을 먹었다.

3 운동 경기 앞

We played **baseball** yesterday. 우리는 어제 야구를 했다.

cf. She was playing **the piano** then. 그녀는 그때 피아노를 연주하고 있었다.

4 관직이 보어나 동격으로 쓰일 때

We elected Mr. Kim **President** of Korea. 우리는 Mr. Kim을 한국의 대통령으로 선출했다.

Mr. Kim, **captain** of our team, is very brave. 우리 팀의 주장인 Mr. Kim은 매우 용감하다.

5 건물, 시설물 등이 본래의 목적으로 쓰일 때

They go to **school** on weekdays. 그들은 평일에 학교에 간다.

My parents go to **church** on Sundays. 나의 부모님들은 일요일마다 교회에 가신다.

* 본래의 목적이 아닌 다른 목적으로 쓰일 때는 관사를 붙인다.

I went to **the school** to meet my friend. 나는 친구를 만나러 학교에 갔다.

뽐쌤의 야무진 Tip!

그 밖에 관사를 쓰지 않는 경우

❶ 「by + 교통 수단」: by bus[train, car] 버스[기차, 자동차]로
I went to the store by bus. 나는 버스를 타고 그 가게에 갔다.

❷ 「by + 통신 수단」: by telephone[letter] 전화[편지]로
She will contact me by letter. 그녀는 나에게 편지로 연락할 것이다.

A. 다음 빈칸에 a나 an, the 중 알맞은 것을 쓰시오. 필요 없는 곳에는 x를 하시오.

① Can you close _____ door?

② _____ earth is round.

③ He comes to work by _____ bus.

④ Will you have _____ lunch with me?

⑤ Would you like _____ cup of tea?

⑥ We don't go to _____ school on Sundays.

⑦ I study English twice _____ week with Jane.

⑧ She is learning how to play _____ badminton.

⑨ I bought _____ notebook and three pencils.

⑩ Her house is on _____ 23rd floor.

⑪ It takes _____ hour and _____ half.

⑫ My favorite subject is _____ math.

⑬ Mary and I have _____ same skirt.

⑭ Practice is _____ only way for us.

⑮ Do you go to _____ church every Sunday?

5.6. There is / There are

1 의미 (~이 있다)

| There is + 단수명사 | There is <u>a doll</u> on the bed. 침대 위에 인형이 있다. |
| There are + 복수명사 | There are <u>many dolls</u> on the bed. 침대 위에 많은 인형이 있다. |

＊ There is + 셀 수 없는 명사: 셀 수 없는 명사는 단수 취급하여 There is를 쓴다.

There is some water in the bottle. 병 안에 약간의 물이 있다.

2 부정문 (~이 없다)

| There is not[isn't] ~ | **There isn't** <u>a ball</u> in the box. 상자 안에 공이 없다. |
| There are not[aren't] ~ | **There aren't** <u>birds</u> in the tree. 나무에 새들이 없다. |

3 의문문 (~이 있나요?)

| Is[Are] there ~?
−Yes, there is[are].
−No, there isn't[aren't]. | **Is there** <u>a cup</u> on the table? 탁자 위에 컵이 있나요?
-Yes, there is. 네, 있습니다.
-No, there isn't. 아니요, 없습니다. |

뽐쌤의
야무진
Tip!

❶ Here is/are: 여기에 ~있다

There is[are] ~와 비슷하게 Here is[are]도 사용할 수 있다.
Here is a book. 여기 책이 있다.
Here you are. 여기 있어. (물건을 건넬 때)
Here we are. 다 왔어. (장소에 도착했을 때)

❷ there의 다른 의미

❶ 형식상의 주어 there: 특별한 의미는 없고, 문장을 이끄는 역할을 한다.
There is a dog in the room. 방에 개가 한 마리 있다.
❷ 장소의 there: '거기에'란 뜻의 부사
They go there every night. 그들은 그곳에 매일 밤 간다.

A. 다음 괄호 안에서 알맞은 것을 고르시오.

① There (is, are) a giraffe in the zoo.

② There (is, are) a lot of books in the library.

③ (Is, Are) there many benches in the park?

④ There (is, are) a boy in front of the school gate.

⑤ There (is, are) a hat on the shelf.

⑥ There (is, are) visitors in the lobby.

B. 다음 문장에서 어법상 어색한 부분을 찾아 바르게 고치시오.

① There is only four passengers in the express bus.

② Are there any juice in the glass?

③ Is there flowers in the vase?

④ There is many foreigners in Seoul.

⑤ There are a problem with her washing machine.

⑥ There is many gyms and a lot of parks in this town.

C. 다음 문장을 괄호 안에 지시대로 바꾸어 쓰시오.

① There is a cat on the table. (부정문으로)

➡ _____

② There is a bag next to the bed. (의문문으로)

➡ _____

③ There are oranges in the refrigerator. (의문문으로)

➡ _____

④ There was a house in the woods. (부정문으로)

➡ _____

⑤ There are three cups on the table. (의문문으로)

➡ _____

1. 다음 중 명사의 복수형이 <u>잘못된</u> 것은?

① dog – dogs
② bus – buses
③ child – children
④ life – lives
⑤ baby – babys

2. 다음 중 빈칸에 a나 an을 쓸 수 <u>없는</u> 것은?

① This is _____ album.
② That is _____ pencil.
③ It's _____ apple.
④ Tom is _____ student.
⑤ Mr. Kim is _____ my teacher.

3. 다음 빈칸에 알맞은 것은?

I have a dog. _____ dog is very cute.

① A
② An
③ The
④ Three
⑤ One

4. 다음 빈칸에 알맞은 말을 쓰시오.

Sam is _____ engineer.

5. 다음 빈칸에 알맞지 <u>않은</u> 것은?

There are _____ in the room.

① a TV set
② two chairs
③ some books
④ a few boys
⑤ lots of balls

6. 다음 중 어법상 옳지 <u>않은</u> 것은?

① a glass of coffee
② a glass of juice
③ a cup of tea
④ a slice of cheese
⑤ a glass of water

7. 다음 빈칸에 알맞지 <u>않은</u> 것은?

I have three _____.

① milk
② pencils
③ books
④ friends
⑤ children

8. 다음 중 어법상 옳은 것은?

① five cups of coffee
② two glass of milks
③ three pair of shoes
④ a pieces of pizza
⑤ ten slice of cheeses

[9–10] 다음 대화의 빈칸에 알맞은 것은?

9.

A: Is there a watch on the desk?
B: _____ It's in the box.

① Yes, it is.
② Yes, there is.
③ No, it isn't.
④ No, there aren't.
⑤ No, there isn't.

10.

A: Are there laptops on the table?
B: Yes, _____.

① I have
② there are
③ there is
④ it is
⑤ she is

1. 다음 중 밑줄 친 부분의 쓰임이 나머지와 <u>다른</u> 것은?

① <u>There</u> are many people in the park.
② We can see many flowers <u>there</u>.
③ Are <u>there</u> any boys in the room?
④ Is <u>there</u> a map in your living room?
⑤ <u>There</u> is a dog on the floor.

2. 다음 중 어법상 옳은 것은?

① There is many books in this room.
② There is some money on the table.
③ There is four seasons in Korea.
④ There is ticket machines in the stations.
⑤ Is there any famous places in your country?

3. 다음 보기 에서 어법상 맞는 것의 개수는?

보기

- I like to count animals at night! One Ⓐ sheep, two Ⓑsheep!
- I lost one Ⓒteeth, but you lost many Ⓓ tooth.
- My cat ate a Ⓔmouse, but your cat ate many Ⓕmice.
- I will make one egg Ⓖsandwich and three cheese Ⓗsandwiches.
- One ⒾJapanese is walking, but two Ⓙ Japanese are running.
- We heard stories about the big Ⓚwolf. But Ⓛwolves were not really big.

① 2개   ② 3개   ③ 4개
④ 8개   ⑤ 10개

4. 다음 중 명사의 복수형이 <u>잘못된</u> 것은?

① She washes the <u>dishes</u>.
② I sometimes fight bad <u>people</u> in my dreams.
③ We play <u>games</u> together in the evening.
④ Do you do any special family <u>activityes</u>?
⑤ Sometimes I see <u>fireflies</u>!

5. 다음 중 빈칸에 a가 들어갈 수 <u>없는</u> 것은?

① My mother has _____ beautiful handbag.
② There is _____ pencil case on the desk.
③ We have _____ audio in our room.
④ She is _____ nurse.
⑤ He doesn't have _____ laptop computer.

6. 다음 중 셀 수 없는 명사의 단위가 알맞지 <u>않은</u> 것은?

① I want to drink a glass of water.
② Tom is looking for a loaf of paper.
③ He gave me a cup of coffee.
④ Sally ate a piece of cheese this morning.
⑤ You need to add a spoonful of sugar.

7. 다음 중 어법상 <u>어색한</u> 부분을 고치시오.

❶ My sister wears an uniform.
❷ Jim goes to school by a bus.
❸ I have the dinner with my best friends.

8. 다음 우리말을 영어로 바르게 옮긴 것은?

> 수영장에 많은 사람들이 있다.

① There is many people in the pool.
② There is some people in the pool.
③ There are many people in the pool.
④ There is a lot of people in the pool.
⑤ There aren't many people in the pool.

9. 다음 중 밑줄 친 부분이 옳은 것은?

① <u>Sheeps</u> give us wool.
② Those <u>boxs</u> are very heavy.
③ Los Angeles is a busy <u>cities</u>.
④ I want three <u>bottle</u> of waters.
⑤ You should brush your <u>teeth</u>.

10. 다음 중 빈칸에 the가 필요한 것은?

① I can play _____ basketball.
② Sumi plays _____ violin.
③ She doesn't like to play _____ tennis.
④ He plays _____ soccer with his friends.
⑤ They play _____ baseball after school.

11. 다음 빈칸에 공통으로 들어갈 단어를 쓰시오.

> - This is a dog. _____ dog is so cute.
> - _____ moon is bright at night.
> - _____ book on the table is mine.

12. 다음 중 빈칸에 들어갈 be동사가 나머지와 <u>다른</u> 것은?

① There _____ some milk in the glass.
② There _____ some toys in the box.
③ There _____ three pencils on the desk.
④ There _____ many candies in the basket.
⑤ There _____ two computers in his room.

13. 다음 중 어법상 옳은 것은?

① They need five pieces of papers.
② We drank four cups of coffees.
③ I want three bottles of juice.
④ I had two piece of pizzas for lunch.
⑤ Will you bring me a glass of waters?

14. 다음 빈칸에 알맞지 <u>않은</u> 것은?

> There are _____ in the park.

① lots of trees　　② a fountain
③ many benches　　④ two playgrounds
⑤ many children

15. 다음 그림을 보고, 빈칸에 알맞은 말을 쓰시오.

❶ A: Is there a cell phone on the chair?

　B: _____ , _____ _____ .

❷ A: Are there any cups on the desk?

　B: _____ , _____ _____ .

16. 다음 중 I로 알맞은 것은?

> - I am a girl.
> - I am a student.
> - I am from Korea.

① 　②

③ 　④

⑤

17. 다음 중 주어진 그림을 알맞게 설명한 것은?

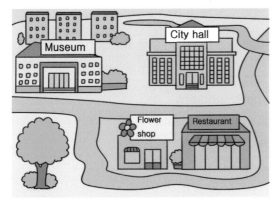

① There are some people in the picture.
② There is a city hall behind the trees.
③ There are museums in the picture.
④ There is a clock tower in front of the museum.
⑤ There is a flower shop next to the restaurant.

18. 다음 중 밑줄 친 부분이 잘못된 것은?

① I play the guitar.
② The earth is round.
③ The dog is smart.
④ Open the door, please.
⑤ We have the lunch at noon.

19. 다음 중 주어진 그림을 알맞게 설명한 것은?

① There are two dogs in the box.
② There is a dish under the table.
③ There is a cup next to the table.
④ There are three cookies in the box.
⑤ There are two books under the table.

20. 다음 문장에서 틀린 곳을 찾아 바르게 고치시오.

> Tony drinks three glass of milk a day.

21. 다음 중 빈칸에 many가 들어갈 수 없는 것은?

① I read _____ comic books.
② She has _____ friends in England.
③ Yuna has _____ CDs in her room.
④ My uncle buys _____ cute dolls.
⑤ My father eats _____ meat.

1. 다음 글의 밑줄 친 부분 중 어법상 적절한 것의 개수는?

I have old <u>photos</u> here. There are some <u>Japanese</u> around a table. Five <u>womans</u>, three boys, and two <u>babyes</u> are eating <u>sandwiches</u>. Some of them are using <u>knifes</u>. Their <u>tooth</u> are very white.

① 2개   ② 3개   ③ 4개
④ 5개   ⑤ 6개

2. 다음 중 밑줄 친 부분의 쓰임이 나머지와 <u>다른</u> 것은?

① I go <u>there</u> on Christmas.
② <u>There</u> are many cars in New York.
③ Is <u>there</u> a pencil on the desk?
④ <u>There</u> is a book under the chair.
⑤ Are <u>there</u> many people in the zoo?

3. 다음 질문에 대한 대답으로 알맞지 <u>않은</u> 것은?

A: Is there anything on the table?
B: _____

① Yes, my cup is there.
② Yes, your book is on it.
③ No, there is nothing there.
④ Yes, the cat is playing there.
⑤ Yes, I am going to sleep there.

4. 다음 빈칸에 순서대로 알맞은 것은?

This is _____ album. It is my _____ first album. I like looking over _____ album in my free time.

① the – X – the   ② an – the – X
③ an – X – the   ④ an – the – the
⑤ the – the – X

5. 다음 중 보기의 밑줄 친 부분과 쓰임이 가장 같은 것은?

보기 Practice English for an hour <u>a</u> day.

① Here's <u>a</u> list.
② I have <u>a</u> little brother.
③ I want to meet <u>a</u> kind teacher.
④ I go to the library once <u>a</u> week.
⑤ I'm feeling <u>a</u> little under the weather.

6. 다음 빈칸에 알맞지 <u>않은</u> 것은?

There are _____ in the shopping mall.

① lots of shoppers
② many workers
③ a few restaurants
④ a huge toy store
⑤ a lot of clothes stores

7. 다음 중 어법상 옳지 <u>않은</u> 것은?

① I drink a cup of tea every morning.
② She buys a glass of milk at lunch.
③ I want three slices of cheese.
④ He drinks eight glasses of water a day.
⑤ Give me two peices of cakes, please.

8. 다음 중 밑줄 친 곳에 a 또는 an이 들어갈 수 있는 것의 개수는?

(가) Can I have ⓐ_____ biscuits and ⓑ _____ cups of milk, please?

(나) I'd like ⓒ_____ sausages and ⓓ_____ eggs, please.

(다) The are 352 calories in ⓔ_____ cheese and ham sandwich.

(라) I want to buy ⓕ_____ cups of coffee and ⓖ_____ bottles of coke.

(마) How do you like your tea? I need to add ⓗ_____ cream.

(바) I'd like ⓘ_____ hamburgers, ⓙ_____ apple pie and ⓚ_____ green salad.

(사) How ⓛ_____ sugar do you have in your coffee?

(아) Would you like ⓜ_____ strawberries or ⓝ_____ grapes?

(자) I want ⓞ_____ jam and ⓟ_____ butter for my toast, please.

① 2개   ② 3개   ③ 4개
④ 5개   ⑤ 6개

9. 다음 중 빈칸에 부정관사 an이 올 수 있는 것은?

① Do you play _____ piano well?
② I want _____ pie for lunch.
③ A dog is _____ royal animal.
④ They buy _____ apples and tomatoes.
⑤ I study social science for _____ hour at night.

10. 다음 보기 에서 어법상 옳은 문장끼리 묶인 것은?

보기
ⓐ She teaches a math to us.
ⓑ I'll buy you some snacks.
ⓒ I'll make three sandwichs.
ⓓ He will give a gift to me.
ⓔ She feels happily these days.
ⓕ I have two dogs and three cat.
ⓖ My uncle will give me his camera.
ⓗ I had 2 pieces of pizza for lunch.

① ⓐ, ⓒ, ⓖ   ② ⓑ, ⓓ, ⓖ, ⓗ
③ ⓓ, ⓖ, ⓗ   ④ ⓔ, ⓕ, ⓖ, ⓗ
⑤ ⓒ, ⓓ, ⓖ, ⓗ

11. 다음 중 빈칸에 들어갈 관사가 나머지와 <u>다른</u> 하나는?

① Suji plays _____ guitar well.
② Please pass me _____ pepper, Dad.
③ _____ water in this bottle is dirty.
④ Brad Bitt is _____ famous actor in the world.
⑤ _____ moon shines brightly at night.

12. 다음 우리말과 뜻이 같도록 빈칸에 알맞은 말을 쓰시오.

❶ 나의 엄마는 아침에 물을 많이 마신다.
⇒ My mom drinks _____ _____ in the morning.

❷ 그들은 매일 자전거를 타고 학교에 간다.
⇒ They go to school _____ _____ every day.

1. 다음 주어진 단어를 사용하여 우리말 뜻에 맞게 영어 문장을 완성하시오.

❶ 내 방에는 커다란 침대 하나가 있다.

(there, big, is, a, in, bed, my room)

⇒ _____

❷ 이 나라에는 많은 산들이 있다.

(in, there, many, are, this country, mountains)

⇒ _____

❸ 그 밥에는 콩이 많이 들어있다.

(in, the rice, beans, there, are, many)

⇒ _____

❹ 탁자 위에는 작은 분홍색 꽃병이 있다.

(vase, there, is, small, the table, on, a, pink)

⇒ _____

❺ 그녀는 일주일에 네 번 운동을 한다.

(four, exercise, week, she, a, times)

⇒ _____

2. 다음 그림을 보고 질문에 알맞은 답을 쓰시오.

❶ A: How many books are there on the table?

B: _____ _____ _____ _____. (4단어)

❷ A: Is there an apple on the book?

B: _____, _____ _____. (3단어)

3. 다음 문장들의 어색한 부분을 바르게 고치시오.

❶ He is a English teacher.

❷ There are seven days in week.

❸ That is a old book.

❹ She has a nice friend. A friend is Korean.

❺ The sun is larger than a moon.

4. 다음 대화에서 밑줄 친 우리말을 4단어의 영어로 쓰시오.

A: How often do you cook?
B: 일주일에 세 번.

5. 다음 주어진 그림을 묘사하는 문장을 조건에 맞게 2개 쓰시오.

조건

- 각 문장은 There is ~ 또는 There are ~로 시작할 것
- 각 문장에 in / on / next to / behind / in front of / under 중 하나는 반드시 넣되, 문장당 한 번만 쓸 것

❶ _____

❷ _____

Chapter 6
대명사

6.1. 지시대명사

))) 지시대명사란? 특정한 사람이나 사물을 가리키는 말이다.

1 this / these

))) '이것' / '이것들'이라는 뜻으로, 말하는 이와 가까이에 있는 대상을 가리킨다. this는 단수이며, these는 복수이다.

This is my bag. 이것은 나의 가방이다.

These are my pencils. 이것들은 나의 연필들이다.

2 that / those

))) '저것' / '저것들'이라는 뜻으로, 말하는 이와 멀리 있는 대상을 가리킨다. that은 단수이며, those는 복수이다.

That is my watch. 저것은 나의 시계이다.

Those are my rings. 저것들은 나의 반지들이다.

3 지시대명사의 의문문

))) this나 that으로 물으면 it, these나 those로 물으면 they로 대답한다.

Is **that** your bag? –Yes, **it** is. / No, **it** isn't. 저것은 네 가방이니? -응, 내 거야. / 아니, 내 것이 아니야.

Are **these** your bags? –Yes, **they** are. / No, **they** aren't. 이것들은 네 가방이니? -응, 내 거야. / 아니, 내 것이 아니야.

뿜쌤의 야무진 Tip!

❶ this/these와 that/those의 품사 변화!

this/these와 that/those는 형용사로 사용되어 명사를 앞에서 꾸며주기도 한다.

This book is so interesting. 이 책은 아주 흥미롭다.

Those shoes are mine. 저 신발은 나의 것이다.

❷ this의 다양한 쓰임

❶ 누군가를 소개할 때

Suji, **this** is my friend, John. 수지, 이 사람은 나의 친구인 John이야.

❷ 전화상에서 전화를 건 사람과 받는 사람을 가리킬 때

Hello, **this** is Sue. Who is **this**? 여보세요, 저는 Sue인데 누구시죠?

A. 다음 우리말과 뜻이 같도록 빈칸에 알맞은 말을 쓰시오.

① 저것들은 나의 개와 고양이다.

➡ _____ are my dogs and cats.

② 여보세요, 저는 수지인데요. Brown 씨 있나요?

➡ Hello, _____ is Suji. Is Mr. Brown there?

③ 저것은 그녀의 사진이니?

➡ _____ _____ her picture?

④ 이것은 당신의 책인가요?

➡ _____ _____ your book?

⑤ 저것들은 아름다운 꽃들이야!

➡ _____ _____ beautiful flowers!

⑥ 저 분들은 Tim의 고모들이다.

➡ _____ _____ Tim's aunts.

⑦ 이 사람은 나의 친구, Junsu야.

➡ _____ _____ my friend, Junsu.

⑧ 이것들은 너의 신발들이니?

➡ _____ _____ your shoes?

⑨ 저것들은 낯선 동물들이구나.

➡ _____ _____ strange animals.

B. 다음 빈칸에 알맞은 지시대명사를 쓰시오.

① A: Is this your ticket?   B: Yes, _____ is.

② A: Who are these little boys?   B: _____ are my brothers.

③ A: Is that John's dog?   B: No, _____ isn't.

④ A: Are those your shorts?   B: No, _____ aren't.

6.2. 부정대명사 (1)

>>> 부정대명사란? 범위가 정해지지 않은 막연한 사람이나 사물을 가리키는 말이다.

Do you have a pen? –Yes, I have **one**. 너 펜 있니? -응, 한 개 있어.

I don't have **any** free time. 나는 자유 시간이 전혀 없다.

1 one

❶ 앞에 언급된 명사와 같은 종류의 불특정한 사람이나 사물을 가리킬 때

(하나인 경우는 one, 두 개 이상인 경우는 ones를 쓴다.)

I lost my wallet. I need to buy **one**. (one = a wallet) 나는 지갑을 잃어버렸다. 나는 하나 살 필요가 있다.

He bought red shoes and I bought blue **ones**. (ones = shoes)

John은 빨간 신발을 샀고 나는 파란 신발을 샀다.

❷ 일반적인 사람을 가리킬 때

One should keep the rules. 사람들은 규칙을 지켜야 한다.

* One은 특정인이 아닌 일반적인 사람을 뜻하기 때문에, '사람들은 규칙을 지켜야 한다.'로 해석된다.

뽐쌤의
야무진
Tip!

one vs it

one이 불특정한 대상을 가리킨다면 it은 앞에 나온 특정 대상을 가리킬 때 사용한다.

I don't have a cellphone. I'll buy one. (one=cellphone)
나는 휴대폰이 없다. 나는 하나 살 것이다.

Where is my cellphone? –It's on the table. (It=the cellphone)
내 휴대폰이 어디에 있지? 그건 탁자 위에 있어.

2 some, any

>>> '다소, 약간의, 얼마간'이라는 의미로 대명사 또는 형용사로 쓰인다.

❶ some

긍정의 평서문, 권유의 뜻을 나타내는 의문문에서 사용된다.

There are **some** apples on the table. 탁자 위에 약간의 사과들이 있다.

Will you have **some** tea? –No, thanks. I already had **some**.

차를 좀 드시겠어요? -아니요, 괜찮습니다. 이미 좀 마셨습니다.

❷ any

부정문, 의문문, 조건문에서 사용된다.

Do you have **any** questions? –No, I don't have **any** (questions). 질문이 있습니까? -아니요, 없습니다.

A. 다음 빈칸에 one, ones 또는 it을 적절하게 쓰시오.

❶ My shoes are old. I need new _____.

❷ I make a doll and give _____ to her.

❸ Suji wears a pink skirt, but a yellow _____ is her favorite.

❹ I love San Francisco. _____ is a very beautiful city.

❺ I like the bag. Please buy _____ for me.

B. 다음 대화의 빈칸에 one 또는 ones를 써 넣으시오.

❶ A: Do you have a pet?   B: Yes, I have _____.

❷ A: Which are Ted's shoes?   B: The green _____.

❸ A: May I borrow your pen?   B: Sure. You can take _____.

❹ A: Would you like some cookies? B: Yes. I'll have blueberry _____.

❺ A: Do you live in hanok?   B: Yes, but it's small _____.

C. 다음 괄호 안에서 알맞은 것을 고르시오.

❶ I need an eraser. Do you have (it / one)?

❷ (One / Ones) should keep promises.

❸ Don't throw the paper away. We can use (it / one) again.

❹ I don't like red roses. I will buy yellow (them / ones).

❺ I live in Osaka. (It / One) is a big city.

D. 다음 빈칸에 some과 any 중 알맞은 것을 쓰시오.

❶ We are having cookies. Would you like _____?

❷ I cannot find _____ of them.

❸ Jenny doesn't have _____ brothers.

❹ _____ of them are teenagers.

❺ I don't want _____ of these books.

6.3. 부정대명사 (2)

>>> 일부를 뺀 나머지를 말할 때는 another, others, the other(s)을 사용할 수 있다. 특정한 것을 가리킬 때 the를 붙인다.

1 another

>>> 「an + other」로, '또 다른 하나'를 의미한다.
I don't like this skirt. Can you show me **another?** 이 셔츠는 맘에 안 들어요. 저에게 또 다른 것을 보여줄래요?

2 one ~, the other …

>>> '(둘 중에서) 하나는 ~, 다른 하나는 …'
He has two bags. **One** is red, and **the other** is blue. 그는 두 개의 가방을 가지고 있다. 한 개는 빨간색, 다른 한 개는 파란색이다.

3 one ~, another …, the other …

>>> '(셋 중에서) 하나는 ~, 다른 하나는 …, 나머지 하나는 …'
He has three bags. **One** is red, **another** is blue, and **the other** is yellow. 그는 세 개의 가방을 가지고 있다. 한 개는 빨간색, 다른 한 개는 파란색, 나머지 한 개는 노란색이다.

4 one ~, the others …

>>> '(셋 이상에서) 하나는 ~, 나머지는 …'
He has seven bags. **One** is red, **the others** are pink. 그는 7개의 가방을 가지고 있다. 한 개는 빨간색, 나머지는 분홍색이다.

5 some ~, others …

>>> '(셋 이상에서) 몇몇은 ~, 다른 사람[것]들은[나머지 일부는] …'
Some students like math. **Others** like English. 몇몇 학생들은 수학을 좋아한다. 다른 학생들은 영어를 좋아한다.

6 some ~, the others …

>>> '(셋 이상에서) 몇몇은 ~, 다른 사람[것]들은[나머지 전부는] …'
Some students like math. **The others** like English. 몇몇 학생들은 수학을 좋아한다. 나머지 학생들은 영어를 좋아한다.

A. 다음 괄호 안에서 알맞은 것을 고르시오.

① There are two cupcakes. One is mine and (other, the other) is my sister's.

② Mr. Johnson wants to read (another, other) book.

③ I have four skirts. (One, the one) is short, and the others are long.

④ Some of the dresses are clean, but (other, the others) are not.

⑤ I'm tired of my job. I'm going to look for (other, another) job soon.

⑥ I have two bags. One is big, and (the other, other) bag is small.

⑦ There are three dogs. One is brown, (other, another) is white, and (other, the other) is black.

⑧ They did well in some courses, but they didn't do well in (other, others) courses.

⑨ Some people are honest, but (other, others) are dishonest.

⑩ I've finished this book. Can I borrow (another, ones)?

B. 다음 보기 에서 알맞은 말을 골라 빈칸에 써 넣어 문장을 완성하시오.

보기 one   the other   the others   another

① The cup is too dirty. Give me a clean _____.

② I don't like this bag. Can you show me _____?

③ I like two colors. _____ is pink, and _____ is blue.

④ We got three gifts. _____ is for Dad, _____ is for Mom and _____ is for my sister.

⑤ There are many tomatoes in the box. One is fresh, and _____ are bad.

⑥ I bought two kinds of cake. One is chocolate cake, and _____ is blueberry cake.

⑦ There are three cups. One is red and _____ are white.

⑧ I have two sisters. _____ is 8 years old and the other is 10 years old.

⑨ There are ten students in the class. _____ is a boy, and _____ are girls.

⑩ One of the two children sings well, and _____ doesn't.

6.4. 비인칭 주어 it

>>> 비인칭 주어 it은 시간, 날짜, 요일, 계절, 날씨, 거리, 명암을 나타내는 문장의 주어로 사용되며, '그것'이라고 해석하지 않는다.

❶ 시간

What time is it? –It's seven o'clock. 몇 시야? -7시야.

❷ 날짜

What date is it today? –It's June 21st. 오늘 며칠이야? -6월 21일이야.

❸ 요일

What day is it today? –It's Friday. 오늘 무슨 요일이야? -금요일이야.

❹ 계절

It's summer. 여름이다.

❺ 날씨

It's hot and humid. 덥고 습하다.

❻ 거리

How far is it from here to the station? –It is about 2 miles.
여기에서 그 역까지 얼마나 멀어? -약 2마일이야.

❼ 명암

It's getting dark. 어두워지고 있다.

뽐쌤의
야무진
Tip!

비인칭 주어 it vs 대명사 it

비인칭 주어 it은 해석을 따로 하지 않는다.
It's rainy today. 그것은 오늘 비가 온다. (X) → 오늘 비가 온다.

대명사 it은 '그것'이라고 해석한다.
There is a bag on the table. It's mine. (It=the bag)
탁자 위에 가방이 있다. 그것은 내 것이다.

A. 다음 문장의 밑줄 친 it의 용법이 '비인칭 주어'이면 (비), '대명사'이면 (대)를 쓰시오

   ① What does <u>it</u> mean?

   ② <u>It</u>'s sunny and clear.

   ③ <u>It</u> is September 18th.

   ④ <u>It</u>'s between the flower shop and the bank.

   ⑤ What time is <u>it</u>?

   ⑥ What a pretty doll <u>it</u> is!

   ⑦ <u>It</u> is seven thirty.

   ⑧ <u>It</u>'s Saturday.

   ⑨ <u>It</u> helps me keep my health.

   ⑩ <u>It</u> rains a lot in summer.

   ⑪ I like <u>it</u> very much.

   ⑫ How far is <u>it</u>?

   ⑬ <u>It</u>'s very dark outside.

   ⑭ <u>It</u> was a cold winter day.

   ⑮ <u>It</u> takes five minutes on foot.

B. 다음 빈칸에 it을 쓸 수 있으면 쓰고, 없으면 x를 쓰시오.

   ① My grandfather has an old watch, and I have a new _____.

   ② That is Tommy's shirt. _____ is his new uniform.

   ③ A: How's the weather in winter?

      B: _____ is very cold.

   ④ _____ is summer in Korea now.

   ⑤ Jisu has a blue hairpin and I like _____ very much.

6.5. 재귀대명사

>>> 재귀대명사란? 인칭대명사의 소유격 또는 목적격에 −self/−selves가 붙어 '…자신'이란 뜻이 되는 대명사이다. 동사나 전치사의 목적어로 사용되어 주어의 동작이 주어 자신에게 돌아옴을 나타내거나, 주어의 행위를 강조하기도 한다.

인칭	단수	복수
1인칭	myself	ourselves
2인칭	yourself	yourselves
3인칭	himself/herself/itself	themselves

1 재귀용법

>>> 주어의 행동이 스스로에게 미칠 때 (생략불가)

❶ 동사의 목적어: 「동사 + 재귀대명사」

They call **themselves** heroes. 그들은 자신들을 영웅이라고 부른다.

She introduced **herself** to me. 그녀는 나에게 자신을 소개시켜 주었다.

❷ 전치사의 목적어: 「전치사 + 재귀대명사」

Take care of **yourself**. 네 자신을 돌보아라.

She made a promise to **herself**. 그녀는 스스로에게 약속을 했다.

2 강조용법

>>> '직접, 스스로'라는 뜻으로 주어의 행동을 강조할 때 (생략가능)

* 강조용법의 재귀대명사는 강조하고자 하는 말의 바로 뒤, 혹은 문장의 맨 뒤에 쓴다. 강조용법의 재귀대명사는 주어 외에 목적어나 보어도 강조하여 사용할 수 있다.

She **(herself)** made it. = She made it **(herself)**. 그녀는 스스로 그것을 만들었다.

I **(myself)** am a famous singer. 나 자신은 유명한 가수이다.

뽐쌤의
야무진
Tip!

다양한 관용표현

help oneself 마음껏 먹다	enjoy oneself 즐기다	for oneself 혼자 힘으로, 스스로
introduce oneself 자기 소개하다	in itself 본래	by oneself 홀로(oneself)
kill oneself 자살하다	of itself 저절로	

A. 다음 괄호 안에서 알맞은 것을 고르시오.

① Sometimes Suji talks to (myself, herself).

② She was angry at (herself, myself).

③ Let me introduce (myself, ourselves).

④ Jack thought to (herself, himself).

⑤ A lot of people know about (itself, themselves).

⑥ Many people enjoyed (yourselves, themselves) at the party.

⑦ I feel proud of (me, myself).

⑧ We (ourselves, themselves) got very exhausted.

⑨ The weather (it, itself) doesn't matter.

⑩ Mina (her, herself) wrote a letter to me.

⑪ I think of (me, myself) as a positive person.

⑫ My father made this food (him, himself).

B. 다음 보기 에서 알맞은 말을 골라 재귀대명사를 이용하여 문장을 완성하시오.

보기 wash   be proud of   grow   close

① Jonathan and I don't buy carrots. We _____ _____ _____.

② The wind was strong. The window _____ by _____.

③ Susan broke her leg. So she cannot _____ _____.

④ Don't be shy. You should _____ _____ _____ _____.

C. 다음 밑줄 친 재귀대명사가 재귀용법이면 (재), 강조용법이면 (강)이라고 쓰시오.

① She was there <u>herself</u>.

② I <u>myself</u> like your sister.

③ We should look after <u>ourselves</u>.

④ She loves <u>herself</u> too much.

1. 다음 대화의 빈칸에 우리말에 맞게 알맞은 것은?

> (Phone rings.)
> John: Hi, Mina. _____ John. (나는 John 야.)
> Mina: Hi, John.
> John: It's raining in Busan. How's the weather in Osaka?
> Mina: Oh, it's warm and sunny. I'm taking a walk now.

① This is   ② They are   ③ She is
④ He is   ⑤ It is

2. 다음 우리말을 영어로 바르게 옮긴 것은?

> Oh, no. 9시 30분이네. I'm late.

① It's 9:30.
② This is 9:30.
③ That is 9:30.
④ You are 9:30.
⑤ They are 9:30.

3. 다음 재귀대명사 표를 완성하시오.

단수	재귀대명사	복수	재귀대명사
1인칭		1인칭	
2인칭		2인칭	
3인칭		3인칭	

[4-5] 다음 중 밑줄 친 It의 의미가 나머지와 다른 것은?

4.

① It's cool today.
② It's nine ten.
③ It's mine.
④ It's October 7.
⑤ It's Sunday.

5.

① It's summer.
② It's 10 o'clock.
③ It's two kilometers.
④ It's a bag.
⑤ It's 32 degrees.

6. 다음 빈칸에 알맞은 재귀대명사를 쓰시오.

❶ She loves _____ so much.
❷ They are very proud of _____.

7. 다음 빈칸에 알맞은 것은?

> I have two sisters. One is talkative, but _____ is very quiet.

① other   ② other   ③ another
④ the other   ⑤ the others

8. 다음 중 어법상 어색한 것은?

① This is my backpacks.
② That is her watch.
③ It is July first.
④ It is too lighter here.
⑤ These are my brother's.

9.

A: What's the date?

B: _____ is October second.

① That   ② This   ③ It

④ Those   ⑤ There

10.

A: Are those your pants?

B: Yes, _____.

① it is   ② those are

③ there are   ④ they are

⑤ these are

단원평가   실전대비

1. 다음 글의 빈칸 ⓐ, ⓑ에 순서대로 알맞은 것은?

You have three flowers. ⓐ(   ) of them is pink, and ⓑ(   ) are white.

	ⓐ	ⓑ
①	One	the other
②	Two	the others
③	Some	others
④	One	the others
⑤	Two	others

2. 다음 중 밑줄 친 It의 쓰임이 나머지와 <u>다른</u> 것은?

① <u>It</u>'s 10:00.

② <u>It</u>'s not yours.

③ <u>It</u>'s Friday.

④ <u>It</u>'s going dark outside.

⑤ <u>It</u>'s windy today, isn't it?

[3-5] 다음 빈칸에 알맞은 것은?

3.

She decided to live by _____ in the country.

① her   ② hers   ③ herself

④ she   ⑤ herselves

4.

They enjoyed _____ a lot at the party.

① theyself   ② theirselves

③ themselves   ④ themself

⑤ himself

5.

I help my grandparents a lot. I feel proud of _____.

① myself   ② herself   ③ himself

④ yourself   ⑤ ourselves

6. 다음 중 빈칸에 it[It]이 들어갈 수 없는 것은?

① What time is _____?
② Where is my pen? Did you see _____?
③ Look at the dog. _____ is really cute.
④ I don't have a pen. Do you have _____?
⑤ I like this book. _____ is very funny.

7. 다음 우리말을 영어로 바르게 옮긴 것은?

> I don't like this skirt. 다른 것을 보여주세요.

① Show me one.
② Show me some.
③ Show me any.
④ Show me another.
⑤ Show me the other.

8. 다음 빈칸에 들어갈 알맞은 말로 짝지어진 것은?

> My teacher has three sons. _____ is an elementary school student, and _____ are middle school students.

① It – one   ② One – the other
③ One – the others ④ One – it
⑤ The other – one

9. 다음 대화의 ⓐ가 의미하는 것은?

> A: Do you want a green tie or a red tie? I don't like the green ⓐone.
> B: I don't know about the color.

① tie   ② bag   ③ book
④ color   ⑤ school

10. 다음 우리말과 뜻이 같도록 빈칸에 알맞은 것은?

> 그녀는 잠시 혼잣말로 중얼거렸다.
> ⇒ She said to _____ for a moment.

① her   ② herself   ③ oneself
④ them   ⑤ themselves

11. 다음 문장의 주어를 복수형으로 바꾸어 빈칸을 채우시오.

> This is a computer.
> ⇒ _____ _____ computers.

12. 다음 중 밑줄 친 부분의 쓰임이 나머지와 다른 것은?

① He himself cooked it.
② You must make it yourself.
③ I myself finished the project.
④ She did her homework herself.
⑤ They are talking about themselves.

13. 다음 밑줄 친 it이 비인칭 주어로 쓰였으면 '비', 지시대명사로 쓰였으며 '지'라고 쓰시오.

❶ It's Christmas today. ( )
❷ It is windy and cold outside. ( )
❸ Is it too big for me? ( )

14. 다음 대화의 빈칸에 알맞은 것은?

> A: Is this your bike?
> B: _____ It's my sister's.

① Yes, it is.　　② No, it isn't.
③ Yes, they are.　④ No, they aren't.
⑤ No, this isn't.

15. 다음 중 어법상 옳은 것은?

① The other are yours.
② There is chilly in autumn.
③ This babies are cute.
④ These cookies is very delicious.
⑤ You should know about yourself.

16. 다음 대화의 밑줄 친 부분과 바꿔 쓸 수 있는 것은?

> A: I'm looking for a clock.
> B: What type of clock do you want?
> A: I want a yellow, round clock.

① it　　　② one　　　③ ones
④ some　　⑤ any

17. 다음 중 밑줄 친 부분이 잘못된 것은?

① It's not very cold today.
② Let me introduce me to you.
③ I don't have a dog, but he has one.
④ I ride my new bike. I like it very much.
⑤ How far is it from here to there?

18. 다음 중 밑줄 친 부분을 생략할 수 있는 것은?

① I love myself.
② She finishes her homework by herself.
③ My brother himself cleans his room.
④ We enjoyed ourselves at the park.
⑤ My mother often talks to herself.

19. 다음 빈칸에 알맞은 대명사를 쓰시오.

> I have two aunts. _____ is a doctor, and
> _____ is a fashion designer.

20. 다음 대화의 밑줄 친 it과 쓰임이 같은 것은?

> A: Do you have my pen?
> B: Yes, I have it.

① It's my sister's.
② It's four forty-five.
③ It's foggy in London.
④ Is it dark there?
⑤ How far is it to the next station?

21. 다음 중 우리말을 영어로 잘못 옮긴 것은?

① 그는 종종 혼잣말을 한다.
⇒ He often talks to himself.

② Kelly는 그녀 자신을 싫어한다.
⇒ Kelly hates herself.

③ 이 쿠키들을 마음껏 드세요.
⇒ Please help yourself to these cookies.

④ 그녀는 거울 속의 그녀 자신을 본다.
⇒ She looks at her in the mirror.

⑤ 나는 직접 쿠키를 굽는다.
⇒ I myself bake cookies.

1. 다음 중 밑줄 친 부분이 잘못된 것은?

① She tells <u>herself</u>, "You can do it."
② Please help <u>yourself</u> to this soup.
③ There are wonderful <u>themselves</u> teachers.
④ I made it <u>myself</u>.
⑤ We ate all the cake <u>ourselves</u>.

2. 다음 괄호 안에 주어진 말의 형태가 바르게 짝지어진 것은?

> The teacher introduced (she). She wanted to know more about (us).

① her – us
② herself – us
③ her – ourselves
④ herself – ourself
⑤ himself – ourselves

3. 다음 보기 에서 it의 쓰임이 같은 문장끼리 묶인 것은?

> 보기
> ⓐ What is it?
> ⓑ What time is it now?
> ⓒ How far is it from here to the park?
> ⓓ It's spring in Korea.
> ⓔ I like it a lot.
> ⓕ I'm good at it.
> ⓖ It takes five minutes by bike.
> ⓗ I can't solve it.

① ⓐ, ⓒ, ⓓ
② ⓐ, ⓔ, ⓖ, ⓗ
③ ⓑ, ⓒ, ⓓ, ⓖ
④ ⓒ, ⓓ, ⓔ
⑤ ⓔ, ⓖ

4. 다음 글에서 날씨 변화를 우리말로 순서대로 쓰시오.

> Today it was sunny. So Minho and I went on a picnic. We went to the Olympic park. But suddenly it became cloudy and windy. And then it rained. We didn't have umbrellas. We were all wet. Today the weather changed a lot.

_____ ⇒ _____ and _____

⇒ _____

5. 다음 중 밑줄 친 재귀대명사의 쓰임이 나머지와 다른 것은?

① Sue caught a cold <u>herself</u>.
② Alex can ride a horse <u>himself</u>.
③ I <u>myself</u> solved the problem.
④ I covered <u>myself</u> with a blanket.
⑤ He <u>himself</u> lent the book to me yesterday.

6. 다음 중 표의 내용과 일치하지 <u>않는</u> 대화는?

도시	Seoul	London	Moscow	Taipei	Chicago
날씨	sunny	rainy	snowy	cloudy	windy
기온	16℃	9℃	-45℃	32℃	17℃

① A: How's the weather in Seoul?
  B: It's sunny and cool.
② A: What's the weather like in London?
  B: It's rainy and cool.
③ A: Is it cloudy and cold in Taipei?
  B: Yes, it is.
④ A: How's the weather in Moscow?
  B: It's snowy and cold.
⑤ A: Is it sunny in Chicago?
  B: No. It's windy and cool.

7. 다음 글의 Ⓐ, Ⓑ에 순서대로 알맞은 것은?

(Ⓐ) little dog decided to visit (Ⓑ).

      Ⓐ   Ⓑ
① One – anothers
② One – other
③ One – others
④ Another – the other
⑤ Another – other

[8-9] 다음 빈칸에 순서대로 알맞은 것은?

8.

- She studied Chinese _____ herself.
- The door opened _____ itself.

① in – of   ② for – of
③ by – in   ④ of – of
⑤ for – for

9.

- I have two cars. One is at home and _____ is in my office building.
- I will visit three countries this year. One is China, another is Japan, and _____ is India.

① the other – the other
② another – another
③ the other – another
④ another – the other
⑤ the other – the others

[10-11] 다음 중 밑줄 친 부분이 잘못된 것은?

10.

① I am going to buy <u>some</u> clothes.
② Can I have <u>some</u> coffee?
③ Is there <u>any</u> good news?
④ There isn't <u>some</u> ice in the fridge.
⑤ Would you like <u>some</u> milk?

11.

① <u>It</u>'s very near from here.
② Let me introduce <u>myself</u> to you.
③ I don't have a camera, but he has <u>one</u>.
④ I ride my new bike. I like <u>one</u> very much.
⑤ She got angry at <u>herself</u>.

12. 다음 중 빈칸에 들어갈 단어가 나머지와 다른 것은?

① A: What's the date today?
   B: _____ is January 25th.
② A: Do you like my new shirt?
   B: Yes, I love _____.
③ A: Is this your favorite skirt?
   B: No, I like the pink _____.
④ A: How's the weather outside?
   B: _____ is freezing.
⑤ A: How about that movie?
   B: Oh, _____ is so boring.

[1-4] 다음은 세계 여러 도시의 어느 날 날씨이다. 질문에 알맞은 말을 쓰시오.

City	Weather
Jeonju	☀
Paris	☁
Moscow	❄
Manila	🌧

1. How's the weather in Jeonju?

⇒ _____

2. How's the weather in Paris?

⇒ _____

3. How's the weather in Moscow?

⇒ _____

4. How's the weather in Manila?

⇒ _____

5. 다음 대화의 빈칸에 알맞은 말을 쓰시오.

A: Is this a laptop computer?
B: No, _____ _____.

6. 다음 우리말과 일치하도록 괄호 안의 단어를 알맞게 배열하여 쓰시오.

❶ 이것은 장난감 자동차이다. (toy, is, a, car, this)

_____

❷ 이것들은 인형들이 아니다. (are, dolls, not, these)

_____

❸ 저것이 네 집이니? (your, house, that, is)

_____

7. 다음 우리말과 뜻이 같도록 괄호 안에 말을 이용하여 문장을 완성하시오.

❶ 나는 혼자서 숙제를 끝냈다. (finish, myself)

_____

❷ 그녀는 자신의 얼굴을 거울로 비춰보고 있다. (look at, herself)

_____ in the mirror.

8. 다음 문장을 우리말로 옮기시오.

❶ It's getting dark.

_____

❷ It is very cold today.

_____

❸ How far is it from Ulsan to Seoul?

_____

9. 다음 표를 보고, 대화의 빈칸에 알맞은 말을 쓰시오.

날짜	9월 6일
요일	수요일
현재시각	9 a.m.

Suji: Hello, John.

John: Hi, Suji. What's the date today?

Suji: _____

John: Is it Tuesday?

Suji: No, it isn't. _____

John: _____

Suji: It's 9 o'clock.

Joh: Thanks, Suji.

10. 다음 그림을 보고, 빈칸에 들어갈 단어를 바르게 쓰시오.

Look at those two girls. _____ is singing, and _____ is dancing.

11. 다음 우리말과 뜻이 같도록 빈칸을 완성하시오.

❶ 도서관에 너의 반 친구들이 있니?

⇒ _____ _____ your classmates in the library?

❷ 저 소녀들은 내 친구가 아니다.

⇒ _____ _____ _____ not my friends.

12. 다음 달력을 보고, 질문에 대한 답변을 쓰시오.(숫자는 영어로 쓰시오.)

September						
월	화	수	목	금	토	일
				1	2	3
④	5	6	7	8	9	10
11	12	13	14	15	16	17
18	19	20	21	22	23	24
25	26	27	28	29	30	

A: When is Andy's birthday?

B: _____

13. 다음 그림을 보고, 글의 빈칸에 알맞은 말을 쓰시오.

There are two apples. One is red and _____ _____ _____ _____.

Chapter 7
의문사

7.1. who, what, which

>>> 의문사란? 의문을 나타내는 말로 누가(who), 무엇을(what), 언제(when), 어디서(where), 왜(why), 어떻게 (how)를 물어볼 때 사용한다.

>>> 의문사의 특징

❶ 문장의 맨 앞에 온다.

❷ 의문사가 있는 의문문은 Yes/No로 대답하지 않는다. 예) Who is he? – He is my cousin.

>>> 의문사가 있는 의문문의 어순

「의문사 + be동사/조동사/do(es)] + 주어 ~?」

1 who

>>> '누구'라는 뜻으로 사람에 대해(이름, 신분) 물을 때 쓴다.

Who is she? –She is **Jenny Brown**. 그녀는 누구니? -그녀는 Jenny Brown이야.

Who helped you? –**Kate** helped me. (의문사가 주어 역할을 하는 경우) 누가 너를 도와줬니? -Kate가 도와줬어.

2 what

>>> '무엇'이라는 뜻으로 사람의 직업이나 사물을 물을 때 쓴다.

What is that? –That's **my desk**. 저것은 무엇이니? -저것은 내 책상이야.

What does she do? –She is **a doctor**. 그녀는 무엇[어떤 일]을 하니? -그녀는 의사야.

What do you do in your free time? –I usually **read books**.

너는 여가 시간에 무엇을 하니? -나는 주로 책을 읽어.

3 which

>>> '어느 것'이라는 뜻으로 선택을 물을 때 쓴다.

Which is faster, a bus or a train? 버스와 기차 중 어느 것이 더 빠르니?

Which do you like better, tea or coffee? 차와 커피 중 어느 것을 더 좋아하니?

뽐쌤의 야무진 Tip!

의문형용사 what / which

명사 앞에 위치하여 명사를 수식하는 형용사로도 쓰인다.

What sport do you like? 너는 무슨 스포츠를 좋아하니?

Which shoes are yours? 어느 신발이 너의 것이니?

A. 다음 대화의 빈칸에 알맞은 의문사를 쓰시오.

① A: _____ are you?   B: I am Yuna.

② A: _____ do you do?   B: I am a soccer player.

③ A: _____ one is cheaper?   B: That one.

④ A: _____ can I do for you?   B: I'm looking for pants.

⑤ A: _____ time is the party?   B: Seven o'clock in the evening.

⑥ A: _____ does your uncle do?   B: He is a computer programmer.

⑦ A: _____ do you want, juice or milk?   B: Juice, please.

⑧ A: _____ are you going to do today?   B: Nothing special.

⑨ A: _____ is she?   B: She is Miss Brown.

⑩ A: _____ did you do yesterday?   B: I went fishing.

⑪ A: _____ is she?   B: She is my classmate.

⑫ A: _____ sports do you like?   B: I like soccer.

⑬ A: _____ are they?   B: They are my teachers.

⑭ A: _____ time shall we make it?   B: Let's meet at two.

⑮ A: _____ season do you like better, summer or winter?

     B: I like summer better.

⑯ A: _____ is the matter with you?   B: I have a headache.

⑰ A: _____ is this?   B: It's a clock.

⑱ A: _____ is that girl?   B: She is my niece.

B. 다음 의문문에 맞는 본인의 답을 쓰시오.

① What is your favorite color?

➡ _____

② What did you do last weekend?

➡ _____

7.2. when, where, why

1 when

>>> '언제'라는 뜻으로 때나 시간을 물을 때 쓴다.

When is your birthday? –It's **July 14**. 너의 생일은 언제니? -7월 14일이야.

When[=What time] do you go to bed? –I go to bed **at ten**.

너는 몇 시에 잠자리에 드니? -나는 10시에 잠자리에 들어.

* 시간을 묻는 when일 경우, what time으로 바꿔 쓸 수 있다. 단, what time은 좀 더 구체적인 시간을 물어본다.

2 where

>>> '어디서, 어디에'라는 뜻으로 위치나 장소를 물을 때 쓴다.

Where do you live? –I live **in Seoul**. 너는 어디에 사니? -나는 서울에 살아.

Where does your sister study? –She studies **at home**. 너의 여동생은 어디에서 공부하니? -그녀는 집에서 공부해.

3 why

>>> '왜'라는 뜻으로 이유를 물을 때 쓴다.

Why were you late for school? –**Because I got up late**.

너는 왜 학교에 늦었니? -늦게 일어났기 때문이야.

Why do you go there? –**Because I need to meet my teacher there**.

너는 왜 거기에 가니? -그곳에서 선생님을 만나야 하기 때문이야.

뽐쌤의
야무진
Tip!

권유를 나타내는 why don't you ~? 와 why don't we ~?

❶ why don't you ~?: '~하는 게 어때?' 상대방에게 권유하는 표현
Why don't you take a rest? You look sick. 너 쉬는 게 어때? 아파 보여.

❷ why don't we ~?: '우리 ~하지 않을래?' 상대방에게 제안하는 표현으로 Let's ~ 와 비슷하다.
Why don't we go to see a movie tonight? 우리 오늘 밤 영화 보러 가지 않을래?

A. 다음 대화의 빈칸에 알맞은 의문사를 쓰시오.

① A: _____ do you like him?　　　B: Because he is kind.

② A: _____ is the party?　　　B: It's the day after tomorrow, October 9th.

③ A: _____ are bees useful to people?　B: Because they make honey.

④ A: _____ are you from?　　　B: I am from Tokyo.

⑤ A: _____ did you visit your aunt?　B: Last week.

⑥ A: _____ is the subway station?　B: It's two blocks away from here.

⑦ A: _____ is Suji?　　　B: She is in her mother's room.

⑧ A: _____ is your school?　　　B: It's next to the library.

⑨ A: _____ can we go there?　　　B: How about next Saturday?

⑩ A: _____ do you have supper?　B: In the cafeteria.

⑪ A: _____ _____ is it?　B: It's 5 o'clock.

⑫ A: _____ don't you join us?　　B: I'm sorry, I can't.

⑬ A: _____ is the grocery store in this town?

　　B: It's across from the flower shop.

⑭ A: _____ is Parents' Day in Korea?　B: It's May 8th.

⑮ A: _____ don't we go camping?　B: Sure. Why not?

⑯ A: _____ are you in a hurry?　B: Because I'm late for the meeting.

B. 다음 질문에 대한 올바른 답변을 찾으시오.

보기　① They were held in Rome.　　　② It was held in Korea.

　　　③ They were held in 1988.　　　④ It was held in 1930.

① When was the first World Cup held?

② Where were the first Olympic Games held?

③ When were the Seoul Olympic Games held?

④ Where was the World Cup held in 2002?

7.3. how

1 how

>>> '어떤, 어떻게'라는 뜻으로 상태, 정도, 방법이나 수단을 물어볼 때 쓴다.

How are you? –I'm **great**. 어떻게 지내? -잘 지내.

How do you go to school? –I go to school **by subway**.

너는 어떻게 학교에 가니? -나는 지하철을 타고 학교에 가.

2 how + 형용사/부사

❶ how old ~? '얼마나 오래된, 몇 살', 나이를 물을 때

How old are you? –I am **fourteen years old**. 너는 몇 살이니? -나는 14살이야.

❷ how long ~? '얼마나 오랫동안, 얼마나 긴', 길이나 기간을 물어볼 때

How long is the river? –It's **twenty kilometers long**.

그 강은 얼마나 기니? -그것은 20킬로미터야.

How long did you stay in New York? –**About 2 months**.

너는 뉴욕에 얼마나 오래 머물렀니? -약 2달 동안.

❸ how often ~? '얼마나 자주', 빈도와 횟수를 물어볼 때

How often do you exercise? –**Every day**. 너는 얼마나 자주 운동을 하니? -매일.

❹ how many + 셀 수 있는 명사의 복수형 ~? '얼마나 많은 수', 개수를 물어볼 때
   how much + 셀 수 없는 명사 ~? '얼마나 많은 양', 양이나 가격을 물어 볼 때

How many brothers do you have? –I have **two brothers**.

너는 얼마나 많은 남자 형제가 있니? -나는 두 명의 남자 형제가 있어.

How much time do you need? –I need just **five minutes**.

너는 얼마나 많은 시간이 필요하니? -나는 5분 정도만 필요해.

뽐쌤의
야무진
Tip!

❶ 그 외의 다양한 how + 형용사/부사

❶ how tall ~?: 키, 높이 ❷ how far ~?: 거리 ❸ how high ~?: 높이
❹ how fast ~?: 속도 ❺ how deep ~?: 깊이 ❻ how wide ~?: 너비

❷ How[What] about + 명사/v-ing ~?는 '~하는 게 어때?'라는 뜻
의 권유 표현이다.

How[What] about eating lunch together? –That sounds great.
같이 점심 먹는 게 어때? -그거 좋은데.

A. 다음 대화의 빈칸에 알맞은 말을 보기에서 고르시오.

보기: How   How many   How much   How tall
        How long   How far   How old   How often

① A: _____ is your sister?   B: She's fine.

② A: _____ uncles do you have?   B: I have two.

③ A: _____ is this bag?   B: It is 10 dollars.

④ A: _____ are you?   B: I'm 160 centimeters tall.

⑤ A: _____ can I get to the hospital?   B: Just turn left.

⑥ A: _____ is this bridge?   B: It's 15 kilometers long.

⑦ A: _____ does it take to your school?   B: It takes about ten minutes.

⑧ A: _____ is it from here to the post office?   B: It's about two miles from here.

⑨ A: _____ is your mother?   B: She's 45 years old.

⑩ A: _____ do you go to the hair salon?   B: Once a month.

B. 다음 밑줄 친 부분이 대답이 될 수 있는 질문을 만드시오.

① It's twenty dollars.

➡ _____

② I studied for two hours.

➡ _____

③ It is only four blocks away.

➡ _____

④ She goes jogging every day.

➡ _____

⑤ He is thirteen years old.

➡ _____

1. 다음 대화의 빈칸에 알맞은 것은?

A: _____ is the woman in the first picture?
B: She is my English teacher.

① Who   ② How   ③ When
④ What   ⑤ Where

2. 다음 질문에 대한 대답으로 알맞은 것은?

Who's the girl in the library?

① She is pretty.
② She is my best friend.
③ She is 13 years old.
④ She plays the cello well.
⑤ She is looking for math books.

3. 다음 대화의 빈칸에 알맞은 것은?

A: _____ are you so late?
B: I got up late, so I missed the school bus.

① What   ② Why   ③ Who
④ When   ⑤ Where

4. 다음 두 문장의 의미가 같도록 빈칸에 알맞은 것은?

What time do you go to bed?
= _____ do you go to bed?

5. 다음 우리말을 영어로 바르게 옮긴 것은?

당신은 키가 얼마입니까?

① What tall are you?
② What are you tall?
③ How long you are?
④ How tall are you?
⑤ How you are tall?

6. 다음 대화의 빈칸에 알맞은 것은?

A: Excuse me. _____
B: It's 12 dollars.
A: Good. I will take this.

① How do you like it?
② What is your hobby?
③ May I take your order?
④ How much is this shirt?
⑤ What kind of food can you cook?

7. 다음 질문에 대한 대답으로 알맞은 것은?

A: How often do you cook?
B: _____

① I like cooking.
② I cook for her.
③ Three times a week.
④ I am good at cooking.
⑤ My favorite food is spaghetti.

8.

> A: I'm from America. _____
> B: I'm from Japan.

① Whose is this?　　② How are you?
③ What's your name?　④ What do you do?
⑤ Where are you from?

9.

> A: _____ about throwing a party?
> B: That's a good idea.

① Where　　② Why　　③ Who
④ When　　⑤ How

10.

> A: _____ is the dog?
> B: It's next to the door.

① What　　② Who　　③ When
④ Where　　⑤ Why

단원평가　실전대비

1. Choose the best question for the answer.

> I like baseball.

① What sports do you like?
② What subject do you like?
③ What is your favorite snack?
④ What is your favorite movie?
⑤ What kind of music do you like?

2. 다음 대화의 빈칸에 공통으로 알맞은 것은?

> - A: _____ is this man in the picture?
>   B: He is my father.
> - A: _____ are you looking for?
>   B: I am looking for my sister.

① Who　　② Why　　③ What
④ When　　⑤ Where

3. 다음 대화의 밑줄 친 부분의 의미로 알맞은 것은?

> A: My name is Charlie. What's your name?
> B: I'm Susan. Where are you from?
> A: I'm from Kenya. <u>How about you?</u>
> B: I'm from the Philippines.

① What's your name?
② Where do you live?
③ What are you doing?
④ Where are you from?
⑤ What's your favorite country?

4. 다음 중 짝지어진 대화가 <u>어색한</u> 것은?

① A: Where is Eric?
　B: He is over there.
② A: Where are you?
　B: I'm at home.
③ A: Where are you going?
　B: I am going to the store.
④ A: Where is he?
　B: He is sick.
⑤ A: Where is the bus stop?
　B: It's in front of the bank.

5. 다음 질문에 대한 대답으로 가장 <u>어색한</u> 것은?

> How do you study English?

① I keep a diary in English.
② I don't study English.
③ I listen to pop songs.
④ I make a word book.
⑤ I chat with Korean friends.

6. 다음 중 짝지어진 대화가 <u>어색한</u> 것은?

① A: Where are you from?
　 B: I'm from Brazil.
② A: What grade are you in?
　 B: I'm in the seventh grade.
③ A: When is it?
　 B: It's at Tom's restaurant.
④ A: Where do you practice?
　 B: I practice at home.
⑤ A: What's your favorite subject?
　 B: I like music.

7. 다음 두 대화의 빈칸에 공통으로 알맞은 것은?

> - A: I'm looking for Jim. _____
>   B: He's in the library.
> - A: John is not at home. _____
>   B: He's in the gym.

① Where is he?
② What is he like?
③ Which one is he?
④ How is he doing?
⑤ What is he looking for?

8. 다음 대답에 대한 질문으로 가장 <u>어색한</u> 것은?

> A: _____
> B: Go down one block. It's on your left.

① Where is the museum?
② Where can I find the museum?
③ How can I get to the museum?
④ How do you go to the museum?
⑤ Can you show me the way to the museum?

9. How many are there in Jessica's family?

> Hi. This is my family. Dad, mom, my older brother John, my little brother Joshua and me. My dad is a computer programmer and my mom is a teacher. I love my family.

① There are five.　　② She's fourteen.
③ She's a nurse.　　④ He's an engineer.
⑤ There are six.

10. 다음 중 빈칸에 들어갈 의문사가 나머지와 <u>다른</u> 것은?

① _____ tall are your sister?
② _____ much is this pencil case?
③ _____ time is it?
④ _____ old is your grandfather?
⑤ _____ many candies do you want?

11. 다음 광고문을 통해서 대답할 수 <u>없는</u> 것은?

Come and Enjoy the ABC Shopping Mall

Location: 140, Main Street
Opening hours: 10 a.m. - 10 p.m.
Special Event: a present for every family with children

① What is the name of the mall?
② Where is the mall?
③ When does the mall open?
④ Who will get a present?
⑤ What is a present?

12. 다음 질문에 대한 대답으로 알맞은 것은?

A: Which do you like better, sports or music?
B: _____

① Yes, I do.
② I like music better.
③ Yes, it's music.
④ I like to play volleyball.
⑤ No, I don't like music.

[13-14] 다음 대화의 빈칸에 순서대로 알맞은 것은?

13.

Jim: _____ do you want to be?
Suji: I want to be a movie director.
Jim: Sounds great. _____ do you want to be a movie director?
Suji: I like movies.

① Why – What   ② What – Why
③ What – How   ④ How – Why
⑤ How – What

14.

A: Excuse me. Is there a bookstore nearby?
B: Yes, there is. There's one next to the bank.
A: _____ is it from here?
B: It is only three blocks away.
A: _____ can I get there?
B: Go straight three blocks and turn right. It is on your right.

① How long – Where   ② How often – How
③ How long – How   ④ How far – How
⑤ How far – Where

15. 다음 중 대화의 빈칸 ⓐ~ⓔ에 순서대로 알맞은 것은?

A: (ⓐ) did you visit your grandmother?
B: Last month.
A: (ⓑ) did you go last week?
B: I went to Jeonju.
A: (ⓒ) did you go there?
B: I went there by car.
A: (ⓓ) did you go with?
B: I went there with my younger sister.
A: (ⓔ) did you eat?
B: I ate a hamburger and coke.

① ⓐ How   ② ⓑ Where   ③ ⓒ Who
④ ⓓ What   ⑤ ⓓ When

16. 다음 중 빈칸에 What이 들어갈 수 <u>없는</u> 것은?

① _____ is your name?
② _____ is your mother?
③ _____ is this in English?
④ _____ do you do after school?
⑤ _____ does your father do for a living?

17. 다음 중 짝지어진 대화가 <u>어색한</u> 것은?

① A: Who's the girl with a dog?
   B: She's my sister.
② A: What's your best friend like?
   B: He is very smart.
③ A: Who's the woman over there?
   B: She is my aunt.
④ A: Who are the men in the park?
   B: They're very kind.
⑤ A: What's your new teacher like?
   B: She is very funny.

18. 다음 중 어법상 옳지 <u>않은</u> 것은?

① How tall is Barbie?
② How long is that rope?
③ How old is your brother?
④ How many sisters do you have?
⑤ How much is it from here to your school?

19. 다음 중 밑줄 친 의문사가 알맞지 <u>않은</u> 것은?

① <u>Who</u> is the boy in the picture?
② <u>Why</u> do you like the children?
③ <u>What</u> does Jinny get up in the morning?
④ <u>Where</u> is the police station?
⑤ <u>When</u> is your birthday?

20. 다음 대답에 대한 질문으로 알맞은 것은?

I go to Seoul middle school.

① Where do you live?
② What is your name?
③ When do you go to school?
④ What school are you go?
⑤ What school do you go to?

1. 다음 중 밑줄 친 부분을 When으로 바꿀 수 <u>없는</u> 것은?

① <u>What time</u> is it now?
② <u>What time</u> is the party?
③ <u>What time</u> shall we make it?
④ <u>What time</u> do you go to school?
⑤ <u>What time</u> do you have dinner?

2. 다음 보기 의 빈칸에 들어갈 수 <u>없는</u> 것은?

> 보기
> ⓐ A: How _____ are you?
>   B: I'm thirteen.
> ⓑ A: How _____ is this pencil?
>   B: It is two dollars.
> ⓒ A: How _____ children do you have?
>   B: I have three sons.
> ⓓ A: How _____ do you go to the movies?
>   B: About once a week.
> ⓔ A: How _____ does it take to go to Ulsan?
>   B: It takes about four hours.

① long　　② far　　③ often
④ much　　⑤ many

3. 다음 중 빈칸에 들어갈 말이 나머지와 <u>다른</u> 하나는?

① _____ is he doing?
② _____ do you go to work?
③ _____ was your holiday?
④ _____ much is that laptop?
⑤ _____ invited Jimmy to the party?

4. 다음 대화의 빈칸에 순서대로 알맞은 것은?

> A: _____ do you do after school?
> B: I usually go to my violin lesson.
> A: _____ time does the lesson end?
> B: At six o'clock.
> A: _____ do you do your homework?
> B: Usually after dinner.
> A: You have a busy day.

① What – What – When
② What – When – When
③ What – When – What
④ When – What – What
⑤ When – When – What

5. 다음 글의 (A), (B), (C)에 들어갈 말로 바르게 짝지어진 것은?

> Please come to my family concert.
> (A) _____ is playing?
> Victoria's Family Band
> (B) _____ is the concert?
> This Saturday at 7 p.m.
> (C) _____ is the concert held?
> Victoria's House: 24 Holy Circle Drive

① (A) – Who   (B) – Where   (C) – When
② (A) – Who   (B) – When   (C) – Where
③ (A) – What   (B) – When   (C) – Where
④ (A) – What   (B) – Where   (C) – When
⑤ (A) – When   (B) – Who   (C) – Where

6. 다음 대화의 ⓐ~ⓔ 중 내용상 적절하지 <u>않은</u> 것은?

> A: What are you doing?
> B: ⓐ <u>I am studying math.</u>
> A: What is your mother doing?
> B: ⓑ <u>She is cleaning the living room.</u>
> A: Where can I see your brother?
> B: ⓒ <u>He swims very well.</u>
> A: ⓓ <u>Is he swimming now?</u>
> B: ⓔ <u>No, he is just sitting by the pool.</u>

① ⓐ   ② ⓑ   ③ ⓒ
④ ⓓ   ⑤ ⓔ

7. 다음 글을 읽고 답할 수 있는 질문 2개는?

> My name is Jessica Alba. I live in New York, USA. I like soccer and music. I like K-pop very much. I have a big family. There are six of us: Grandma, Dad, Mom, two sisters, and me. We have two dogs, too. My dogs' names are Happy and Spotty.

① What does Jessica do?
② How many people are there in Jessica's family?
③ Where does Jessica want to live?
④ What is Jessica good at?
⑤ What is Jessica's family name?

8. 다음 보기에서 자연스러운 대화의 개수는?

보기

ⓐ A: What is your mother's name?
   B: She is a doctor.
ⓑ A: What does your aunt look like?
   B: She is very kind.
ⓒ A: What's his personality like?
   B: He is very friendly.
ⓓ A: Who's the girl with short hair?
   B: She still studies.
ⓔ A: Who's the woman in the black skirt?
   B: She is my art teacher.

① 1개   ② 2개   ③ 3개
④ 4개   ⑤ 5개

9. 다음 중 짝지어진 대화가 자연스러운 것은?

① A: Where do you meet?
   B: We meet every Sunday.
② A: When do you meet?
   B: We meet in the baking room.
③ A: How much is this jacket?
   B: Yes, it is.
④ A: How can I join the club?
   B: We have cookies and bread.
⑤ A: How long do you bake?
   B: We bake for 2 hours.

10. 다음 주어진 대답에 알맞은 질문은?

I like coffee better.

① What did you drink?
② When do you usually drink tea?
③ How do you like your tea?
④ Why do you like tea and coffee?
⑤ Which do you like better, tea or coffee?

11. 다음 중 대화의 밑줄 친 부분에 대한 질문으로 알맞지 않은 것은?

① It is mine.
   ⇒ Whose bag is this?
② He is my classmate.
   ⇒ Who is that boy?
③ He is from Japan.
   ⇒ Where is he from?
④ She is very sick.
   ⇒ Why does Julia look bad?
⑤ I go there on foot.
   ⇒ When do you go to park?

12. 다음 생일파티 초대장을 보고 내용을 알 수 없는 것은?

INVITATION

To: Olivia
Date: September 1st
Time: 3 o'clock
Place: Charlie's Restaurant

① Who gets the invitation card?
② What time is the party?
③ When is the birthday party?
④ Where is the party?
⑤ How long is the party?

13. 다음 중 밑줄 친 부분의 쓰임이 나머지와 다른 것은?

① What happened next?
② What does she want?
③ What is his address?
④ What will come after this?
⑤ What is your favorite subject?

1. 다음 표를 보고 질문에 답을 완성하시오.

	Monday	Tuesday
Bob	study Math	swim
Minju	study Science	swim

❶ What does Bob do on Monday?

⇒ _____ _____ _____ on Monday.

❷ When do Bob and Minju swim?

⇒ _____ _____ _____ _____.

2. 다음 보기에서 알맞은 표현을 찾아 대화를 완성하시오.

보기
① Three times a week.
② Usually spaghetti.
③ I cook.
④ Yes. I'm good at it.
⑤ No, I'm not.

❶ A: What do you do in your free time?

B: _____

❷ A: What kind of food do you cook?

B: _____

❸ A: Do you cook Italian food?

B: _____

❹ A: How often do you cook?

B: _____

3. 다음 문장의 의미가 같도록 알맞은 말을 쓰시오.

❶ What is her job?

= _____ does she do?

❷ What time do you go to school?

= _____ do you go to school?

❸ Pardon me?

= _____ did you say?

❹ What is the weather like?

= _____ is the weather?

❺ Where are you from?

= Where do you _____ from?

4. 다음 Emma의 자기소개 글을 바탕으로 질문에 답하시오.

My name is Emma. I'm from Shanghai. I'm fifteen years old. I go to Edmonds Middle School. I'm in the eighth grade. I live in Washington now. Nice to meet you.

❶ Where is she from?

⇒ She _____.

❷ What school does Emma go to?

⇒ She _____.

❸ Where does she live?

⇒ She _____.

5. 다음 주어진 단어를 이용하여 대화를 완성하시오.(필요하면 어형을 변화 가능)

A: What time does she have dinner?
B: _____
   (have, usually, 6:30).

6. 다음 대화의 밑줄 친 우리말을 영어로 쓰시오.

A: Who is the woman in brown skirt?
B: She's my grandmother.
A: ❶ 그녀는 연세가 어떻게 되시니?
B: She is 63 years old.
A: ❷ 그녀의 직업은 무엇이니?
B: She is a nurse.
A: ❸ 그녀는 왜 여기에 계시니?
B: Because I forgot to bring my lunch box.

❶ _____

❷ _____

❸ _____

7. 다음 밑줄 친 ⓐ, ⓑ를 우리말로 바르게 해석하시오.

A: ⓐ Why didn't you buy the book?
B: I didn't have enough money.
A: ⓑ Why don't you borrow it from the library?
B: That's a good idea.

ⓐ _____

ⓑ _____

8. 다음 학급 시간표를 보고, 대화를 완성하시오.

	Mon	Tue	Wed
9:00~9:45	과학	영어	영어
10:00~10:45	국어	체육	수학
11:00~11:45	체육	체육	과학
13:00~13:45	음악	국어	음악
14:00~14:45	영어	수학	미술
15:00~15:45		사회	

A: _____ does the first class begin?
B: It begins at nine.
A: _____ _____ classes do you have on Tuesday?
B: We have _____ _____.
A: _____ subject is the last class on Monday?
B: It is _____.

9. 다음 글을 읽고, 주어진 질문에 완전한 문장으로 대답하시오.

Minji loves pets. She has a cat, three dogs, and two hamsters. She also has three snakes.

Q: How many pets does Minji have?
A: _____

Chapter 8
문장의 종류

8.1. 부가의문문

>>> 부가의문문이란? 평서문 끝에 간단하게 「동사 + 주어」를 덧붙여 상대방의 동의나 확인을 구할 때 쓴다.

1 부가의문문 만들기

앞의 평서문	부가의문문
긍정	isn't / aren't / don't / doesn't / didn't / 조동사n't + 주어의 대명사?
부정	is / are / do / does / did / 조동사 + 주어의 대명사?

>>> 앞문장이 긍정이면 부정, 부정이면 긍정으로 한다.
You like pizza, don't you? 너는 피자를 좋아해, 그렇지 않니?
You don't like pizza, do you? 너는 피자를 안 좋아해, 그렇지?

>>> 앞문장의 동사가 be동사이면 be동사를, 조동사면 조동사를, 일반동사면 do/does를 쓴다.
He can't speak English, can he? 그는 영어를 못해, 그렇지?
You are tired, aren't you? 너는 피곤해, 그렇지 않니?

>>> 인칭과 시제를 일치시킨다.
She likes math, doesn't she? 그녀는 수학을 좋아해, 그렇지 않니?
He wasn't at home, was he? 그는 집에 없었어, 그렇지?

>>> 주어는 꼭 대명사로 쓴다.
Jim loves you, doesn't he? 짐은 너를 사랑해, 그렇지 않니?

>>> 부가의문문의 부정형은 반드시 줄임말을 쓴다.
Tom knows the answer, doesn't he? 탐은 답을 알아, 그렇지 않니?

* 예외적인 경우: 명령문에는 will you?, 권유문(Let's ~)에는 shall we?를 쓴다.
Clean the room, will you? 방을 청소해라, 알았지?
Let's go swimming, shall we? 수영하러 가자, 그럴래?

2 부가의문문의 대답

>>> 긍정이면 Yes, 부정이면 No로 답한다.
The movie was interesting, wasn't it? 그 영화는 흥미로웠어, 그렇지 않니?
–Yes, it was. 응, 흥미로웠어. / **No, it wasn't.** 아니, 흥미롭지 않았어.

A. 다음 괄호 안에서 알맞은 것을 고르시오.

① Miss Johnson is a good dancer, isn't (she, Miss Johnson)?

② You go to school at 7 o'clock, (do, don't) you?

③ She plays the piano well, (don't, doesn't) she?

④ Kevin doesn't study hard, (do, does) he?

⑤ Let's go fishing, (will, shall) we?

⑥ You don't like apples, (don't, do) you?

⑦ It's a beautiful flower, (isn't, is) it?

⑧ You won't leave me alone, (will, will not) you?

⑨ Nick has a great smile, (does, doesn't) he?

⑩ She is an early bird, (is, isn't) she?

⑪ Mina, open the door, (will, shall) you?

⑫ He can't tell a lie, (can, can't) he?

⑬ Picasso was a great artist, (was, wasn't) he?

⑭ Let's have lunch, (don't, shall) we?

B. 다음 빈칸에 알맞은 말을 쓰시오.

① You are thirteen years old, _____ _____?   – Yes, _____ _____.

② They will not go to Seoul, _____ _____?   – No, _____ _____.

③ She can ride a horse, _____ _____?   – No, _____ _____.

④ My father likes a dog, _____ _____?   – Yes, _____ _____.

⑤ His father was a great actor, _____ _____?   – Yes, _____ _____.

⑥ We will have good time there, _____ _____?   – Yes, _____ _____.

⑦ Jack doesn't look like his father, _____ _____?– No, _____ _____.

⑧ It rained cats and dogs, _____ _____?   – No, _____ _____.

1 부정의문문

》》》 부정으로 묻는 의문문을 말하며 '~하지 않(았)니?'라고 해석한다. 대답은 우리말에 상관없이 긍정이면 Yes, 부정이면 No로 한다.

❶ be동사: Be동사 not + 주어 ~?

Aren't you busy? 너는 바쁘지 않니?

–Yes, I am. 응, 바빠. / No, I'm not. 아니, 바쁘지 않아.

❷ 조동사: 조동사 not + 주어 ~?

Won't you go there? 그곳에 가지 않을 거니?

–Yes, I will. 응, 갈 거야. / No, I won't. 아니, 안 갈 거야.

❸ 일반동사: Don't[Doesn't, Didn't] + 주어 + 동사원형 ~?

Don't you think so? 너는 그렇게 생각하지 않니?

–Yes, I do. 응, 그렇게 생각해. / No, I don't. 아니, 그렇게 생각하지 않아.

Doesn't she have a pet? 그녀는 애완동물이 있지 않니?

–Yes, she does. 응, 가지고 있어. / No, she doesn't. 아니, 가지고 있지 않아.

Didn't she study well? 그녀는 공부를 잘하지 않았니?

–Yes, she did. 응, 잘했어. / No, she didn't. 아니, 잘하지 않았어.

2 선택의문문

》》》 or을 써서 한쪽의 선택을 요구하는 의문문으로 대답은 Yes/No로 하지 않고, 제시된 것 중에서 하나를 선택하여 대답한다.

❶ 의문사가 없는 선택의문문

Is the man a singer **or** an actor? 그 남자는 가수이니, 배우이니?

–He is a singer. 그는 가수야.

❷ 의문사 which가 있는 선택의문문

Which do you like more, coffee **or** tea? 너는 커피와 차 중에 어느 것을 더 좋아하니?

–I like coffee more. 나는 커피를 더 좋아해.

A. 다음 문장을 부정의문문으로 바꿀 때 괄호 안에서 알맞은 것을 고르시오.

① Tom will change his cellphone.

➡ (Doesn't, Won't) Tom change his cellphone?

② You like ice cream.

➡ (Don't, Doesn't) you like ice cream?

③ Mary goes to school on Saturdays.

➡ (Didn't, Doesn't) Mary go to school on Saturdays?

B. 다음 질문에 대한 답을 보기 를 참고하여 우리말에 맞게 쓰시오.

보기 Don't you like English?
➡ Yes, I like English. (응, 나는 영어를 좋아해.)
➡ No, I don't like English. (아니, 나는 영어를 좋아하지 않아.)

① Don't you want to go to a mountain?

➡ _____ (아니, 나는 산에 가는 걸 원하지 않아.)

② Aren't you going to see a movie?

➡ _____ (응, 나는 영화 보러 갈 거야.)

③ Didn't you have dinner?

➡ _____ (아니, 나는 먹지 않았어.)

C. 다음 문장을 보기 와 같이 바꿔 쓰시오.

보기 Do you like coffee? + Do you like tea?
➡ Do you like coffee or tea?

① Do you like summer? + Do you like winter?

➡ _____

② Will you go to the mountain? + Will you go to the river?

➡ _____

》》》 감탄문이란? 강한 기쁨이나 슬픔, 놀람, 감탄 등의 강한 감정을 나타내는 문장으로 '참 ~하구나'라는 의미를 가지며 how나 what으로 시작한다.

1 How로 시작하는 감탄문

》》》 평서문에서 형용사나 부사를 강조할 때 how로 시작하는 감탄문을 쓴다.

> How + 형용사/부사 (+ 주어 + 동사)!

This cake is very **delicious**. 이 케이크는 매우 맛있다.
➡ **How delicious** this cake is! 이 케이크는 참 맛있구나!
The concert was very **exciting**. 그 콘서트는 매우 신났다.
➡ **How exciting** the concert was! 그 콘서트는 참 신났어!

2 What으로 시작하는 감탄문

》》》 평서문에서 명사를 강조할 때 what으로 시작하는 감탄문을 쓴다.

> What + a(n) + 형용사 + 명사 (+ 주어 + 동사)!

It's **a very nice car**. 그것은 매우 좋은 차다.
➡ **What a nice car** it is! 그것은 참 좋은 차구나!

》》》 모음으로 시작하는 형용사 앞에는 an을 쓴다.
What **an honest girl** she is! 그녀는 참 정직한 소녀구나!

》》》 명사가 복수형이면 a(n)을 쓰지 않고 복수명사를 쓴다.
What honest **girls** they are! 그들은 참 정직한 소녀들이구나!

* 일상생활에서 감탄문을 쓸 때 주어와 동사를 종종 생략한다.
How pretty! 참 예쁘구나!
What a handsome boy! 참 잘생긴 소년이구나!

A. 다음 빈칸에 How 또는 What 중 알맞은 말을 쓰시오.

① _____ pretty you are!

② _____ a small animal this is!

③ _____ sweet juice this is!

④ _____ funny his face is!

⑤ _____ beautiful girls they are!

⑥ _____ tall trees they are!

⑦ _____ hard he works!

⑧ _____ slow the horse is running!

⑨ _____ cute toys the babies have!

⑩ _____ an interesting book this is!

⑪ _____ well Amy sings!

⑫ _____ short pencils they are!

⑬ _____ a nice car it is!

⑭ _____ a scary story it is!

B. 다음 두 문장의 의미가 같도록 빈칸을 채우시오.

① Jane is very smart.   ➡ How _____!

② The boy is very honest.   ➡ How _____!

③ My first trip was very interesting.   ➡ How _____!

④ It's a very adorable doll.   ➡ What _____!

⑤ She wears very colorful pants.   ➡ What _____!

⑥ It is a very old house.   ➡ What _____!

⑦ This is a very beautiful flower.   ➡ What _____!

⑧ That singer is so young.   ➡ How _____!

⑨ He has a very small calender.   ➡ What _____!

⑩ That dog has a very long tail.   ➡ What _____!

8.4. 명령문

>>> 명령문이란? 상대방에게 명령, 권유, 요구를 하는 문장을 의미하며, 보통 주어(You)를 생략하고 동사원형으로 시작한다.

1 일반 명령문

종류	형태	의미
긍정	Be ~	~이어라
	동사원형 ~	~해라
부정	Don't 동사원형 ~	~하지 마라
	Never 동사원형 ~	절대 ~하지 마라 (강한 부정)

Be kind. 친절해라.

Open the door. 문을 열어라.

Don't swim here. 여기서 수영을 하지 말아라.

Never give up on your dreams. 절대 너의 꿈을 포기하지 말아라.

* 부탁이나 요청을 공손하게 말할 때, 문장의 앞이나 뒤에 please를 붙인다.

Pass me the salt **please**. (= Please pass me the salt.) 소금 좀 건네 주세요.

2 권유의 명령문

종류	형태	의미
긍정	Let's 동사원형	~하자
부정	Let's not 동사원형	~하지 말자

Let's play tennis after school. 학교 끝나고 테니스를 치자.

= **Why don't we play** tennis after school? = **Shall we play** tennis after school?

= **How about playing** tennis after school?

Let's not have a party on Saturday. 토요일에 파티를 하지 말자.

권유의 명령문에 대한 대답

❶ 동의: Yes, let's. / OK. / All right. / That's a good idea. / Of course. / No problem. / That sounds good.

❷ 거절: No, let's not. / Sorry, I can't.

A. 다음 괄호 안에서 알맞은 것을 고르시오.

❶ Suji, (come, comes) here.

❷ (Don't, Not) swim here.

❸ Bob, (don't, doesn't) eat too much.

❹ (Do, Be) kind to others, John.

❺ (Don't, Be) go outside. It's snowing.

❻ Let's (not, no) play tennis here.

❼ (Never, None) cross the street here.

B. 다음 주어진 문장을 지시대로 쓰시오.

❶ You change the rule. (명령문으로)

➡ _____

❷ You speak clearly. (please를 붙여 명령문으로)

➡ _____

❸ You turn off the computer. (명령문으로)

➡ _____

❹ You are scared of the dog. (부정 명령문으로)

➡ _____

❺ You make a noise. (부정 명령문으로)

➡ _____

C. 다음과 같이 학급 규칙을 만들 때 Let's 또는 Let's not 중 알맞은 말을 쓰시오.

❶ _____ fight with friends.

❷ _____ run around.

❸ _____ listen to the teacher.

❹ _____ help each other.

❺ _____ throw paper in the wastebasket.

1. 다음 중 어법상 옳지 <u>않은</u> 것은?

① Don't is late for school.
② Turn off the TV.
③ Close the door.
④ Water the plants.
⑤ Don't open the window.

2. 다음 빈칸에 알맞은 것은?

_____ shy.

① Do
② Don't
③ Don't be
④ Never
⑤ Don't you

3. 다음 대화의 빈칸에 알맞은 것은?

A: Let's go to a movie this Wednesday.
B: _____ I have a test on Thursday.

① Yes, let's.
② Sounds great.
③ Sorry, I can't.
④ No, I don't.
⑤ That's a good idea.

4. 다음 중 짝지어진 대화가 <u>어색한</u> 것은?

① A: I'm tired.   B: Take a rest.
② A: I'm thirsty.   B: Drink some water.
③ A: It's cold.   B: Put on your coat.
④ A: I'm sleepy.   B: Go to bed.
⑤ A: It's hot.   B: Have something hot.

[5–6] 다음 대화의 빈칸에 알맞은 것은?

5.

Suji: Oh. You really like soccer, don't you?
Jiho: _____ Soccer is my favorite sport.

① Yes, I am.   ② No, I don't.
③ Yes, I do.   ④ No, I won't.
⑤ Yes, I will.

6.

A: The question was difficult, _____?
B: Yes, it was.

① was it   ② was they   ③ wasn't it
④ did it   ⑤ didn't it

[7–8] 다음 우리말을 영어로 바르게 옮긴 것은?

7.

정말 재미있는 사진이구나!

① What funny it is!
② How a funny photo is it!
③ How a funny photo it is!
④ What a funny photo is it!
⑤ What a funny photo it is!

8.

너는 행복하지 않니?

① Doesn't you happy?
② Don't you happy?
③ Isn't you happy?
④ Aren't you happy?
⑤ Can't you happy?

9. 다음 중 어법상 옳은 것은?

① Can't she sings?
② Don't she drive a car?
③ Isn't she a doctor?
④ Aren't you like soda?
⑤ Isn't you sleepy?

10. 다음 질문에 대한 대답으로 알맞은 것은?

> Don't you have a pet?

① No, I do.　　② Yes, I am.
③ Yes, I do.　　④ Yes, I don't.
⑤ No, I'm not.

단원평가　실전대비

1. 다음 중 주어진 문장과 의미가 같은 것은?

> Don't make a noise in the library.

① You will make a noise in the library.
② You may make a noise in the library.
③ You won't make a noise in the library.
④ You must not make a noise in the library.
⑤ Let's make a noise in the library.

2. 다음 중 어법상 옳은 것은?

① Never give up.
② Not be careful.
③ Turns on the light.
④ Do kind to your friends.
⑤ Don't talks with your friend.

3. 다음 질문에 대한 대답으로 알맞은 것은?

> Q: Isn't that Big Ben in the picture?
> A: _____

① It's a big ben.
② Yes, it's not.
③ No, it's Big Ben.
④ It's in the picture.
⑤ Yes, it is.

4. 다음 중 밑줄 친 부분이 옳은 것은?

① She isn't studying, <u>isn't she</u>?
② You found your dog, <u>didn't you</u>?
③ They didn't help you, <u>do they</u>?
④ The girl was at the party, <u>was the girl</u>?
⑤ You can speak Japanese, <u>will you</u>?

[5–6] 다음 우리말과 일치하도록 빈칸에 알맞은 말을 쓰시오.

5.

> A: Don't you like candies?
> B: Yes, I _____. (응, 좋아해.)
> / No, I _____. (아니, 안 좋아해.)

6.

> A: Don't you like animals?
> B: _____, _____ _____. (좋아합니다.)

7. 다음 중 어법상 옳은 것을 모두 고르면?

① Never go there!
② Be plant tulips!
③ Don't late for school!
④ Water the flowers!
⑤ Jane, watches out!

8. 다음 질문에 대한 대답으로 알맞은 것은?

> Q: You cannot see bacteria, can you?

① No, we can.
② No, we can't.
③ Yes, we can't.
④ Why can we see them?
⑤ It's because we can't see them.

9. 다음 빈칸에 알맞지 않은 것은?

> You _____, don't you?

① like pizza
② play football
③ are handsome
④ do exercise every day
⑤ go to school early

10. 다음 빈칸에 순서대로 알맞은 것은?

> - _____ quiet in class, please.
> - _____ swim in the river. It's very dirty.

① Be – Don't   ② Don't – Don't
③ Don't – Be   ④ Be – Doesn't
⑤ Doesn't – Don't

11. 다음 중 어법상 옳지 않은 것은?

① What handsome boys they are!
② How wonderful you are!
③ What a great play it is!
④ How delicious the dinner was!
⑤ How scary was the movie!

12. 다음 대화의 빈칸에 순서대로 알맞은 것은?

> A: You like sports, _____?
> B: Yes, I do. I like baseball.
> A: Baseball is your favorite sport, _____?
> B: Yes, you're right.

① do you – is it
② don't you – is it
③ doesn't you – isn't it
④ don't you – isn't it
⑤ do you – isn't it

13. 다음 중 빈칸에 들어갈 말이 나머지와 다른 것은?

① _____ funny the story is!
② _____ a cute cat it is!
③ _____ pretty sisters they are!
④ _____ an old gentleman he is!
⑤ _____ small puppies they are!

14. 다음 우리말과 뜻이 같도록 빈칸에 알맞은 말을 쓰시오.

> A: 너는 커피와 녹차 중 어떤 것이 더 좋니?
> B: I like coffee better.

⇒ _____ do you like better, coffee _____ green tea?

15. 다음 영화관에 게시할 안내문의 빈칸에 공통으로 들어갈 한 단어를 쓰시오.

> • _____ bring smelly food inside.
> • _____ talk on the phone.
> • _____ take pictures.

16. 다음 빈칸에 들어갈 알맞은 부가의문문을 쓰시오.

> ❶ Junk food isn't good for our health,
> _____ _____?
> ❷ Most countries have their own
> languages, _____ _____?

17. 다음 대화의 밑줄 친 부분 중 어법상 옳지 <u>않은</u> 것은?

> A: I <u>don't</u> <u>like</u> carrots.
>   ①   ②
> B: <u>Not</u> <u>say</u> that. <u>They're</u> good for your eyes.
>   ③   ④   ⑤

18. 다음 중 어법상 옳은 것은?

① You can keep a secret, don't you?
② She is a teacher, is she?
③ You are Korean, aren't you?
④ He doesn't like it, doesn't he?
⑤ Sue can't cook well, does she?

19. 다음 빈칸에 순서대로 알맞은 것은?

> - Minho is your brother, _____?
> - You like music, _____?

① is he – do you
② isn't he – do you
③ isn't he – don't you
④ is not he – do not you
⑤ isn't Minho – doesn't you

20. 다음 대화의 빈칸에 알맞은 것은?

> A: Jim likes music, doesn't he?
> B: _____ he can do all kinds of
>   music.

① Yes, he is.
② No, he isn't.
③ Yes, he does.
④ No, he doesn't.
⑤ Yes, he doesn't.

단원평가 　고난도

1. 다음 중 두 문장의 의미가 <u>다른</u> 것은?

① Be careful! = Watch out!
② Slow down! = Don't run fast!
③ That's not right. = That's wrong.
④ That's surprising! = I can believe it!
⑤ You must go there. = You have to go there.

2. 다음 주어진 단어만을 사용하여 문장을 완성할 때 (★)에 오는 단어는?

> 너의 코를 막고, 승강기를 타지 마라.
> = Cover (　) (　) (　) (★) (　)
> 　(　) (　).
> (take / and / nose / elevator / don't / your / the)

① and 　　② don't 　　③ take
④ your 　　⑤ elevator

3. 다음 중 환경보호의 실천방안을 제안한 것으로 <u>어색한</u> 것은?

① We waste paper.
　⇒ Let's cut trees.
② We waste much food.
　⇒ Let's eat all the food on our plates.
③ We often use plastic bags.
　⇒ Let's use paper bags.
④ There are too many cars.
　⇒ Let's ride a bike.
⑤ We make too much garbage.
　⇒ Let's try to recycle.

4. 다음 글의 빈칸에 알맞은 것은?

> Today is Saturday. It is sunny and clear. Father, Mother, my younger sister and I are going on a picnic. Everyone is very happy.
> _____

① How a wonderful day!
② How wonderful day!
③ What a wonderful day!
④ What wonderful day!
⑤ How a wonderful day!

5. 다음 중 어법상 옳지 <u>않은</u> 것은?

① The box is Minho's, isn't he?
② She understood everything, didn't she?
③ Your cousin is good at swimming, isn't she?
④ My mom didn't tell you anything, did she?
⑤ Bob and Mira are good friends, aren't they?

6. 다음 중 의미가 나머지와 <u>다른</u> 것은?

① She is very old.
② How old is she?
③ How old she is!
④ What an old woman she is!
⑤ She is a very old woman.

7. 다음 중 평서문을 감탄문으로 바꾼 것 중 옳은 것은?

① He is so handsome.
　⇒ How handsome is he!
② It's a very sunny day.
　⇒ What sunny day it is!
③ Your cat is so smart.
　⇒ How smart your cat is!
④ This is a really nice present.
　⇒ How a nice present this is!
⑤ These are great jeans!
　⇒ What a great jeans these are!

8. 다음 밑줄 친 부분을 바르게 고치시오.

❶ <u>Do</u> touch! It's hot.
　⇒ _____ _____ touch! It's hot.

❷ <u>Are</u> nice to your friends.
　⇒ _____ nice to your friends.

9. 다음 중 밑줄 친 부분이 옳지 않은 것은?

① He was right, <u>wasn't he</u>?
② Talk to your friends, <u>won't they</u>?
③ You won't be late, <u>will you</u>?
④ Tomorrow the exam is over, <u>isn't it</u>?
⑤ You and your friends want a party, <u>don't you</u>?

10. 다음 대화의 빈칸에 알맞지 않은 것은?

Mom: What are you doing?
Jinny: I'm watching my favorite show.
Mom: You have school tomorrow.
_____
Jinny: Alright, Mom.

① Go to bed early.
② Stay up late, Jinny.
③ Don't stay up too late.
④ Make sure you go to bed early.
⑤ Get enough sleep for tomorrow.

11. 다음 주어진 상황에 알맞은 말은?

You are studying with your friend in the library. Your friend's cell phone is on his desk. It keeps ringing, and it bothers you. In this situation, what would you say to your friend?

① Study harder.
② Let's go have lunch.
③ Turn on your cell phone, please.
④ Stand up and get out.
⑤ Turn off your cell phone, please.

12. 다음 대화의 빈칸에 들어갈 말이 바르게 짝지어진 것은?

A: _____ careful!
B: What's wrong?
A: Look at the sign. This river is so deep. _____ swim here.
B: Oh, I didn't see it. Thank you for telling me.

① Do – Let's
② Be – Don't
③ Do – Never
④ Be – Let's
⑤ Do – Let's not

13. 다음 대화에서 어색한 문장을 찾아 바르게 고쳐 문장을 다시 쓰시오.

A: Look at Sam! He is helping the sick.
B: What kind he is!

⇒ _____

14. 다음 우리말과 뜻이 같도록 빈칸에 알맞은 말을 쓰시오.

❶ Can't she play the cello?
_____, she _____.
(응, 할 수 있어.)

❷ Aren't you're a high school student?
_____, I _____.
(아니, 그렇지 않아.)

❸ Didn't Eric watch a movie last night?
_____, he _____.
(아니, 안 봤어.)

1. 친구에게 다른 나라의 식사 예절에 대한 에티켓을 조언해 주려고 한다. 다음에 제시된 세 나라의 상황을 주어진 단어나 어구를 활용하여 '~ 하라, ~ 하지 마라'라고 조언하는 메시지를 완전한 문장으로 작성하시오.

China	France	Thailand
eat all the food on your plate	put your arms on the table	eat too fast

❶ _____

❷ _____

❸ _____

2. 다음은 수업 시간에 지켜야 할 규칙들이다. 주어진 내용을 명령문을 활용하여 영어 문장으로 쓰시오.

❶ _____
(지각하지 않기)

❷ _____
(떠들지 않기)

❸ _____
(휴대폰 사용하지 않기)

❹ _____
(숙제 가져오는 것 잊지 않기)

3. 다음 예시를 참고하여 그림이 의미하는 것을 영어 문장으로 쓰시오.

예시

⇒ Don't be late.　　⇒ Stop.

❶ Don't _____.

❷ Be _____.

❸ _____ ride a bike.

❹ Don't _____ here.

4. 다음 빈칸에 들어갈 알맞은 부가의문문을 쓰시오.

❶ Jane and John had lunch, _____?

❷ Your mother washes the dishes,

_____?

❸ Peter can play basketball, _____?

5. 다음 문장을 보기와 같이 주어진 낱말로 시작하여 쓰시오.

> **보기**
>
> This car is very nice.
> ⇒ How nice this car is!
> ⇒ What a nice car this is!

❶ This is a very beautiful flower.

⇒ How _____!

⇒ What _____!

❷ These are very wonderful toys.

⇒ How _____!

⇒ What _____!

6. 다음 단어들을 배열하여 문장을 완성하시오.

❶ like, you, don't, to, listen to, music, you

⇒ _____,

_____?

❷ are, good, a, you, you, aren't, dancer

⇒ _____,

_____?

❸ sing, Susan, can't, she, can, well, very

⇒ _____,

_____?

❹ didn't, you, did, you, homework, your

⇒ _____,

_____?

7. 다음 문장의 밑줄 친 부분을 어법에 맞게 고쳐 쓰시오.

❶ You are sad, will you?

❷ You are hungry, are you?

❸ Read the comic books, shall we?

❹ Get to the hospital now, don't you?

❺ You can't understand me, don't you?

❻ He really enjoyed this cake, he didn't?

❼ Let's speak in Japanese for several minutes, will you?

8. 다음 세 문장의 의미가 같도록 빈칸을 완성하시오.

> Why don't we eat out for dinner?
> = _____ _____ eating out for dinner?
> = _____ _____ _____ for dinner.

memo

Chapter 9
문장의 형태

9.1. 문장의 형식

① 목적어를 가지지 않는 문장 (자동사가 있는 문장)

》》》 1형식: S + V (주어 + 동사)

I laughed. 나는 웃었다.
주어　　동사

> ※ 1형식 문장은 부사(구)와 함께 쓰이기도 한다.
> ※ 「There + be동사(V) + 주어(S)」 는 '~이 있다' 라고 해석하며 be동사 뒤에 나오는 명사가 주어가 된다.
>   There is a cat on the table. 탁자 위에 고양이 한 마리가 있다.

》》》 2형식: S + V + S.C. (주어 + 동사 + 주격보어)

She looks beautiful. 그녀는 아름다워 보인다.
주어　　동사　　주격보어

> ※ be, become, get, turn 등이 주로 2형식 문장의 동사로 사용된다.
> ※ 2형식 문장에서는 감각동사(look, sound, taste, smell, feel)등이
>   자주 함께 쓰이며, 이 동사의 뒤에는 반드시 형용사가 온다.

② 목적어를 가지는 문장 (타동사가 있는 문장)

》》》 3형식: S + V + O (주어 + 동사 + 목적어)

I opened the window. 나는 창문을 열었다.
주어　　동사　　목적어

》》》 4형식: S + V + I.O. + D.O. (주어 + 동사 + 간접목적어 + 직접목적어)

She gave me a pretty doll. 그녀는 나에게 예쁜 인형을 주었다.
주어　　동사　간접목적어　　직접목적어

> ※ 4형식에 쓰이는 동사는 간접목적어(I.O.) '~에게' 와
>   직접목적어(D.O.) '~을' 에 해당하는 두 개의 목적어를
>   갖는데 이런 동사를 수여동사라고 한다.

》》》 5형식: S + V + O + O.C. (주어 + 동사 + 목적어 + 목적격보어)

He makes me happy. 그는 나를 행복하게 만든다.
주어　　동사　목적어　목적격보어

> ※ 목적격보어 자리에는 명사(구)/형용사(구), to부정사, 동사원형을 활용할 수 있다.

**뽐쌤의
야무진
Tip!**

다시 한 번 정리해보는 문장의 기본 요소

❶ 주어(Subject): 문장에서 동작을 행하는 주체로, '~은(는), ~이(가)'로 해석한다.
❷ 동사(Verb): 주어의 상태나 동작을 나타내는 말로 '~이다, ~하다'로 해석한다.
❸ 목적어(Object): 주어가 하는 동작의 대상이 되는 말로 '~을(를), ~에게'라고 해석한다.
❹ 보어(Complement): 주어와 목적어를 보충 설명하는 말로, 주어를 설명하는 것을 주격보어, 목적어를 설명하는 것은 목적격보어라고 한다.

A. 다음 문장에서 주어에 밑줄을 그으시오.

1. I wanted to see a movie.
2. This gift shop is very popular.
3. My favorite season is summer.
4. He has no money.
5. The man in the park looks handsome.
6. Mary found the book boring.

B. 다음 문장에서 동사에 밑줄을 그으시오.

1. I always get up early.
2. John goes to Hawaii every summer.
3. The girl with a skirt stands next to me.
4. My parents drink soda.
5. He walked to school yesterday.
6. This soup smells great.

C. 다음 문장에서 목적어에 밑줄을 그으시오.

1. We pay electric bill.
2. I bought some new shoes.
3. You must wear your seat belt.
4. Susan met her old friend last weekend.
5. He knows my name and number.
6. Boys play soccer in the yard.

D. 다음 문장에서 보어에 밑줄을 그으시오.

1. I am a student.
2. The class is boring.
3. The news made us shocked.
4. My mom made me clean the room.
5. I found Jolie famous.
6. She became a model.

E. 다음 보기 와 같이 주어진 문장의 문장 형식과 밑줄 친 단어에 해당하는 각각의 문장 성분을 쓰시오.

> 보기 I   drink   a glass of water. [3형식]
>
> 주어   동사   목적어

1. She arrives at the museum.
2. Ted collects a lot of stamps as a hobby.
3. Her explanation sounds easy.
4. He saw John ride a bike in the park.

9.2. 감각동사 + 형용사

>>> 감각동사란? look, feel, smell, sound, taste와 같이 사람의 감각을 표현하는 동사

❶ look + 형용사: ~하게 보이다

He **looks happy**. 그는 행복해 보인다.

You **look exhausted** today. 너는 오늘 지쳐 보인다.

❷ feel + 형용사: ~하게 느끼다

He **feels tired** after a long walk. 그는 오래 걸은 후 피곤하게 느낀다.

She **felt sad** about the news. 그녀는 그 소식에 슬프게 느꼈다.

❸ smell + 형용사: ~한 냄새가 나다

This bread **smells delicious**. 이 빵은 맛있는 냄새가 난다.

Her perfume **smells nice**. 그녀의 향수는 좋은 냄새가 난다.

❹ sound + 형용사: ~하게 들리다

This music **sounds beautiful**. 이 음악은 아름답게 들린다.

Let's go out for a walk. –That **sounds great**. 산책하러 나가자. -그거 좋겠다.

❺ taste + 형용사: ~한 맛이 나다

This milk **tastes a little sour**. 이 우유는 약간 신 맛이 난다.

It **tastes so sweet**. 그것은 매우 단 맛이 난다.

* 중요! 감각동사 다음에는 부사를 쓰지 않도록 주의한다.

He looks happy. (o)   He looks happily. (x)

뽐쌤의 야무진 Tip!

감각동사 + like + 명사

look like (~처럼 보이다)   She <u>looks like</u> <u>a doll</u>. 그녀는 인형처럼 보인다.

feel like (~처럼 느끼다)   This paper <u>feels like</u> <u>silk</u>. 이 종이는 실크처럼 느껴진다.

sound like (~처럼 들리다)   That <u>sounds like</u> <u>a good idea</u>. 그것은 좋은 생각처럼 들린다.

smell like (~같은 냄새가 나다)   It <u>smells like</u> <u>roses</u>. 그것은 장미 같은 냄새가 난다.

taste like (~와 같은 맛이 나다)   Does turkey <u>taste like</u> <u>chicken</u>? 칠면조는 닭과 같은 맛이 나니?

A. 다음 괄호 안에서 알맞은 말을 고르시오.

❶ You look (health, healthy).

❷ It (looks, looks like) snow.

❸ That sounds (interesting, interest).

❹ This soup smells (terrible, terribly).

❺ Susan (looks, looks like) her mom.

❻ The roses smell (sweet, sweetly).

❼ The song sounds (beautiful, beautifully).

B. 다음 우리말과 뜻이 같도록 주어진 단어를 이용하여 빈칸을 채우시오.

❶ 그 책들은 무거워 보여. (heavy)

The books _____ _____.

❷ 네 향수는 냄새가 강해. (strong)

Your perfume _____ _____.

❸ 이 스웨터는 감촉이 부드럽다. (soft)

This sweater _____ _____.

❹ 그 뮤지컬은 재미있어 보인다. (interesting)

The musical _____ _____.

❺ 이 샐러드는 맛이 신선하다. (fresh)

This fruit _____ _____.

C. 다음 밑줄 친 부분을 어법에 맞게 고쳐 쓰시오.

❶ Does the man look <u>smartly</u>?

❷ Her voice sounded <u>differently</u>.

❸ This cloth <u>feels</u> wood.

❹ You <u>look like</u> happy today.

❺ John looks <u>sleep</u>.

9.3. 수여동사 + 직접목적어 + 간접목적어

》》 수여동사란? '~에게 …을 주다'라는 의미로, 간접목적어(~에게)와 직접목적어(~을)를 취하는 4형식 문장에 쓰이는 동사

He   teaches   us   English. 그는 나에게 영어를 가르친다.

주어   수여동사   간접목적어   직접목적어

1 수여동사의 종류

》》 give(주다), send(보내다), teach(가르치다), tell(말하다), show(보여주다), write(쓰다), make(만들다), buy(사다), cook(요리하다), get(얻다, 구하다), find(찾다), ask(묻다) 등

2 4형식 문장의 3형식 전환

》》 목적어가 두 개인 4형식 문장은 간접목적어와 직접목적어의 위치를 바꾸고, 간접목적어 앞에 전치사를 넣어 3형식 문장으로 전환할 수 있다.

4형식: She gave **me some flowers**. 그녀는 나에게 약간의 꽃을 주었다.

3형식: She gave **some flowers to me**.

》》 「전치사 + 간접목적어」는 부사구가 되어 3형식 문장이 되며 전치사는 동사에 따라 결정된다.

to를 쓰는 동사	give, tell, teach, send, bring, show, write, offer, pass, owe, promise, tell, read etc.	He told me the news. → He told the news **to** me. 그는 나에게 그 소식을 말했다.
for를 쓰는 동사	buy, make, find, get, cook, leave, build, choose, order etc.	I bought him a cooking book. → I bought a cooking book **for** him. 나는 그에게 요리책을 사주었다.
of를 쓰는 동사	ask, beg, inquire, require etc.	I asked her some questions. → I asked some questions **of** her. 나는 그녀에게 약간의 질문을 했다.

* 직접목적어가 대명사인 경우는 4형식 문장으로 만들 수 없으므로 3형식 문장으로 표현한다.

I gave her it. (x)   I gave it to her. (o)

A. **다음 4형식 문장을 3형식으로 전환하여 문장을 완성하시오.**

1. They will tell him the story.

   ➡ They will tell _____.

2. Can I ask you a favor?

   ➡ Can I ask _____?

3. My dad got me a concert ticket.

   ➡ My dad got _____.

4. Susan cooked me ramen.

   ➡ Susan cooked _____.

B. **다음 괄호 안에 말을 알맞은 자리에 넣어 4형식 문장을 만드시오.**

1. I gave two postcards. (my friend)

   ➡ _____

2. Grace taught children at the community center. (English)

   ➡ _____

3. My father bought a diamond ring. (my mother)

   ➡ _____

C. **다음 괄호 안에 단어들을 바르게 배열하여 문장을 완성하시오.**

1. A: Does the baby want more milk?

   B: Yes. _____. (more, give, him, milk)

2. A: Can you _____? (me, some, make, sandwiches)

   B: Sure. I'll make them for you.

3. A: Is this your pen?

   B: Yes. It's mine. Can you _____? (to, pass, it, me)

>>> 5형식 문장의 순서는? 주어(S) + 동사(V) + 목적어(O) + 목적격보어(O.C.)

>>> 목적격보어란? 목적어의 성질/상태를 보충해주는 말로 명사(구), 형용사(구), to부정사(구), 동사원형 혹은 분사가 온다.

1 명사(구)/형용사(구)를 목적격보어로 취하는 동사

>>> find, call, keep, turn, make, think 등

I **named my dog 'Dongki'.** 나는 내 개에게 '동키'라고 이름을 지어줬다.

(목적격보어 자리에 명사가 오는 경우, 목적어=목적격보어)

I **found the book interesting.** 나는 그 책이 재미있다는 것을 알았다.

(목적격보어 자리에 형용사가 오는 경우, 목적격보어는 목적어의 상태/성질을 나타낸다.)

2 to부정사를 목적격보어로 취하는 동사

>>> want, ask, tell, order, advise, expect 등

She **told me to clean** the room. 그녀는 나에게 청소를 하라고 말했다.

I **want him to be** quiet. 나는 그가 조용히 하길 원한다.

* help는 목적격보어로 to부정사와 동사원형을 모두 쓸 수 있다.

Thomas **helped me do** my homework. Thomas는 내가 숙제를 하는 것을 도와주었다.

= Thomas **helped me to do** my homework.

3 동사원형/분사를 목적격보어로 취하는 동사

❶ 사역동사 make, let, have + 목적어 + 동사원형

She **made me feel** uncomfortable. 그녀는 나를 편하게 만들었다.

He **has me wash** the dishes. 그는 나를 설거지를 하게 한다.

❷ 지각동사 see, watch, hear, feel, listen to, smell 등 + 목적어 + 동사원형/분사

I **saw him run.** 나는 그가 달리는 것을 보았다.

I **saw him running.** (현재분사를 쓰면 진행의 의미가 강조됨)

She **felt the ground shake.** 그녀는 땅이 흔들리는 것을 느꼈다.

Tom **watched Suji singing** on the stage. Tom은 Suji가 무대에서 노래하는 것을 지켜보았다.

A. 다음 괄호 안에서 알맞은 것을 고르시오

1. Your smile makes your parents (happy, happily).

2. The coat will keep you (warm, warmly).

3. I told him (open, to open) the door.

4. We saw the dog (wag, to wag) its tail.

5. His father made him (sit, sat) at the desk for two hours.

6. Mrs. Brown (let, allowed) her son fix the car.

7. I thought the movie (interesting, interestingly).

B. 다음 보기 와 같이 문장의 사선(/)으로 끊어진 부분을 우리말로 옮기시오.

> 보기 We elected / him / president.
>   우리는 선출했다   그를   대통령으로

1. I called / him / a fool.

2. Her mother made / her / a famous musician.

3. I believe / her / very friendly.

4. We painted / the door / a different color.

C. 다음 우리말과 뜻이 같도록 괄호 안에 주어진 말을 이용하여 문장을 완성하시오.

1. 나는 그를 겁쟁이라고 부른다. (call, a coward)

   I _____ _____ _____ _____.

2. 그 책은 그녀를 졸리게 했다. (make, sleepy)

   The book _____ _____ _____.

3. 그 문을 계속 열어 두어라. (open)

   Keep _____ _____ _____.

4. 나는 네가 그와 함께 춤추는 것을 보았다. (see, dance with)

   I _____ _____ _____ _____ _____.

1. 다음 대화의 빈칸에 알맞은 것은?

> A: How does Susan look in the picture?
> B: She looks _____.

① sing ② bake ③ draw
④ speak ⑤ happy

2. 다음 중 어법상 옳지 <u>않은</u> 것은?

① She looks happy.
② It tastes yummy.
③ Pizza smells good.
④ I feel very hungry.
⑤ The drum sounds loudly.

[3-4] 다음 빈칸에 알맞은 것은?

3.

> I met my friend, Jessica, today. She looked _____.

① calmly ② angrily ③ lovely
④ happily ⑤ strangely

4.

> Minho _____ some flowers for me.

① gave ② sent ③ showed
④ bought ⑤ brought

[5-6] 다음 빈칸에 알맞지 <u>않은</u> 것은?

5.

> Jim _____ his son a basketball.

① liked ② gave ③ passed
④ showed ⑤ bought

6.

> My friend sent _____ some flowers.

① me ② him ③ your
④ her ⑤ Minho

7. 다음 질문에 대한 대답으로 알맞은 것은?

> A: What does your teacher look like?
> B: _____

① She is tall and thin.
② She looks happy today.
③ She is from London.
④ She is looking at the mirror.
⑤ She is an English teacher.

8. 다음 밑줄 친 happy의 알맞은 형태를 쓰시오.

❶ He looks <u>happy</u> today.
❷ She gave me <u>happy</u>.

[9-10] 다음 빈칸에 알맞은 것은?

9.

> Mira _____ me help her with homework.

① wanted   ② made   ③ told
④ asked   ⑤ advised

10.

> My parents want me _____ a good singer.

① be   ② to be   ③ being
④ to being   ⑤ been

단원평가 / 실전대비

1. 다음 대화의 빈칸에 알맞지 <u>않은</u> 것은?

> A: How do you feel about the first day of middle school?
> B: I feel _____.

① worried   ② excited   ③ happy
④ kind   ⑤ pleased

2. 다음 중 밑줄 친 부분이 <u>잘못된</u> 것은?

① It tastes <u>sweetly</u>.
② They taste <u>delicious</u>.
③ You look <u>happy</u> today.
④ The cat looks <u>hungry</u>.
⑤ The boy looks <u>sad</u>.

3. 다음 대화의 A, B에 순서대로 알맞은 것은?

> M: He looks (A).
> W: No, he feels (B). His best friend moved to another city.

① bored – sadly   ② sick – lone
③ sickly – sad   ④ sadly – tired
⑤ sick – lonely

4. 다음 두 문장의 빈칸에 공통으로 알맞은 것은?

> - The baby looks _____ an angel.
> - The pie smells _____ an apple.

① like   ② in   ③ at
④ for   ⑤ around

5. 다음 중 밑줄 친 부분이 <u>잘못된</u> 것은?

① The lemon tastes <u>sour</u>.
② The girl looks <u>fashionable</u>.
③ The boy looks <u>cold</u>.
④ The music sounds <u>sleep</u>.
⑤ Bibimbab looks <u>delicious</u>.

6. 다음 중 빈칸에 알맞지 <u>않은</u> 것은?

> Mrs. Brown _____ us a book.

① gave   ② sent   ③ bought
④ wanted   ⑤ showed

7. 다음 우리말을 영어로 바르게 옮긴 것은?

> 우리는 병원에 있는 아픈 아이들에게 음악을 가르쳐.

① We teach children sick music in the hospital.
② We teach sick children music to the hospital.
③ We teach sick children music in the hospital.
④ We teach music sick children in the hospital.
⑤ We teach sick music to children in the hospital.

8. 다음 중 어법상 옳지 <u>않은</u> 문장 두 개는?

① Jim read her Yuan's letter.
② Did she show you her pictures?
③ Minho sent an e-mail his friends.
④ John's mother made dinner his son.
⑤ Give her sister a hamburger.

9. 다음 중 두 문장의 의미가 같은 것은?

① She had a serious look on her face.
   = She looks seriously.
② I gave my sweet smile to everybody.
   = I gave everybody my sweet smile.
③ Because he failed the test, his voice was sad.
   = He failed the test. So his voice sounded sadly.
④ Sam bought Anne a present.
   = Sam bought a present to Anne.
⑤ Mom made me a pretty doll.
   = Mom made a pretty doll to me.

10. 다음 중 문장의 형식이 나머지와 <u>다른</u> 것은?

① I studied math yesterday.
② The woman asked me a question.
③ My brother made me a hamburger.
④ Mr. Choi bought her a ring.
⑤ Hyosup showed me his picture.

11. 다음 중 어법상 옳지 <u>않은</u> 것은?

① He saw Kate and gave her a ride.
② The man showed nice shoes Amy.
③ Tom's grandmother made him a cake.
④ Mira's mom bought a computer for her.
⑤ Mira showed Yunho a picture of her family.

12. 다음 빈칸에 들어갈 전치사가 순서대로 짝지어진 것은?

> (A) He always asks funny questions _____ me.
> (B) She showed some pictures _____ me.
> (C) My father bought a puppy _____ us.

	(A)	(B)	(C)
①	to	for	of
②	to	of	for
③	of	for	to
④	of	to	for
⑤	for	to	to

13. 다음 중 밑줄 친 부분이 <u>잘못된</u> 것은?

① This music makes me <u>calm</u>.
② A contest makes me <u>nervously</u>.
③ This painting makes me <u>lonely</u>.
④ Baseball games make people <u>excited</u>.
⑤ School trips make me <u>tired</u>.

14. 다음 중 주어진 문장과 형식이 같은 것은?

> I will give all my things to the cleverest son.

① Give him a good-bye kiss.
② He sent him the ball to the north.
③ Please send me some pictures of our house.
④ She gave our class the letter to say sorry.
⑤ I want to show them to my friends in Korea.

15. 다음 중 빈칸에 to가 들어갈 수 있는 문장 두 개는?

① Lucy told her secret _____ her mom.
② Mr. Choi taught his son _____ how to ride a bike.
③ Ella cooked lunch _____ her husband.
④ Sofia asked many personal questions _____ the teacher.
⑤ Mina sent a thank-you card _____ her English teacher.

16. 다음 빈칸에 순서대로 알맞은 것은?

> Tom looked at me _____. He said, "You look _____ today. You look _____".

① happy – beautiful – an angel
② happily – beautiful – an angel
③ happy – beautiful – like an angel
④ happily – beautiful – like an angel
⑤ happy – beautifully – like an angel

17. 다음 중 빈칸에 들어갈 말이 나머지와 <u>다른</u> 것은?

① She made a kite _____ him.
② He showed his book _____ me.
③ Mina sent a letter _____ her mom.
④ We gave a dollar _____ him.
⑤ She told the news _____ them.

18. 다음 중 밑줄 친 부분의 쓰임이 나머지와 <u>다른</u> 것은?

① Just call me <u>Bomi</u>.
② I found him <u>a fool</u>.
③ I threw the boy <u>a big ball</u>.
④ They named their son <u>Carl</u>.
⑤ We elected Mr. Lee <u>president</u>.

[19–20] 다음 빈칸에 알맞은 것은?

19.

> His mother made him _____ at the desk for two hours every day.

① sit   ② sits   ③ sat
④ sitting   ⑤ to sit

20. (정답 2개)

> I heard a baby _____ late at night.

① cry   ② cries   ③ cried
④ crying   ⑤ to cry

1. 다음 보기에서 어법상 맞는 문장을 말한 학생의 수는?

보기

지윤: The cake looks delicious.
지나: The coffee smells well.
민호: This steak tasted so good.
효섭: Her perfume smells nicely.
진석: The music sounds beautifully.
형식: My girlfriend looks upset.
경훈: The noodle smelled spicy.

① 2명　　　② 3명　　　③ 4명
④ 5명　　　⑤ 6명

2. 다음 보기에서 빈칸에 들어가는 말이 같은 것끼리 묶은 것은?

보기

look / look like (어법에 맞게 변형할 수 있음)

a. Sam _____ tired.
b. The movie _____ boring.
c. The cookies _____ delicious.
d. My little brother _____ a cute bear.
e. The pictures _____ very nice.
f. Jessica and Linda _____ movie stars.

① a, e　　　② b, d　　　③ d, f
④ a, c, d　　⑤ b, d, f

3. 다음 중 3형식으로의 전환이 올바른 것은?

① She made me this cake.
⇒ She made this cake to me.
② You can ask him this question.
⇒ You can ask this question for him.
③ Ms. Brown can teach us science.
⇒ Ms. Brown can teach science of us.
④ Dad will send mom some flowers.
⇒ Dad will send some flowers for mom.
⑤ He will give Elena this ring.
⇒ He will give this ring to Elena.

4. 다음 중 빈칸에 be동사가 들어갈 수 <u>없는</u> 것은?

① Aria _____ a nurse.
② She _____ playing the piano.
③ Your English _____ very good.
④ Jim _____ painted a picture.
⑤ Taeyoen _____ surprised at the news.

5. 다음 중 그림을 올바르게 표현한 것은?

① She showed her student the picture.

② My grandfather passed a pen for me.

③ She bought a new computer of me.

④ Grandma made me for a birthday cake.

⑤ He taught his children to korean.

6. 다음 보기에서 문장의 형식이 같은 것을 찾아 번호를 쓰시오.

> **보기**
> ① There is an apple on the table.
> ② She is a famous dancer.
> ③ I know how to ride a bike.
> ④ Will you pass me the pepper?
> ⑤ We call her Britney.

❶ I found this book interesting.　　(　)
❷ My teacher asked me a question.　(　)
❸ The door opens slowly.　　　　(　)
❹ This cake is delicious.　　　　(　)
❺ I think that she is kind.　　　　(　)

7. 다음 중 주어진 문장과 문장의 형식이 같은 것은?

> He made his daughter a doll.

① The boy made me laugh.
② I'll make you a good suit.
③ He will make a good doctor.
④ They make cars in the factory.
⑤ The old lady made John her secretary.

8. 다음 두 문장이 같은 뜻이 되도록 빈칸을 채우시오.

> The man said to us, "Don't touch these paintings."
> = The man told us _____ _____ _____ these paintings.

9. 다음 중 밑줄 친 낱말의 뜻이 서로 같은 것은?

① Jonathan <u>is</u> a great actor.
　The pen <u>is</u> in his right hand.
② He <u>became</u> a famous soccer player in 2002.
　This dress <u>becomes</u> you well.
③ I <u>felt</u> hungry and sleepy.
　Are you <u>feeling</u> all right, Elena?
④ He <u>grows</u> his hair and now his hair is longer than mine.
　The sun <u>grew</u> so hot that we stopped working.
⑤ My mother's black hair <u>turned</u> gray.
　Hyosup <u>turned</u> to Jina and began to talk.

10. 다음 중 어법상 옳지 <u>않은</u> 것은?

① He has me laugh all the time.
② John helped me to wash the dishes.
③ They let us to go outside to play soccer.
④ Mrs. Lee had her children do the laundry.
⑤ Every morning, Helen makes pancakes to feed her children.

1. 다음 빈칸에 들어갈 말을 보기에서 골라 알맞은 형태로 쓰시오. (보기의 단어 변형 가능)

> 보기 tired feel hear like taste sound

❶ He exercised too much. He looks _____.

❷ A: Why don't you go to the movies?

  B: It _____ _____ a good idea!

❸ My mom made an apple cake. It _____ sweet.

2. 다음 주어진 문장을 영어로 옮길 때 괄호 안에 알맞은 것을 쓰시오.(한 괄호에 한 단어씩만 사용)

> 숙제는 나에게 너무 많은 스트레스를 준다.
> = Homework (   ) (   ) (   ) (   ) (   ) me.

3. 다음 괄호 안에 주어진 단어들을 활용하여 질문에 대한 알맞은 답을 쓰시오.

> A: What did Minho and Minji do on Parents' Day?
> B: ❶ Minho _____.
>   (주어포함 6단어) (send / a card / his mom)
>   Minji ❷ _____.
>   (주어포함 7단어) (make / her mom / a cake)

4. 다음 두 문장이 같은 뜻이 되도록 빈칸에 알맞은 말을 쓰시오.

❶ The woman allowed us to come in.

  = The woman _____ us come in.

❷ He forced the boy to listen to the story.

  = He _____ the boy listen to the story.

5. 다음 문장에서 잘못된 부분을 찾아 고친 후 올바른 문장 전체를 다시 쓰시오.

❶ Suji sent she some cookies.

  _____

❷ John's dad showed John's many photos.

  _____

❸ Please get some water me.

  _____

6. 다음 대화를 괄호 안에 단어를 모두 사용하여 완성하시오. (단, 필요한 경우, 형태를 변형)

❶ A: Can I help you?

  B: Yes. _____

  (me / bring / cups / two / coffee / of)

❷ A: How was your interview?

  B: Not bad. _____

  (many / ask / they / me / questions / of)

7. 다음 문장을 3형식이 되도록 빈칸에 알맞은 말을 쓰시오.

❶ Nobody showed him the ticket.

= Nobody showed the ticket _____.

❷ Mr. Kim bought his wife a nice hat.

= Mr. Kim bought a nice hat _____.

8. 다음 문장에서 어법상 <u>어색한</u> 부분을 찾아 바르게 고치시오.

❶ This cloth feels smoothly.

❷ He told Minji share the room with his sister.

❸ My mom made me to study math during the vacation.

9. 다음 두 문장을 한 문장으로 만들 때 빈칸에 알맞은 말을 쓰시오.

❶ I saw John. He was walking a dog.

⇒ I saw John _____.

❷ Minho heard the dog. It was barking loudly at night.

⇒ Minho heard the dog _____.

10. 다음 밑줄 친 부분에 주의하여 우리말로 옮기시오.

❶ Mina found the book <u>easily</u>.

⇒ _____

❷ Mina found the book <u>easy</u>.

⇒ _____

11. 다음 4형식 문장을 3형식으로 바꿔 쓰시오.

❶ Jenny gave me useful information.

⇒ _____

❷ Jim's uncle sent him a gift.

⇒ _____

❸ My father bought me a bike.

⇒ _____

❹ Ms. Kim teaches us math.

⇒ _____

12. 다음 주어진 문장을 4형식 문장으로 바꿔 쓰시오.

❶ He wrote a card to his teacher.

⇒ _____

❷ Father cooked dinner for us.

⇒ _____

❸ Helen bought skates for him.

⇒ _____

13. 다음 보기 와 같이 바꿔 쓸 때 빈칸에 알맞은 말을 쓰시오.

> 보기 "Turn off the computer, Jiho."
> ⇒ I told Jiho <u>to turn off the computer.</u>

❶ "Be quiet in the classroom, Susan."

⇒ I told Susan _____.

❷ "Take care of your sister, Minho."

⇒ I told Minho _____.

Chapter 10
형용사와 부사

10.1. 형용사의 역할

》》 형용사란? 사람이나 사물의 모양, 상태, 크기, 성질 등을 나타내는 말이다. be동사 뒤에 쓰이거나 명사를 앞이나 뒤에서 꾸며준다.

1 한정적 용법

》》 명사나 대명사의 앞이나 뒤에서 직접 수식한다.

I have a **nice house**. 나는 멋진 집을 가지고 있다.

She wants to drink **something hot**. 그녀는 뜨거운 무언가를 마시길 원한다.

* -thing, -body, -one으로 끝나는 대명사는 형용사가 반드시 뒤에서 수식을 한다.

Give me cold something. (x)   Give me something cold. (o)

2 서술적 용법

》》 주어나 목적어를 설명하는 보어로 쓰이며 명사나 대명사를 간접 수식한다.

The boy is **wise** and **handsome**. (주격보어) 그 소년은 현명하고 잘생겼다.

I kept my room **clean**. (목적격보어) 나는 내 방을 깨끗하게 유지했다.

* 서술적 용법에만 쓰이는 형용사: alive(살아 있는), afraid(두려워하는), alone(혼자), asleep(잠이 든), alike(비슷한), aware(알고 있는), ashamed(부끄러운), glad(기쁜), drunk(술이 취한) 등

3 형용사의 어순

》》 형용사가 두 개 이상인 경우 「지시형용사 + 수량형용사(수, 양, 정도) + 성질형용사(성질, 상태, 모양)」 순으로 쓴다.

I like **those two cute** dogs. <지시 + 수량 + 성질> 나는 저 두 마리의 귀여운 개들을 좋아한다.

He has **four big red** bags. <수량 + 성질(크기) + 성질(색깔)> 그는 네 개의 큰 빨간색 가방을 가지고 있다.

4 수량형용사

》》 명사의 수나 양을 나타낸다.

	셀 수 있는 명사(수)	셀 수 없는 명사(양)	둘 다 씀(수/양)
많은	many	much	a lot of / lots of / plenty of
조금 있는(긍정)	a few	a little	some (긍정문, 권유문) / any (부정문, 의문문)
거의 없는(부정)	few	little	-

I have **many(=a lot of, lots of, plenty of)** friends. 나는 많은 친구들이 있다.

She drinks **much(=a lot of, lots of, plenty of)** water every day. 그녀는 매일 많은 물을 마신다.

다음 밑줄 친 형용사의 용법으로 올바른 것을 고르시오.

① My girlfriend is <u>pretty</u> and <u>kind</u>.   (한정/서술)

② She kept the door <u>open</u>.   (한정/서술)

③ I'm looking for something <u>nutty</u>.   (한정/서술)

④ He is <u>afraid</u> of snakes.   (한정/서술)

⑤ Jimmy raises a <u>cute</u> puppy.   (한정/서술)

⑥ Ann is a <u>diligent</u> student.   (한정/서술)

⑦ The long story was <u>interesting</u>.   (한정/서술)

⑧ Susan felt <u>nervous</u> about the future.   (한정/서술)

B. **다음 우리말과 뜻이 같도록 괄호 안에 단어들을 배열하시오.**

① 나는 매운 것을 원한다. (something, spicy)

I want _____.

② 이 두 마리의 사랑스러운 새들을 봐. (these, lovely, two, birds)

Look at _____.

③ 그녀의 신작 소설은 흥미롭다. (new, is, novel, interesting)

Her _____.

④ 나는 오늘 중요한 회의가 있다. (important, an, meeting, today)

I have _____.

C. **다음 괄호 안에 알맞은 말을 고르시오**

① He doesn't have (many, much) time.

② She drinks (many, much) milk every day.

③ We had (many, much) rain last summer.

④ Do you have (many, much) money?

⑤ She writes (a few, a little) letters every week.

⑥ Please call again in (a few, a little) minutes.

10.2. 부사의 역할

>>> 부사란? 동사, 형용사, 다른 부사 또는 문장 전체를 수식하는 말이다.

1 부사의 형태

❶ 원래 부사인 경우

very, well, now, then, here, there

❷ 대부분의 경우: 「형용사 + -ly」

quick → quickly, careful → carefully, new → newly, sure → surely, kind → kindly, great → greatly, beautiful → beautifully

❸ 「자음 + y」로 끝나는 경우: y를 i로 바꾸고 + -ly

happy → happily, easy → easily, lazy → lazily

❹ [-ue]로 끝나는 경우: -ue를 -uly로

true → truly

❺ [-le]로 끝나는 경우: -le를 -ly로

gentle → gently, terrible → terribly, simple → simply

❻ 형용사와 형태가 같은 부사

pretty	(형)예쁜 (부)꽤	fast	(형)빠른 (부)빠르게
early	(형)이른 (부)일찍	late	(형)늦은 (부)늦게
hard	(형)어려운 (부)열심히	high	(형)높은 (부)높게
near	(형)가까운 (부)가까이	right	(형)바른 (부)곧장, 바로

❼ 형태는 비슷하지만 의미가 다른 부사

late(늦게) – lately(최근에), high(높게) – highly(매우), near(가까이) – nearly(거의), hard(열심히) – hardly(거의 ~않다)

2 부사의 용법

❶ 동사 수식   He runs **fast**. 그는 빠르게 달린다.
❷ 형용사 수식   The girl is **very** tall. 그 여자 아이는 키가 매우 크다.
❸ 부사 수식   She speaks English **very** well. 그녀는 영어를 매우 잘 한다.
❹ 문장 전체 수식   **Luckily**, he passed the exam. 운좋게도, 그는 시험에 통과했다.

A. 다음 형용사를 부사로 만드시오.

① careful ➡ _____

② good ➡ _____

③ quick ➡ _____

④ fast ➡ _____

⑤ new ➡ _____

⑥ true ➡ _____

⑦ easy ➡ _____

⑧ happy ➡ _____

⑨ great ➡ _____

⑩ wonderful ➡ _____

B. 다음 문장의 밑줄 친 부분이 형용사이면 '형', 부사이면 '부'라고 쓰시오.

① She is an early bird.

② Don't go out in the late evening.

③ My father works hard for my family.

④ I can jump high.

⑤ We can see these flowers in the early spring.

C. 다음 문장의 밑줄 친 부분이 수식하는 말을 찾아 동그라미 하시오.

① He wakes up early in the morning.　　　(동사, 형용사, 부사, 문장)

② The flowers are really beautiful.　　　(동사, 형용사, 부사, 문장)

③ Julia eats very quickly.　　　(동사, 형용사, 부사, 문장)

④ Mr. Simpson looked at me angrily.　　　(동사, 형용사, 부사, 문장)

⑤ Strangely, he didn't invite her.　　　(동사, 형용사, 부사, 문장)

>>> 빈도부사란? 어떤 일이 얼마나 자주 일어나는지 빈도를 나타내는 부사로 be동사나 조동사 뒤, 일반동사의 앞에 위치한다.

발생빈도

100% ←───→ 0%

always	usually	often		sometimes	seldom	never
항상	보통은, 대개	종종		가끔, 때때로	좀처럼 ~않다	결코 ~아니다

1 빈도부사의 뜻

빈도부사	뜻	예문
always	항상	He **always** comes in time. 그는 언제나 제 시간에 온다.
usually	보통은, 대개	I **usually** go to school on foot. 나는 대개 학교에 걸어서 간다.
often	종종	She is **often** late. 그녀는 종종 늦는다.
sometimes	가끔, 때때로	He is **sometimes** sad at night. 그는 때때로 밤에 슬퍼한다.
seldom	좀처럼 ~않다	The kids can **seldom** watch TV. 그 아이들은 좀처럼 티비를 볼 수 없다.
never	결코 ~아니다	She will **never** be busy. 그녀는 절대 바쁘지 않을 것이다.

2 빈도부사의 위치

❶ be동사나 조동사의 뒤

His room <u>is</u> **always** clean. 그의 방은 언제나 깨끗하다.
We <u>may</u> **often** change the plan. 우리는 종종 계획을 바꿀 수도 있다.

❷ 일반동사의 앞

She **sometimes** <u>drives</u> too fast. 그녀는 가끔 차를 너무 빠르게 몬다.
I **never** <u>ride</u> a rollercoaster. 나는 절대 롤러코스터를 타지 않는다.

A. 다음 주어진 빈도부사를 넣어 문장을 다시 쓰시오.

❶ She is honest. (always)

_____

❷ Minho makes fun of me. (always)

_____

❸ My dad comes home late in the evening. (usually)

_____

❹ I sleep for about 8 hours every night. (usually)

_____

❺ She can't sleep well. (often)

_____

❻ I break my promise. (never)

_____

❼ I drink coffee at night. (seldom)

_____

❽ I will miss the chance. (never)

_____

❾ He feels tired in the morning. (often)

_____

❿ I hang out with my friends after school. (sometimes)

_____

10.4. 비교급/최상급 변화

1 규칙 변화

원급	비교급	최상급	예
대부분	+ er	+ est	old - older - oldest long - loner - longest
-e로 끝날 때	+ r	+ st	large - larger - largest nice - nicer - nicest
「자음 + y」로 끝날 때	y를 i로 고치고 + er	y를 i로 고치고 + est	pretty - prettier - prettiest busy - busier - busiest
「단모음 + 단자음」으로 끝날 때	자음 반복 + er	자음 반복 + est	big - bigger - biggest fat - fatter - fattest
3음절 이상이거나, -ful, -ous, -ish, -less, -ive, -ing으로 끝나는 2음절 형용사	more + 원급	more + 원급	beautiful - more beautiful - most beautiful
「형용사 + ly」로 끝나는 부사	more + 원급	more + 원급	quickly - more quickly - most quickly

2 불규칙 변화

good / well	better	best
bad / ill	worse	worst
many / much	more	much
little	less	least
late	later	latest(최근의)
	latter	last(마지막의)
old	older	oldest(나이)
	elder	eldest(순서)
far	farther	farthest(거리)
	further	furthest(정도)

A. 다음 주어진 단어의 비교급, 최상급을 쓰시오.

① small - _____ - _____　　② large - _____ - _____

③ busy - _____ - _____　　④ big - _____ - _____

⑤ good - _____ - _____　　⑥ many - _____ - _____

⑦ easy - _____ - _____　　⑧ well - _____ - _____

⑨ hot - _____ - _____　　⑩ much - _____ - _____

⑪ little - _____ - _____　　⑫ bad - _____ - _____

⑬ useful - _____ - _____　　⑭ popular - _____ - _____

⑮ interesting - _____ - _____　　⑯ happy - _____ - _____

⑰ beautiful - _____ - _____　　⑱ precious - _____ - _____

⑲ fat - _____ - _____　　⑳ heavy - _____ - _____

B. 다음 괄호 안에 주어진 낱말을 활용하여 빈칸을 완성하시오.

① Russia is _____ than Korea. (cold)

② Suji is _____ than Minho. (short)

③ Geumgangsan is _____ than Seoraksan. (beautiful)

④ This bag is _____ than I thought. (expensive)

⑤ Seoul is the _____ city in Korea. (big)

⑥ Mt. Everest is the _____ mountain in the world. (high)

⑦ Alaska is the _____ country from here. (far)

⑧ Bob is _____ than his sister. (talkative)

10.5. 비교표현 (원급, 비교급)

1 원급을 이용한 비교

>>> 비교되는 두 대상의 정도가 서로 같음을 나타낸다.

❶ as + 형용사/부사의 원급 + as: ~만큼 …한

My hair is **as long as** Mina's. 나의 머리는 미나의 머리만큼 길다.

She eats **as fast as** I. 그녀는 나만큼 빨리 먹는다.

❷ not as[so] + 원급 + as: ~만큼 …하지 않은

Today is **not as hot as** yesterday.

= Yesterday is **hotter than** today.

* 원급비교의 부정: A + not as + 원급 + as B = B + 비교급 than + A

2 비교급을 이용한 비교

>>> 비교급 + than : ~보다 …한

He is **richer than** I (am). 그는 나보다 더 부유하다.

>>> 비교급을 이용한 다양한 비교구문

❶ less + 원급 + than: ~보다 덜 …한

Julia is **less smart than** Mina. = Julia is **not as smart as** Mina. = Mina is **smarter than** Julia.

줄리아는 미나보다 덜 똑똑하다. = 줄리아는 미나만큼 똑똑하지 않다. = 미나는 줄리아보다 더 똑똑하다.

❷ the 비교급, the 비교급: ~하면 할수록 점점 …하다

The higher we go, **the colder** it becomes. 우리가 더 높이 갈수록, 더 추워진다.

❸ get[become, grow] + 비교급: 더 ~해지다

It's **getting darker**. 점점 어두워지고 있다.

❹ get[become] + 비교급 and 비교급: 점점 더 ~해지다 (점진적인 변화를 나타냄)

It's **getting colder and colder**. 점점 더 추워지고 있다.

* 비교급 강조: 비교급 앞에 much, still, even, far, a lot (훨씬)

Jina is **much** younger than Jihee. [훨씬 더 어리다]

A. 다음 괄호 안에서 알맞은 것을 고르시오.

① I am as (tall, taller, tallest) as you.

② Today isn't as (cold, colder, coldest) as yesterday.

③ Brazil is not as (big, bigger, biggest) as Canada.

④ He is (not as, as not) short as his brother.

⑤ The Thames is not as long (as, than) the Amazon.

B. 다음 두 문장을 참고하여 빈칸에 알맞은 말을 쓰시오.

① Jim is short. Hailey is tall.

➡ _____ is taller than _____.

② Mina's cat is big. Junsu's cat is small.

➡ Mina's cat is _____ than Junsu's cat.

③ Claire's pen is very long. Brian's pencil is very short.

➡ Claire's pen is longer than _____.

④ "The Christmas Present" is very interesting. The Little Prince is a little interesting.

➡ "The Christmas Present" is _____ than The Little Prince.

C. 다음 우리말 뜻에 맞게 주어진 말을 이용하여 빈칸에 알맞은 말을 쓰시오.

① 밤이 점점 더 짧아지고 있다.

➡ The nights are getting _____ and _____. (short)

② 더 많이 먹을수록, 더 살이 찐다.

➡ _____ you eat, _____ you become. (much, fat)

③ 날씨가 점점 더 서늘해진다.

➡ It's getting _____. (cool)

④ 나의 영어 실력이 점점 더 향상되고 있다.

➡ My English is getting _____. (good)

10.6. 비교표현(최상급)

1 최상급을 이용한 비교

》》 셋 이상의 대상을 비교한다.

❶ the + 최상급 + in 단수명사(장소, 집단) 〈비교범위〉 '..중에서 가장 ~한'

He is **the tallest** student **in my school**. 그는 학교에서 키가 가장 큰 학생이다.

❷ the + 최상급 + of 복수명사(같은 종류) 〈비교대상〉 '..중에서 가장 ~한'

This bag is **the most expensive of the four**. 이 가방은 그 네 개 중에서 가장 비싸다.

❸ one of the 최상급 + 복수명사 '가장 ~중의 하나'

Tom is **one of the most famous people** in Korea. Tom은 한국에서 가장 유명한 사람 중 한 명이다.

2 여러 가지 최상급 표현

Health is **the most important thing** in the world. 건강이 세상에서 가장 중요한 것이다.

= **Nothing** is **more important than** health in the world.

= **Nothing** is **as important as** health in the world.

= Heath is **more important than any other thing** in the world.

A. 다음 괄호 안에 알맞은 말을 고르시오.

① A bee is one of the (busier, busiest) insects.

② Jack is one of the tallest (boy, boys) in our class.

③ This is the most boring program (of, than) all.

④ Nothing is (the most important, more important) than love.

⑤ I wrote a letter to one of my closest (friend, friends).

⑥ She is the tallest (in, of) her class.

⑦ New York is one of (the beautiful, the most beautiful) cities in the world.

⑧ This is the one of (the deliciouser, the most delicious) bread in this bakery.

⑨ I read (more popular, the most popular) novel of all these days.

⑩ Haesu is more diligent than (anyone, anyones) in my family.

B. 다음 주어진 문장과 같은 뜻이 되도록 빈칸을 채우시오.

① Mary is the most famous actress in France.

➡ No one is _____ _____ _____ Mary in France.

② This tool is the most useful thing for me.

➡ Nothing is _____ _____ than this tool for me.

③ The problem is the most difficult of all.

➡ The problem is _____ _____ than any other problem.

④ Nothing is as precious as time in the world.

➡ Time is _____ _____ _____ in the world.

⑤ She is the best flute player in the orchestra.

➡ She plays the flute _____ _____ all the members in the orchestra.

1. 다음 중 주어진 단어가 들어갈 곳은?

He ① gets ② up ③ at seven ④ in the morning ⑤. (always)

2. 다음 중 형용사와 부사의 연결이 알맞지 <u>않은</u> 것은?

① fast – fastly　　② busy – busily
③ quick – quickly　④ true – truly
⑤ careful – carefully

3. 다음 중 밑줄 친 형용사의 용법이 나머지와 <u>다른</u> 것은?

① He is <u>kind</u>.
② I want a <u>yellow</u> skirt.
③ It's a <u>new</u> bag.
④ She has a <u>big</u> hat.
⑤ She is a <u>good</u> doctor.

4. 다음 빈칸에 알맞지 <u>않은</u> 것은?

He is the _____ boy in his class.

① tallest　　② thinner　　③ fastest
④ smartest　⑤ most famous

5. 다음 두 문장의 의미가 같도록 빈칸에 알맞은 말을 쓰시오.

The boy is kind.
= He is a _____ _____.

6. 다음 중 밑줄 친 부분과 의미가 같은 것은?

He didn't bake <u>a lot of</u> bread.

① few　　② little　　③ many
④ much　⑤ any

7. 다음 우리말과 일치하도록 괄호 안에 주어진 단어를 알맞게 배열할 때, ★에 들어갈 단어는?

_____ _____ <u>★</u> _____ _____.
그는 절대로 돌아오지 않을 것이다.
(never / back / will / he / come)

① never　　② back　　③ will
④ he　　　⑤ come

8. 다음 두 문장의 의미가 같도록 빈칸에 알맞은 것은?

Yuna doesn't go to school on foot at all.
= Yuna _____ goes to school on foot.

① never　　② always　　③ often
④ usually　⑤ sometimes

9. 다음 중 밑줄 친 부분의 위치가 알맞은 것은?

① What time do you <u>usually</u> get up?
② Does <u>sometimes</u> she watch TV?
③ He <u>often</u> is late for school.
④ They go <u>always</u> to church.
⑤ I <u>never</u> can stay up late.

10. 다음 중 밑줄 친 부분이 올바른 것은?

① Soccer is the <u>excitingest</u> game.
② Today was the <u>hotest</u> day of the year.
③ This book is <u>more thicker</u> than that book.
④ Today's weather is <u>nicer</u> than yesterday.
⑤ The blue bag is <u>heavyer</u> than the red one.

단원평가 실전대비

1. 다음 빈칸에 알맞지 <u>않은</u> 것은? (정답 2개)

> The water is _____ cold.

① much   ② very   ③ too
④ so   ⑤ many

2. 다음 우리말을 영어로 바르게 옮긴 것은?

> 저 두 마리의 예쁜 개들을 보아라.

① Look at two pretty those dogs.
② Look at pretty dogs those two.
③ Look at those pretty dogs two.
④ Look at those two pretty dogs.
⑤ Look at dogs those two pretty.

3. 다음 빈칸에 알맞지 <u>않은</u> 것은?

> Susan is _____ prettier than her cousin.

① much   ② even   ③ still
④ very   ⑤ a lot

4. 다음 표의 내용과 일치하는 것은?

	Jim	Andrew	Linda
Age	13	11	12
Weight	56kg	60kg	45kg
Height	155cm	145cm	160cm

① Andrew is taller than Linda.
② Linda is younger than Andrew.
③ Jim is older than Linda.
④ Linda is heavier than Jim.
⑤ Jim is the youngest of all.

5. 다음 중 비교급과 최상급 연결이 <u>잘못된</u> 것은?

① much – more – most
② hot – hotter – hottest
③ small – smaller – smallest
④ early – earlier – earliest
⑤ dangerous – dangerouser – dangerousest

6. 다음 표의 내용과 일치하지 <u>않는</u> 것은?

축구	야구	테니스	농구	배드민턴
25%	16%	12%	38%	9%

① The students like soccer more than tennis.
② The students like baseball more than tennis.
③ The students like basketball more than soccer.
④ The students like badminton more than tennis.
⑤ The students like basketball more than baseball.

7. 다음 주어진 글을 읽고 Sam의 나이를 영어 문장으로 빈칸에 쓰시오.

Sam is two years older than Jack.
Jack is a year older than Susan.
Susan is fourteen years old.

⇒ _____

8. 다음 중 어법상 옳지 <u>않은</u> 것은?

① Time is the most important thing.
② She is the youngest girl of them.
③ Jack is the most strong boy in our class.
④ It's the largest city in that country.
⑤ He climbed the highest mountain in Japan.

9. 다음 중 어법상 옳은 것은?

① Do always you wear pants?
② I never don't catch a cold in winter.
③ He comes usually home late in the evening.
④ We play sometimes badminton together.
⑤ Minho often listens to his friends' problems.

10. 다음 중 밑줄 친 부사의 쓰임이 나머지와 <u>다른</u> 것은?

① Do not talk <u>loudly</u> at night.
② My father speaks Chinese <u>well</u>.
③ The movie is <u>very</u> interesting.
④ The girl smiled <u>happily</u> to me.
⑤ It is raining <u>heavily</u>.

11. 다음 중 어법상 옳지 <u>않은</u> 것은?

① Minho went to bed early.
② She speaks too softly.
③ It is a very nice computer.
④ I practiced singing very hardly.
⑤ It's cold in winter.

12. 다음 중 영어 문장을 바르게 해석한 것은?

① I am never late for school.
나는 보통 학교에 늦지 않는다.
② They sometimes go to a movie.
그들은 때때로 영화를 보러 간다.
③ I usually play computer games at night.
나는 절대 밤에 컴퓨터 게임을 하지 않는다.
④ He is always kind to me.
그는 자주 내게 친절하다.
⑤ Anna often eats breakfast.
Anna는 항상 아침을 먹는다.

13. 다음 중 밑줄 친 부분이 <u>어색한</u> 것은?

① She swims <u>well</u>.
② She is a <u>well</u> dancer.
③ My uncle cooks <u>well</u>.
④ Bob speaks Korean <u>well</u>.
⑤ Joshua plays the piano very <u>well</u>.

14. 다음 중 어법상 옳지 <u>않은</u> 것은?

① She looks taller than her dad.
② She is the most powerful than Iron Man.
③ This book is more expensive than that book.
④ What is the most important thing in your life?
⑤ The red bag is heavier than the yellow one.

15. 다음 두 문장의 의미가 같지 <u>않은</u> 것은?

① Jiho is as smart as his sister.
   = Jiho and his sister have the same intelligence.
② A cheetah can run as fast as a car.
   = A cheetah runs fast like a car.
③ Jinsu eats as much as an elephant.
   = Jinsu eats a large amount of food as an elephant does.
④ Mina is not as tall as the tree in the yard.
   = The tree in the yard is taller than Mina.
⑤ Bob's homework is not as much as Jim's.
   = Bob has more homework than Jim has.

16. 다음 중 주어진 문장과 의미가 같은 것은?

> My sister is heavier than my brother.

① My sister is the heaviest woman.
② My brother is lighter than my sister.
③ My brother is not as light as my sister.
④ My sister is as heavy as my brother.
⑤ My sister is lighter than my brother.

17. 다음 중 밑줄 친 부분의 의미가 <u>틀린</u> 것은?

① I wake up <u>early</u> in the morning. (일찍)
② He will arrive <u>shortly</u>. (곧)
③ <u>Luckily</u>, I passed the exam. (운좋게도)
④ They <u>hardly</u> practiced dancing for the contest. (열심히)
⑤ Junsu didn't get enough sleep <u>lately</u>. (최근에)

18. 다음 빈칸에 공통으로 알맞은 것은?

> - He is interviewing _____ people.
> - We had _____ fun today.

① many   ② much   ③ a few
④ a little   ⑤ a lot of

19. 다음 중 빈칸에 들어갈 말이 나머지와 <u>다른</u> 것은?

① Would you like _____ tea after meals?
② Do you have _____ questions?
③ My aunt gave _____ pocket money to me.
④ Let's make _____ food for dinner.
⑤ _____ like soccer, and others don't

20. 다음 빈칸에 알맞은 것은?

> She is smarter than I. I am _____.

① as smart as her
② not as smart as her
③ as not smart as her
④ the smartest than her
⑤ smarter than her

1. 다음 Elena의 일과표를 보고 보기 에서 알맞은 말을 골라 쓰시오.

하는 일\요일	월	화	수	목	금	토
study math	O	O	O	O	O	O
clean the house		O		O		O
be late for school						

보기 　often　always　never

❶ Elena _____ studies math.

❷ Elena _____ cleans the house.

❸ Elena is _____ late for school.

2. 다음 중 두 문장의 의미가 같지 <u>않은</u> 것은?

① My room is smaller than yours.
= Your room isn't as small as my room.

② You got up earlier than I.
= I didn't get up as early as you.

③ We played better than they.
= They played as well as us.

④ Mt. Everest is the highest mountain in the world.
= Mt. Everest is higher than all the other mountains in the world.

⑤ She is smarter than any other student in her class.
= She is the smartest student in her class.

3. 다음 글의 내용과 일치하는 것은?

Susan goes to school at eight o'clock. School starts at nine o'clock. Susan is never late for school. She likes art and music. Her class usually finishes at three o'clock. She often goes to the library after school.

① 수업은 8시 정각에 시작한다.
② Susan은 가끔 학교에 지각한다.
③ Susan은 영어와 수학을 좋아한다.
④ 수업은 대체로 3시 정각에 끝난다.
⑤ Susan은 항상 방과 후 도서관을 간다.

4. 다음 Bob이 자신의 일생생활에 대해 쓴 글에서 단어의 위치가 <u>잘못된</u> 문장 3개를 바르게 짝지은 것은?

My Daily Life

A. I get up usually at 7:00.
B. I always brush my teeth.
C. I am often hungry in the morning.
D. I exercise never.
E. I sometimes take a shower.
F. I walk to school every day.
G. I never am late.
H. So, my teacher is always happy with me.

① A, C, H　　② A, D, G　　③ D, F, G
④ B, C, H　　⑤ B, E, F

5. 다음 괄호 ⓐ~ⓒ에서 어법상 옳은 표현을 골라 바르게 짝지은 것은?

- This bag is ⓐ(larger / more large) than that one.
- The white bag is ⓑ(heavyer / heavier) than the green one.
- A baseball field is ⓒ(biger / bigger) than a basketball court.

	ⓐ	ⓑ	ⓒ
①	larger	heavier	bigger
②	larger	heavier	biger
③	larger	heavyer	bigger
④	more large	heavyer	biger
⑤	more large	heavyer	bigger

6. 다음은 James의 학급 학생들이 좋아하는 음식에 대한 통계표이다. 이를 해석한 내용으로 적절하지 않은 것은?

spaghetti	1
Bibimbap	3
Bulgogi	5
chicken	7
pizza	9

① Five students like Bulgogi.
② More than half of the students like chicken.
③ Pizza is the most popular food in this class.
④ Only one student likes spaghetti in this class.
⑤ There are twenty five students in this class.

7. 다음 빈칸에 알맞은 말을 보기에서 골라 쓰시오.

보기 very   much   sweeter   sweetest

❶ Susan's jacket is _____ more expensive than mine.

❷ These pieces of cookies are _____ than those chocolate bars.

8. 다음 빈칸에 공통으로 알맞은 것은?

- I don't like to sit on the _____ chairs.
- I studied _____ to pass the exam.
- This game is so _____.

① hot
② hard
③ easy
④ soft
⑤ empty

9. 다음 중 빈칸에 보기의 단어가 들어갈 수 없는 것은?

보기 full   excited   useful   present   waist

① Dad bought me a nice phone as a _____.
② He tied a rope around his _____.
③ Oprah Winfrey's talk show is my favorite _____.
④ I think that this washing machine is very _____.
⑤ Everybody is so _____ about tomorrow's field trip.

1. 다음 주어진 문장을 자신의 입장에서 얼마나 자주 하는지 [보기]의 말을 첨가하여 쓰시오.

> [보기] always, usually, often, sometimes, never

❶ I go to the library after school.

⇒ _____

❷ I go to the movies on Sunday.

⇒ _____

❸ I listen to K-pop in my free time.

⇒ _____

2. 다음 표를 보고 문장을 완성하시오.

	Steak A	Steak B	Steak C
Price	$10	$20	$35
Size			

❶ The price of Steak A is _____ _____ of all.

❷ The size of Steak B is _____ _____ of all.

❸ The price of Steak C is _____ _____ _____ that of Steak B.

❹ The size of Steak C is _____ _____ that of Steak A.

3. 다음 우리말과 일치하도록 빈칸에 알맞은 말을 쓰시오.

❶ 나의 아버지는 늘 신문을 읽는다.

= My father _____ reads a newspaper.

❷ 나는 전혀 조깅을 하지 않는다.

= I _____ go jogging.

❸ 그들은 보통 8시에 저녁을 먹는다.

= They _____ have dinner at 8 p.m.

4. 다음 표를 보고 주어진 표현을 활용하여 문장을 완성하시오.

Sam	57kg	160cm	tall
Dean	65kg	197cm	heavy
Tom	99kg	178cm	

❶ Dean is _____ of all.

❷ Tom is _____ of all.

5. 다음은 기네스북에 기재된 세계기록을 보고 [보기] 와 같이 최상급을 사용하여 문장을 완성하시오.

How	Name
tall	Mr. Kosen(251㎝)
❶ heavy	Mr. Uribe(560㎏)
❷ long	the Amazon River(7,062㎞)

> [보기] The tallest man in the world is Mr. Kosen.

❶ _____

❷ _____

Chapter 11
to부정사와 동명사

>>> to부정사란? 「to + 동사원형」의 형태로 문장에서 명사, 형용사, 부사의 역할을 한다.

1 역할

>>> '~하기', '~하는 것'이라는 뜻으로, 문장 안에서 주어, 목적어, 보어의 역할을 한다.

역할	의미	위치	예문
주어	~하는 것은, ~하는 것이	to부정사 + 동사 * 주로 가주어 it을 주어 자리에 두고 to부정사를 뒤에 쓴다.	**To study** English is fun. =**It** is fun **to study** English. 영어를 공부하는 것은 재미있다.
목적어	~하는 것을	동사 + to부정사 *to부정사를 목적어로 취하는 동사: hope, want, decide, plan, wish, choose, expect, need, promise, refuse, like, love, start, begin 등	I want **to drink** a glass of water. 나는 물 한잔을 마시는 것을 원한다.
보어	~하는 것	주격보어: be동사 + to부정사 목적격보어: 동사 + 목적어 + to부정사 * to부정사를 목적격보어로 취하는 동사: want, advise, tell, expect, ask 등	My hobby is **to read** books. 나의 취미는 책을 읽는 것이다. She wants me **to forgive** him. 그녀는 내가 그를 용서하길 원한다.

2 의문사 + to부정사

what + to부정사	무엇을 ~할지	I don't know **what to wear**. 나는 무엇을 입어야 할지 모른다.
when + to부정사	언제 ~할지	The problem is **when to start** the meeting. 문제는 언제 회의를 시작할 지이다.
where + to부정사	어디서 ~할지	She decided **where to go** on her vacation. 그녀는 어디로 휴가를 가야 할지 결정했다.
how + to부정사	어떻게 ~할지(~하는 방법)	I want to learn **how to swim**. 나는 수영을 하는 방법을 배우고 싶다.
who(m) + to부정사	누구를 ~할지	She knows **whom to meet** today. 그녀는 오늘 누구를 만날지 알고 있다.

3 to부정사의 부정

>>> not[never] + to부정사

I told her **not to wear** my clothes. 나는 그녀에게 내 옷을 입지 말라고 말했다.

A. 다음 빈칸에 알맞은 말을 보기 에서 골라 문장을 완성하시오.

> 보기 ⓐ to take a rest ⓑ to drink a glass of juice
> ⓒ to wear a coat ⓓ to eat a slice of pizza

❶ I am thirsty. I want _____.

❷ I'm cold. I want _____.

❸ I don't feel well. I want _____.

❹ I'm hungry. I want _____.

B. 다음 우리말과 뜻이 같도록 주어진 단어를 배열하시오.

❶ Suji와 나는 피자를 어떻게 만드는지 배울 것이다. (will, pizza, how, to, learn, make)

➡ Suji and I _____.

❷ 나는 초밥을 먹는 방법을 모른다. (sushi, to, how, eat)

➡ I don't know _____.

❸ Nick은 파티를 위해 무엇을 사야할지 알고 싶다. (for, the party, buy, what, to)

➡ Nick wants to know _____.

C. 다음 밑줄 친 틀린 부분을 바르게 고치시오.

❶ To cooking Japanese food is very enjoyable to us.

❷ The photographer taught me how taking good pictures.

❸ Jim didn't know what eating.

D. 다음 주어진 낱말을 올바른 순서로 배열하시오.

❶ to / drive / James / on Sundays / likes

➡ _____

❷ a hamburger / hope / have / I / for lunch / to

➡ _____

❸ Julia / watch / likes / on TV / to / fashion shows

➡ _____

to부정사가 '~할, ~하는'의 뜻으로 형용사의 역할을 하며 명사[대명사]를 뒤에서 수식한다.

명사/대명사 + to부정사

I have a ring **to give** you. 나는 너에게 줄 반지를 가지고 있다.

We need someone **to guide** us. 우리는 우리를 안내할 누군가가 필요하다.

-thing, -one, -body로 끝나는 대명사

-thing, -one, -body로 끝나는 대명사는 형용사와 to부정사가 뒤에서 수식하므로 어순에 주의한다.

대명사 + (형용사) + to부정사

She gave me something <u>to drink</u>. 그녀는 나에게 마실 무언가를 주었다.
She gave me something hot <u>to drink</u>. 그녀는 나에게 마실 따뜻한 무언가를 준었다.

A. **다음 괄호 안에서 알맞은 것을 고르시오.**

① I don't have anyone (believe, to believe).

② She needs (warm something, something warm) to drink.

③ There are lots of interesting (games to enjoy, to enjoy games).

④ Do you have any friends (to help, helping) you?

⑤ There is (nothing to eat fresh, nothing fresh to eat) in the fridge.

B. **다음 우리말과 같은 뜻이 되도록 주어진 단어를 바르게 배열하여 문장을 완성하시오.**

① 나는 해야 할 숙제가 많다. (a lot of, I, have, homework, to do)

➡ _____

② 한국에는 방문할 곳이 많이 있다. (places, there, in Korea, visit, are, to, many)

➡ _____

③ 제게 차가운 마실 것을 주세요. (give, please, something, cold, drink, to, me)

➡ _____

④ 경주는 방문하기에 좋은 장소였다. (Gyeongju, to, visit, a, nice, place, was)

➡ _____

⑤ 할아버지는 네게 해 줄 재미있는 이야기가 있다. (funny stories, has, Grandpa, to, you, tell)

➡ _____

⑥ 수지는 지불해야 할 치과 의사의 청구서를 받았다. (bill, Suji, to, got, pay, the dentist's)

➡ _____

11.3. to부정사의 부사적 용법

>>> to부정사가 문장 안에서 부사처럼 동사나 형용사를 수식하며 목적, 결과, 원인, 이유를 나타낸다.

1 목적

>>> '~하기 위하여, ~을 하러'

I went out **to see** him. 나는 그를 보기 위해 나갔다.

She has to stand in a line **to enter** the theater. 그녀는 극장에 들어가기 위해 줄을 서야 한다.

2 원인, 이유

>>> '~해서, ~하고서'라고 해석하며 주로 glad, happy, sorry, surprised 등과 같은 감정을 나타내는 형용사 뒤에 쓰인다.

I am glad **to see** you. 나는 너를 봐서 기쁘다.

I am sorry **to hear** that. 그 얘기를 들으니 유감이다.

3 결과

>>> '~해서 (결국) …하다'

He grew up **to be** a doctor. 그는 자라서 의사가 되었다.

She lived **to be** 100 years old. 그녀는 살아서 100살이 되었다.(그녀는 100살이 될 때까지 살았다.)

4 형용사/부사 수식

>>> to부정사가 앞에 나온 형용사나 부사를 수식

English is <u>difficult</u> **to speak**. <형용사 수식> 영어는 말하기 어렵다.

She runs <u>fast</u> **to catch** up with me. <부사 수식> 그녀는 나를 따라잡을 만큼 빨리 달린다.

뽐쌤의 야무진 Tip!

to부정사의 관용표현

❶ 형용사/부사 enough to부정사: ~할 만큼 충분히 ~한
She is rich <u>enough to buy</u> that bag. 그녀는 그 가방을 살 만큼 부유하다.
=She is so rich that she can buy that bag.

❷ too 형용사/부사 to부정사: 너무 …해서 ~할 수 없는
He is <u>too young to travel</u> alone. 그는 너무 어려서 혼자 여행할 수 없다.
=He is so young that he can't travel alone.

A. 다음 문장의 빈칸에 알맞은 말을 [보기]에서 골라 괄호 안에 번호를 쓰시오.

[보기]
① to return books   ② to pick up my dad   ③ to buy a present for mom
④ to visit the doctor   ⑤ to play tennis

❶ I am going to the library (   ).

❷ I am going to Dr. Brown's office (   ).

❸ I am calling to my friend (   ).

❹ I am going to the department store (   ).

❺ I am going to airport (   ).

B. 다음 밑줄 친 to부정사의 쓰임을 [보기]에서 골라 쓰고 문장을 해석하시오.

[보기] 목적   원인   결과   형용사/부사 수식

❶ They went to the park <u>to take</u> a walk. (   )

➡ _____

❷ I must hurry <u>to catch</u> the bus. (   )

➡ _____

❸ I'm sorry <u>to call</u> you at night. (   )

➡ _____

❹ He lived <u>to see</u> his son succeed. (   )

➡ _____

❺ This book is difficult <u>to read</u>. (   )

➡ _____

❻ I got angry <u>to hear</u> the news. (   )

➡ _____

❼ Japanese is easy <u>to learn</u>. (   )

➡ _____

>>> 동명사란? 「동사원형 + ing」의 형태로 동사와 명사의 특성을 가진다. '~하기, ~하는 것'이라는 의미로, 명사처럼 문장 안에서 주어, 목적어, 보어로 쓰인다.

1 동명사의 역할

역할	위치	예문
주어 * 동명사가 주어의 역할을 할 경우, 항상 단수 취급한다.	동명사 + 동사	**Brushing** your teeth after meals is important. 식후에 양치질을 하는 것은 중요하다.
목적어	동사 + 동명사 전치사 + 동명사	I like **drinking** milk in the morning. (동사의 목적어) 나는 아침에 우유를 마시는 것을 좋아한다. Thank you for **helping** me. (전치사의 목적어) 나를 도와줘서 고마워.
보어	be동사 + 동명사	His job is **teaching students**. 그의 직업은 학생들을 가르치는 것이다.

2 동명사와 to부정사

>>> 동사에 따라 목적어로 동명사나 to부정사 또는 둘 다를 취한다.

동사	목적어
enjoy, finish, give up, mind, avoid, keep 등	동명사
hope, want, decide, plan, wish, choose, expect, need, promise, refuse 등	to부정사
like, love, hate, begin, start, continue 등	동명사/to부정사

She **enjoys fishing** at the lake. 그녀는 호수에서 낚시하는 것을 즐긴다.

We **hope to see** him again. 우리는 그를 다시 만나길 바란다.

They **started to sell** flowers. 그들은 꽃을 팔기 시작했다.

=They **started selling** flowers.

A. 다음 우리말을 참고하여 빈칸을 완성하시오.

① 일찍 일어나는 것은 건강에 좋다. (get)

_____ up early is good for your health.

② 나는 편지 쓰는 것을 좋아한다. (write)

I like _____ letters.

③ 컴퓨터 게임 하는 것은 재미있다. (play)

_____ computer games is interesting.

④ 나의 직업은 영어를 가르치는 것이다. (teach)

My job is _____ English.

⑤ 그는 영화 보기를 즐긴다. (watch)

He enjoys _____ movies.

B. 다음 괄호 안에 알맞은 말을 고르시오.

① Yura decided (to write, writing) a book.

② My dad gave up (to smoke, smoking).

③ The baby kept (to cry, crying).

④ She is poor at (to play, playing) tennis.

⑤ Would you mind (to open, opening) the window?

⑥ They wish (to ski, skiing) this winter.

⑦ He would like (to plant, planting) flowers.

⑧ I want something hot (to drink, drinking).

⑨ Julia went to the store (to buy, buying) a can of coke.

⑩ Mother was proud of (to help, helping) the poor.

⑪ Before (to finish, finishing) her homework, she went to bed.

⑫ Minho hopes (to get, getting) a latest tablet for Christmas.

⑬ Jina is fond of (to make, making) dolls.

⑭ He was very tired. So he stopped (to take, taking) a rest.

1. 다음 밑줄 친 listen의 공통된 형태를 쓰시오.

- My hobby is <u>listen</u> to music.
- She enjoys <u>listen</u> to pop music.

⇒ _____

2. 다음 중 밑줄 친 부분과 바꿔 쓸 수 있는 것은?

I like <u>to watch</u> movies at home.

① watch   ② watched
③ to watched   ④ watching
⑤ to watching

3. 다음 대화의 빈칸에 공통으로 알맞은 것은?

A: Would you like _____ about Korean culture?
B: Yes, I want _____ about Korean culture.

① know   ② knowing   ③ to know
④ knew   ⑤ to knowing

4. 다음 빈칸에 알맞은 것은?

I want _____ you again soon.

① see   ② to see   ③ seeing
④ saw   ⑤ to seeing

5. 다음 우리말과 일치하도록 빈칸에 알맞은 말을 쓰시오.

I don't know _____ _____

_____.
(나는 수영하는 법을 모른다.)

[6-7] 다음 빈칸에 알맞은 것은?

6.

I'm terribly thirsty. I need _____ first.

① drink   ② to drink
③ to drinking   ④ drank
⑤ drinking

7.

Can you show me how _____ the game?

① play   ② playing
③ played   ④ to play
⑤ to playing

8. 다음 우리말을 영어로 바르게 옮긴 것은?

오늘 저녁에 드라이브 하실래요?

① How about go for a drive tonight?
② How about going for a drive tonight?
③ How about to go for a drive tonight?
④ What about to going for a drive tonight?
⑤ What about will go for a drive tonight?

9. 다음 문장의 <u>어색한</u> 부분을 고치시오.

① I want buy a bag.

② I want to buying a bag.

③ He wants buys a cell phone.

④ He wants to buys a cell phone.

10. 다음 우리말과 같은 뜻이 되도록 빈칸에 알맞은 말을 쓰시오.

나는 해야 할 많은 숙제가 있다.

= I have a lot of homework _____.

단원평가 실전대비

1. 다음 중 밑줄 친 to의 쓰임이 보기와 같은 것은?

보기 I want <u>to</u> buy a new cell phone.

① I like <u>to</u> teach singing.

② I am going <u>to</u> send it to you.

③ Do you have something warm <u>to</u> drink?

④ I studied hard <u>to</u> get a good grade.

⑤ I went to China <u>to</u> see the Great Wall.

2. 다음 중 밑줄 친 부분과 바꾸어 쓸 수 있는 것은?

I studied hard <u>in order to</u> pass the exam.
= I studied hard _____ pass the exam.

① for   ② to   ③ so that
④ instead of   ⑤ so as

3. 다음 중 어법상 옳은 것은?

① I hope see you soon.

② Ride a bike is fun.

③ Do your best is very important.

④ I like to play chess with my dad.

⑤ His hobby is go to the park.

4. 다음 우리말과 뜻이 같도록 빈칸에 알맞은 말을 쓰시오.

나는 어디로 갈지를 결정하지 못했다.

⇒ I didn't decide _____ _____ _____ yet.

5. 다음 중 밑줄 친 부분이 <u>잘못된</u> 것은?

① It began <u>raining.</u>

② My hobby is <u>playing</u> soccer.

③ Thank you for <u>coming.</u>

④ I like <u>to going</u> to the movies.

⑤ <u>Studying</u> English is fun and exciting.

6. 다음 두 문장이 같은 뜻이 되도록 빈칸에 알맞은 말을 쓰시오.

① To learn a foreign language is interesting.

  ⇒ _____ a foreign language is interesting.

② He started to play computer games.

  ⇒ He started _____ computer games.

③ My brother dances well.

  ⇒ My brother is good at _____.

7. 다음 빈칸에 알맞지 <u>않은</u> 것은?

> I _____ doing the work.

① gave up   ② stopped
③ enjoyed   ④ wanted
⑤ finished

8. 다음 중 두 문장의 의미가 같지 <u>않은</u> 것은?

① Speaking French is difficult.
   = To speak French is difficult.
② He wanted to drink coffee.
   = He wanted drinking coffee.
③ I like playing soccer.
   = I like to play soccer.
④ My hobby is collecting stamps.
   = My hobby is to collect stamps.
⑤ It began raining.
   = It began to rain.

9. 다음 두 문장이 같은 뜻이 되도록 빈칸에 알맞은 말을 쓰시오.

❶ I couldn't decide what I should eat first.
   = I couldn't decide _____
   _____ _____ first.

❷ I don't know when I should start.
   = I don't know _____ _____
   _____ .

10. 다음 문장에서 틀린 부분을 찾아 바르게 고치시오.

❶ We need to decide when leaving first.

❷ Do you have anything to wear warm?

11. 다음 주어진 문장의 밑줄 친 부분과 쓰임이 같은 것은?

> My dream is <u>to become</u> a designer.

① <u>To keep</u> a diary is a good habit.
② I hope <u>to make</u> a lot of friends.
③ His job is <u>to treat</u> sick people.
④ Do you know how <u>to cook</u> steak?
⑤ <u>To take</u> a trip abroad is good experience.

12. 다음 주어진 우리말과 뜻이 같도록 괄호 안의 단어를 활용하여 문장을 완성하시오.

❶ 마실 차가운 것 좀 드릴까요?
   Would you like something _____
   _____ _____ ? (cold, drink)

❷ 나는 나를 도와 줄 많은 친구가 있다.
   I have many friends _____
   _____ me. (help).

13. 다음 중 주어진 문장과 의미가 같은 것은?

> To speak English is difficult but interesting.

① It is to speak English difficult but interesting.
② It is to speak difficult but interesting English.
③ That is difficult but interesting to speak English
④ It is difficult but interesting to speak English.
⑤ That is difficult but interesting to English speak.

14. 다음 중 괄호 안에 단어가 들어갈 위치로 가장 적절한 곳은?

> The classic music ① was ② hard ③ to ④ understand ⑤. (too)

15. 다음 두 문장의 의미가 같도록 빈칸에 알맞은 것은?

> I got up too late to have breakfast.
> = I got up so late that I _____ have breakfast.

① can
② can't
③ could
④ couldn't
⑤ was able to

16. 다음 우리말과 뜻이 같도록 빈칸에 알맞은 것은?

> 우산 가져가는 것 잊지 마.
> = Don't forget _____ your umbrella.

① bring
② brought
③ bringing
④ to bring
⑤ to have brought

17. 다음 중 밑줄 친 부분이 잘못된 것은?

① I began collecting stamps three years ago.
② Suji didn't like to speak in public.
③ I hate studying at home.
④ Would you mind to open the window?
⑤ I promise to keep it a secret.

18. 다음 두 문장을 to부정사를 이용하여 한 문장으로 연결하시오.

> Don't eat fast food often. It is bad for your health.
> = _____ is bad for your health.

19. 다음 중 밑줄 친 부분이 잘못된 것은?

① She loves to watch horror movies.
② He enjoys listening to music.
③ We hope seeing you again.
④ They wanted to go on a picnic.
⑤ Suji loves walking her dog.

20. 다음 중 빈칸에 to be가 들어갈 수 없는 것은?

① She wants _____ a teacher.
② Monkeys enjoy _____ with people.
③ You must practice hard _____ a basketball player.
④ What do you want _____ in the future?
⑤ They are going _____ there soon.

21. 다음 빈칸에 순서대로 알맞은 것은?

> - This soup is too cold for me _____.
> - She is clever enough _____.

① to eat – understanding
② to eat – to understand
③ eating – to understand
④ eat – understood
⑤ to be eating – to understanding

1. 다음 보기에서 밑줄 친 부분의 쓰임이 주어진 문장과 같은 것을 모두 고른 것은?

> We are planning to visit Canada soon.

> **보기**
>
> ⓐ I'm happy to be here tonight.
> ⓑ I got up early to climb a mountain.
> ⓒ Sam wished to talk with his friends.
> ⓓ Would you like something to drink?
> ⓔ Alice began to learn Chinese last year.

① ⓐ, ⓒ   ② ⓑ, ⓔ   ③ ⓒ, ⓔ
④ ⓐ, ⓓ, ⓔ   ⑤ ⓑ, ⓒ, ⓓ

2. 다음 중 밑줄 친 부분의 쓰임이 나머지와 <u>다른</u> 것은?

① I study hard to be a judge in the future.
② Tom called to Jessica to say hello.
③ Jim doesn't like to play table tennis.
④ She cleaned the house to please her mother.
⑤ She wrote an email to get a refund.

3. 다음 빈칸에 알맞은 것은?

> I'm looking forward _____ her soon.

① meet   ② met   ③ meeting
④ to meet   ⑤ to meeting

4. 다음 중 밑줄 친 부분의 쓰임이 보기와 같은 것은?

> **보기** I have a lot of homework to do.

① I'm very happy to see your room.
② They need a newspaper to read.
③ She grew up to be a doctor.
④ To live without air is impossible.
⑤ Do you want to play tennis?

5. 다음 우리말을 영어로 바르게 옮긴 것은?

> 그녀는 너무 피곤해서 샤워를 할 수 없었다.

① She was too tired not to take a shower.
② She is tired that she didn't take a shower.
③ She was so tired that she couldn't take a shower.
④ She was so tired that she can't take a shower.
⑤ She is so tired that she can take a shower.

6. 다음 주어진 단어 중 알맞은 것을 골라, 어법에 맞게 대화를 완성하시오.

> play / read / go

❶ A: How about _____ to see a movie tonight.

   B: That's a good idea!

❷ A: Hey, you look tired.

   B: Yes, I enjoyed _____ soccer a lot yesterday.

❸ A: I feel bored now.

   B: _____ comic books can be fun.

7. 다음 대화를 읽고 보기에서 필요한 단어를 골라 문장을 완성하시오.(한 단어를 두 번 이상 사용할 수 있음. 예: a house to live in과 같은 형태로 쓸 것)

Tom: It's time to study English! I'm so happy.
Sam: Me, too. It's my favorite subject.
Tom: Uh oh. There's no chair for me.
Sam: You can bring one from downstairs. Oh no! I forgot to bring my pen.

보기 to, on, for, with, pen, time, chair, sit, write

❶ Tom needs a _____ _____ _____ _____.

❷ Sam needs a _____ _____ _____ _____.

8. 다음 빈칸에 공통으로 알맞지 <u>않은</u> 것은?

- Jessica _____ playing baseball with Tom.
- Jessica _____ to play cards with Tom.

① likes   ② starts   ③ loves
④ begins   ⑤ enjoys

9. 다음 우리말에 맞게 괄호 안에 주어진 단어가 들어갈 곳은?

나는 토요일에 소개팅에 나가지 않기로 결심했다.
I ① decided ② to ③ go ④ out ⑤ on a blind date on Saturday. (not)

10. 다음 문장에 들어갈 알맞은 말을 보기에서 골라 빈칸에 쓰시오.

보기 on   by   with   of   in

❶ Please give me a piece of paper to write _____.

❷ Sam bought a house to live _____.

❸ Yena is looking for a roommate to live _____.

11. 다음 문장의 의미가 통하도록 빈칸에 들어갈 말로 알맞은 것은?

I went to the gym _____.

① to have lunch
② to play table tennis
③ to get some post cards
④ to catch a train
⑤ to buy a book

12. 다음 문장의 빈칸에 들어갈 말로 알맞은 것은?

Emily is too busy _____.

① taking a rest
② to taking a rest
③ to take a rest
④ not to take a rest
⑤ not taking a rest

1. 다음 보기와 같이 자신의 입장에서 질문에 답하시오.

> **보기**
> Q: What do you want to do this Sunday?
> A: I want to go to the movies.

❶ Q: What do you want to do this weekend?

A: _____

❷ Q: What do you want to do this vacation?

A: _____

❸ Q: What do you want to do on your birthday?

A: _____

2. 다음 두 문장을 한 문장으로 쓸 때 빈칸에 알맞은 말을 쓰시오.

❶ She will go to America. She wants to learn English.

⇒ She will go to America _____.

❷ Barbie felt scared. Because she was at home alone.

⇒ Barbie felt scared _____.

❸ He took the subway. He wanted to arrive on time.

⇒ He took the subway _____.

3. 다음 우리말과 뜻이 같도록 괄호 안에 단어를 활용하여 문장을 완성하시오.

❶ 아기가 울기 시작했다.
(start, cry)

⇒ The baby _____.

❷ 나의 아버지는 신문을 읽는 것을 멈췄다.
(stop, read a newspaper)

⇒ My father _____.

❸ 네 생일파티에 초대해 줘서 고마워.
(thank you, invite)

⇒ _____ to your birthday party.

4. 다음 문장에서 어법상 틀린 부분을 찾아 바르게 고치시오.

❶ My sister and I love watch TV on weekends.

❷ Last winter, I had a lot of homework finishing.

5. 다음 보기와 같이 주어진 단어를 이용하여 문장을 만드시오.

> **보기**
> I want something. (eat)
> ⇒ I want something to eat.

❶ I want a book. (read)

⇒ _____

❷ My hometown is a good place. (visit)

⇒ _____

Chapter 12
접속사

12.1. 등위접속사 and, but, or, so

>>> 등위 접속사란? 단어, 구, 절 등을 대등하게 연결하는 <u>접속사</u>

My mother is beautiful **and** kind. → 단어(형용사)와 단어(형용사)를 연결

It is autumn, **but** it is still hot. → 절과 절을 연결

> ※ 접속사란?
> 단어와 단어, 구와 구, 절과 절을 glue(접착제)처럼 연결하는 말

① 등위 접속사의 종류와 쓰임

and (그리고, ~와)	앞, 뒤 내용을 연결한다. I have a cat **and** a dog. 나는 고양이와 개를 기른다.
	셋 이상 나열 시 A, B(,) and C로 쓴다. I have a cat, a dog, **and** a hamster. 나는 고양이와 개, 그리고 햄스터를 기른다.
	and로 연결된 어구가 주어일 때 복수 취급한다. Susan **and** Jennifer **are** my friends. Susan과 Jennifer는 나의 친구들이다.
but (그러나, 하지만)	서로 반대되거나 대조되는 내용을 연결한다. Jack is young, **but** wise. Jack은 어리지만 현명하다. I can see her, **but** I can't see him. 나는 그녀를 볼 수 있지만 그는 볼 수 없다.
or (또는, 혹은)	둘 중 하나를 선택하는 경우 사용한다. Do you go by bus **or** by bike? 너는 버스를 타고 가니 아니면 자전거를 타고 가니? A or B가 주어일 때 동사는 가까운 주어에 일치시킨다. You **or** I **am** wrong. 너 또는 내가 틀렸다.
so (그래서)	결과를 나타낸다. I was sick, **so** I couldn't go to school. 나는 아파서 학교에 갈 수 없었다. I didn't study at all, **so** I failed the exam. 나는 공부를 전혀 안 해서 시험에 떨어졌다.

뿜쌤의
야무진
Tip!

주의해야 할 구문

❶ 명령문 + and: ~해라, 그러면 …할 것이다
Go now, and you won't be late for school.
지금 가라, 그러면 학교에 늦지 않을 것이다.

❷ 명령문 + or: ~해라, 그렇지 않으면 …할 것이다
Go now, or you will be late for school.
지금 가라, 그렇지 않으면 학교에 늦을 것이다.

❸ so ~ that 구문: 너무 ~해서 …하다
I was so tired that I went to bed. 나는 너무 피곤해서 잠자리에 들었다.

A. **다음 괄호 안에서 알맞은 것을 고르시오.**

① I have a piano, a bookshelf, (and, or) a bed in my room.

② Do you have any brothers (or, so) sisters?

③ I was late for school, (and, so) I took a taxi.

④ Wear a coat, (and, or) you won't catch a cold.

⑤ It is too hot, (so, but) I want to drink a lot of water.

⑥ Eat more (and, or) you will be hungry soon.

⑦ Which do you prefer, skirts (or, and) pants?

⑧ Are you good with computers (or, so) other machines?

B. **다음 문장에서 밑줄 친 부분을 자연스럽게 고치시오.**

① It's hot <u>or</u> humid in summer in Korea.

② Richard is smart, <u>but</u> good-looking.

③ She broke her leg <u>but</u> she is in the hospital.

④ Which is better, soccer <u>and</u> badminton?

⑤ Did you play soccer, <u>and</u> were you at church last weekend?

C. **다음 보기와 같이 다음 문장들이 같은 뜻이 되도록 빈칸에 알맞은 단어를 쓰시오.**

> 보기 If you take this medicine, you'll get better.
>
> =Take this medicine, and you'll get better.
>
> =Take this medicine, or you won't get better.

① If you start now, you will catch the bus.

= Start now, _____ you won't catch the bus.

= Start now, _____ you will catch the bus.

② If you practice hard, you will win the game.

= Practice hard, _____ you will win the game.

= Practice hard, _____ you won't win the game.

12.2. 종속 접속사 (때)

>>> 종속 접속사란? 주가 되는 절(주절)과 종속되어 있는 절(종속절)을 연결하는 접속사로, 때, 조건, 이유, 양보 등을 나타낸다.

I didn't go out because it was raining. 비가 오고 있었기 때문에, 나는 밖에 나가지 않았다.

주가 되는 부분(주절)　　　종속이 되는 부분(종속절)

* 종속절이 문장의 앞에 오는 경우, 종속절이 끝나는 자리에 comma(,)를 찍는다.

Because it was raining, I didn't go out. 비가 오고 있었기 때문에, 나는 나가지 않았다.

1 때를 나타내는 종속접속사

when (~할 때) + 주어 + 동사	I had a dog **when** I was young. 나는 어렸을 때, 개를 키웠다. **When** my teacher called me, I stood up. 선생님께서 부르셨을 때, 나는 일어났다.
while (~하는 동안) + 주어 + 동사	**While** she went out, I cleaned her room. 그녀가 나가 있는 동안, 나는 그녀의 방을 청소했다. We ate popcorn **while** we were watching a movie. 우리는 영화를 보는 동안 팝콘을 먹었다.
before (~하기 전에) + 주어 + 동사	**Before** the class ended, he asked a question. 수업이 끝나기 전, 그는 질문을 했다. We should think carefully **before** we speak. 우리는 말하기 전에 신중하게 생각해야 한다.
after (~한 후에) + 주어 + 동사	I washed my hands **after** I came back home. 나는 집에 돌아온 후에 손을 씻었다. **After** Suji watched that soap opera, she became a fan of Eric. Suji는 그 드라마를 본 후에, Eric의 팬이 되었다.
until (~할 때까지) + 주어 + 동사	She couldn't realize the problem **until** I told her. 내가 말해주기 전까지 그녀는 그 문제를 깨닫지 못했다. I waited **until** they called my name. 그들이 내 이름을 부를 때까지 기다렸다.

뿜쌤의
야무진
Tip!

접속사 when과 의문사 when의 구별
❶ 접속사 when (~할 때): When 주어 + 동사, 주어 + 동사
<u>When</u> you arrive at home, please call me. 집에 도착할 때, 내게 전화해 줘.
❷ 의문사 when (언제): When 동사 + 주어?
<u>When</u> is your birthday? 네 생일이 언제니?

A. 다음 문장의 빈칸에 알맞은 말을 보기 에서 골라 번호를 쓰시오.

보기 ① when you are unhappy with school life

② when you climb a mountain

③ when you are worried about your weight

❶ You should get some exercise, (   ).

❷ You should find something interesting in school, (   ).

❸ You should be careful, (   ).

B. 다음 우리말과 뜻이 같도록 괄호 안에 단어를 배열하시오.

❶ 그녀는 박물관에 가고 있을 때, 그를 만났다. (she, when, was, to, going, the museum)

➡ _____, she met him.

❷ 나는 눈이 내린 후 스노우보드를 타러 갔다. (it, after, snowed)

➡ I went snowboarding _____.

❸ 그는 음식을 먹는 동안 스마트폰을 보았다. (eating, was, while, he)

➡ He looked at his smart phone _____.

❹ 나는 죽을 때까지 너를 잊지 않을 것이다. (I, until, die)

➡ I will never forget you _____.

❺ 그의 아버지는 그가 10살 때 돌아가셨다. (was, when, ten years old, he)

➡ His father passed away _____.

❻ 우리는 기차가 출발하기 전 두 시간이 남았다. (before, starts, the train)

➡ We have two hours left _____.

12.3. 종속 접속사 (이유/조건)

1 이유를 나타내는 접속사

because (~이기 때문에) + 주어 + 동사	I didn't feel good **because** I had a bad dream. 나는 나쁜 꿈을 꿔서 기분이 좋지 않았다.
since (~이므로) + 주어 + 동사	**Since** I left home early, I couldn't see her. 나는 집을 일찍 나섰기 때문에, 그녀를 볼 수 없었다.

뽐쌤의 야무진 Tip!

접속사 because와 전치사 because of의 구별

❶ because + 주어 + 동사: ~이기 때문에
  I was absent <u>because I was sick</u>. 나는 아팠기 때문에 결석했다.

❷ because of + 명사(구): ~ 때문에
  I was absent <u>because of my sickness</u>. 나는 아팠기 때문에 결석했다.

2 조건을 나타내는 접속사

》》 if + 주어 + 동사 (만약 ~라면)

If you study hard, you can pass the exam. 공부를 열심히 한다면, 너는 그 시험에 합격할 수 있을 것이다.

＊ 시간이나 조건을 나타내는 부사절에서는 현재시제를 써서 미래의 일을 나타낸다.

If it **rains** tomorrow, I'll stay at home. 내일 비가 온다면 나는 집에 머물 것이다.

If it **will rain** tomorrow, I'll stay at home. (X)

When he **finishes** the work, he will call me. 그는 일을 끝낼 때, 나에게 전화할 것이다.

A. 다음 우리말과 뜻이 같도록 빈칸에 알맞은 말을 쓰시오.

① 비가 오고 있었기 때문에, 나는 밖에 나가지 않았다.

I didn't go out _____ it was raining.

② 일찍 일어나지 않으면 학교에 늦을 것이다.

_____ you don't get up early, you'll be late for school.

③ 네가 만약 노트북이 있다면 나에게 빌려주겠니?

Can you lend me your laptop, _____ you have it?

④ Suji는 아무것도 먹지 않았기 때문에 어지러움을 느꼈다.

Suji felt dizzy _____ she didn't eat anything.

⑤ 만약 그를 보면, 내가 늦는다고 전해줘.

If you _____ him, tell him that I'll be late.

⑥ 그는 독감 때문에 결석했다.

He was absent _____ flu.

B. 다음 문장의 의미가 자연스럽도록 알맞게 연결하시오.

If + ① the weather is sunny,   ⓐ I will call you later.

② you don't start now,   ⓑ I will go to the park.

③ she sends a parcel today,   ⓒ he will receive it tomorrow.

④ you are busy,   ⓓ you will miss the train.

⑤ he comes late,   ⓔ we will go without him.

12.4. 종속 접속사 that

1 that절의 형태

))) 「that + 주어 + 동사」: '~하는 것, ~인 것'

2 that절의 역할

))) 문장에서 주어, 목적어, 보어로 쓰이는 명사절 역할을 한다.

주어	**That** he is handsome is true. 그가 잘생겼다는 것은 사실이다. → It is true **that** he is handsome. * that절이 주어로 쓰일 경우, It(가주어) ~ that(진주어)으로 쓰인다.
목적어	I promise **that** I will come back early. 나는 내일 일찍 돌아올 것을 약속한다. * that절을 목적어로 취하는 동사: think, believe, hope, tell, say, know … * 목적어로 쓰인 that절에서의 that은 생략 가능하다.
보어	Her dream is **that** she will be a doctor. 그녀의 꿈은 의사가 되는 것이다.

A. 다음 밑줄 친 that절의 역할로 알맞은 것에 체크 표시 하시오.

① Mom said <u>that she could make some sandwiches</u>. □ 주어　□ 보어　□ 목적어

② The bad news is <u>that he can't attend the meeting</u>. □ 주어　□ 보어　□ 목적어

③ It's amazing <u>that Jack was able to come on time</u>. □ 주어　□ 보어　□ 목적어

④ The reason we cannot go is <u>that we have a flat tire</u>. □ 주어　□ 보어　□ 목적어

⑤ I told them <u>that they should be careful</u>. □ 주어　□ 보어　□ 목적어

⑥ It is important <u>that we work together</u>. □ 주어　□ 보어　□ 목적어

⑦ Everyone knows <u>that nothing is impossible</u>. □ 주어　□ 보어　□ 목적어

⑧ <u>That she is a world champion</u> is obvious. □ 주어　□ 보어　□ 목적어

⑨ The trouble is <u>that he can't join us</u>. □ 주어　□ 보어　□ 목적어

⑩ We hope <u>that he will recover soon</u>. □ 주어　□ 보어　□ 목적어

B. 다음 보기 와 같이 주어진 단어를 사용하여 문장을 완성하시오.

> 보기 A: Is he a good dancer? (that)
>
> B: Yes, I <u>think that he is a good dancer</u>.

① A: Will it snow soon? (think)

B: Yes, I _____.

② A: Will the Korean team win the game? (hope)

B: Yes, I _____.

③ A: Did you meet him at the party? (remember)

B: Yes, I _____.

④ A: Will she become a good doctor ? (believe)

B: Yes, I _____.

⑤ A: Does he lie every day? (know)

B: Yes, I _____.

1. 다음 우리말에 맞게 빈칸에 알맞은 것은?

_____ I went there, she was dancing.
(내가 거기 갔을 때, 그녀는 춤추고 있었어.)

① When   ② After   ③ Before
④ However   ⑤ Since

2. 다음 두 문장을 when을 사용하여 한 문장으로 쓰시오.

I have a cold. I drink a cup of lemon tea.
⇒ _____

[3-4] 다음 빈칸에 알맞은 것은?

3.

I think _____ this problem is very difficult.

① this   ② it   ③ that
④ but   ⑤ what

4.

Mina is smiling because she
_____.

① lost her cellphone
② broke her leg
③ can't see well
④ did well on the test
⑤ has a hard test tomorrow

5. 다음 ⓐ~ⓔ 중 생략할 수 있는 것은?

I thought that she's my teacher.
ⓐ   ⓑ   ⓒ   ⓓ   ⓔ

① ⓐ   ② ⓑ   ③ ⓒ
④ ⓓ   ⑤ ⓔ

6. 다음 빈칸에 공통으로 알맞은 것은?

- Jim is angry, _____ Sally isn't angry.
- I can't play the cello, _____ I can sing well.

① then   ② or   ③ and
④ but   ⑤ so

7. 다음 대화의 빈칸에 알맞은 접속사를 쓰시오.

A: Why are you so upset?
B: _____ I failed my driving test again.

8. 다음 빈칸에 알맞은 것은?

I am Emily. I am not good at sports, _____ I am good at music.

① and   ② but   ③ because
④ so   ⑤ if

9. 다음 주어진 단어를 이용하여 우리말을 영어로 옮기시오.

> Eric은 오전 7시에 아침을 먹는다. 하지만 Mark는 아침을 먹지 않는다. (eat breakfast, but, 7 a.m.)
> ⇒ _____

10. 다음 빈칸에 공통으로 알맞은 것은?

> - Please come in _____ I call your name.
> - _____ did you come back to Korea?

① as[As]
② when[When]
③ why[Why]
④ what[What]
⑤ how[How]

단원평가 실전대비

1. 다음 글의 빈칸 ⓐ, ⓑ에 들어갈 말로 바르게 짝지어진 것은?

> James: I'm a guitarist in the school band, ⓐ_____ my guitar is important to me. I have three guitars, ⓑ_____ the smallest one is my favorite. It's from France, and it sounds beautiful.

① but – and
② so – and
③ so – but
④ and – so
⑤ but – so

2. 다음 문장의 밑줄 친 부분이 잘못된 것은?

① When ② the movie ③ being over ④ I'll ⑤ call you.

3. 다음 빈칸에 알맞은 것은?

> It's the dry season, _____ it's raining cats and dogs now.

① if
② or
③ so
④ but
⑤ because

4. 다음 중 빈칸에 들어갈 접속사가 보기와 다른 것은?

> 보기 Van Gogh drew a sad old man _____ he was in the hospital.

① She read a book _____ she was waiting for me.
② I don't like winter _____ I like to go skiing.
③ He called me _____ I was in bed.
④ _____ I was in the library, my aunt visited my house.
⑤ He fell asleep _____ he was reading a book.

5. 다음 중 어법상 옳지 않은 것은?

① When I play the violin, I am sad.
② I live with my grandma when I was young.
③ When I am lonely, I am talking with my parents.
④ I went swimming while my parents were asleep.
⑤ How did you feel when you read my story?

6. 다음 중 밑줄 친 when의 쓰임이 나머지와 <u>다른</u> 것은?

① <u>When</u> are you leaving for Seoul?
② I was watching TV <u>when</u> he came back.
③ What were you doing <u>when</u> I called you?
④ <u>When</u> I was eleven, I had a dog named Happy.
⑤ <u>When</u> you were a child, you liked to go fishing.

7. 다음 우리말을 영어로 바르게 옮긴 것은?

> 나는 졸릴 때, 커피를 마신다.

① I am sleepy, when I drink coffee.
② After I feel sleepy, I drink coffee.
③ When I want to sleep, I drink coffee.
④ When I felt sleepy, I drink coffee.
⑤ When I am sleepy, I drink coffee.

8. 다음의 빈칸에 이어질 말로 적절하지 <u>않은</u> 것은?

> I feel happy _____.

① when I eat delicious food
② when my mom is very sick
③ when I read a very interesting book
④ when I get a good grade on my test
⑤ when I play fun games with my family

9. 다음 빈칸에 공통으로 알맞은 것은?

> - We thought _____ it was a deer.
> - I think _____ she is very pretty.

① that   ② who   ③ what
④ as   ⑤ like

10. 다음 중 빈칸에 because가 들어가기 <u>어색한</u> 것은?

① I'll go to bed early _____ I'm so tired.
② My mother was angry _____ I didn't clean my room.
③ I want to be a teacher _____ I like children.
④ Kate doesn't look okay _____ she has a cold.
⑤ It was very cold _____ I didn't go out.

11. 다음 중 짝지어진 대화가 <u>어색한</u> 것은?

① A: Why can't we live on the moon?
   B: Because there is no air there.
② A: Why is your sister so sad?
   B: Because she failed the exam.
③ A: Why do you want to be a doctor?
   B: Because I want to help people.
④ A: Why didn't Minsu come to school today?
   B: Because he studies very hard.
⑤ A: Why are you studying at this late hour?
   B: Because I have a test tomorrow.

12. 다음 중 밑줄 친 that의 쓰임이 나머지와 <u>다른</u> 것은?

① I think <u>that</u> is your bag.
② I believe <u>that</u> he is honest.
③ She said <u>that</u> they like the story.
④ They know <u>that</u> Sarah is always busy.
⑤ I hope <u>that</u> there is a toy store in town.

13. 다음 중 빈칸에 들어갈 말이 나머지와 <u>다른</u> 것은?

① I think _____ it's very scary.
② I went to the dentist _____ I had a toothache.
③ She said _____ it was not a mountain.
④ People believed _____ the Earth was flat.
⑤ He thought _____ she was younger than him.

14. 다음 괄호 안에 주어진 동사의 형태로 알맞은 것은?

> When Frank (grow) up, he will be a famous movie star.

① grow   ② grows   ③ will grow
④ grew   ⑤ is grown

15. 다음 중 밑줄 친 that을 생략할 수 있는 것은?

① I knew <u>that</u> he was wrong.
② <u>That</u> person is my brother.
③ <u>That</u> he is my father is true.
④ It is amazing <u>that</u> she became a famous singer.
⑤ The problem is <u>that</u> we don't have time.

16. 다음 빈칸에 알맞은 것은?

> I could not go out _____.

① as I don't go there
② if he doesn't start now
③ before it gets very dark
④ because I had lots of homework
⑤ when I come back home

17. 다음 중 어법상 옳지 <u>않은</u> 것은?

① I can't go outside because it rains.
② I can't go outside because of the rain.
③ She is happy because of him.
④ She is not happy because her bad score.
⑤ He moved to Busan because he got a new job.

18. 다음 밑줄 친 that을 생략할 수 <u>없는</u> 것을 고르시오.

① I know <u>that</u> he is kind to his friends.
② I hope <u>that</u> you will come to my birthday party.
③ She said <u>that</u> he was an honest boy.
④ I believe <u>that</u> you can come here.
⑤ We think <u>that</u> was the first Thanksgiving Day in America.

19. 다음 중 빈칸에 들어가기에 <u>어색한</u> 것은?
(순서는 상관없음)

> ❶ She is happy because
> _____.
> ❷ He is crying because
> _____.
> ❸ He is in the hospital because
> _____.
> ❹ She was running away because
> _____.

① she saw a bear
② he broke his leg
③ she got good scores on the test
④ he didn't wear a heavy coat
⑤ the movie is so sad

20. 다음 주어진 대화의 빈칸에 들어갈 단어와 같은 말이 들어갈 수 있는 것은?

> A: Why do bears sleep all winter?
> B: That's _____ there is little food in winter and the weather is cold.

① Benjamin is very diligent, _____ I like him so much.
② Emily lost her bag yesterday, _____ she has to buy a bag.
③ Jane is proud of herself _____ she did not do well on the test.
④ He broke his arm, _____ now he's in the hospital.
⑤ She is very happy _____ she got a new puppy.

단원평가 　　고난도

1. 다음 빈칸에 알맞은 것은?

> The weather was sunny yesterday, _____ we went out for a walk.

① or　　　② but　　　③ then
④ so　　　⑤ however

2. 다음 괄호 안에 단어를 배열했을 때 다섯 번째에 오는 단어는?

> He was in the church (looking, his, him, were, for, friends, when).

① were　　　② looking　　　③ him
④ friends　　　⑤ for

3. 다음 주어진 문장의 빈칸에 들어갈 접속사와 같지 않은 것은?

> Last weekend, my plant looked very dry. _____ I watered it but it got worse.

① I have a toothache, _____ I will see a doctor.
② I want to help sick people, _____ I want to be a doctor.
③ It rains a lot today. _____ why don't you wear rain boots?
④ A surprising thing happened _____ I was 10 years old.
⑤ Only a few skaters took part in the race, _____ the race finished early.

4. 다음 중 어법상 옳지 않은 것은?

① Mina is very smart. She began reading when she was four years old.
② Mina is very smart, and she began reading when she was four years old.
③ Because Mina is very smart, she began reading when she was four years old.
④ Mina is very smart. So she began reading when she was four years old.
⑤ Mina is very smart, when she began reading, because she is four years old.

5. 다음 중 보기의 밑줄 친 부분과 의미가 다른 것은?

> 보기 <u>When</u> I met him, he was going home.

① <u>When</u> I ride a bike, I wear a helmet.
② <u>When</u> did you buy the new laptop?
③ Did you see her <u>when</u> she came here?
④ <u>When</u> he was young, he couldn't swim.
⑤ What do you usually do <u>when</u> you are sad?

6. 다음 보기에서 원인과 결과의 관계가 자연스러운 것을 모두 고르면?

> **보기**
> (A) I hate him because he always tells a lie.
> (B) He is fat because he doesn't eat much.
> (C) You must watch carefully because many bags look the same.
> (D) He could sleep well last night because he was so afraid.
> (E) She enjoyed lunch because she had a lot of problems.

① (A), (B)   ② (A), (C)   ③ (B), (D)
④ (B), (D), (E)   ⑤ (C), (D), (E)

7. 다음 중 어법상 옳은 것은?

① I stay home because it was cold.
② I turned on the light because the room was very dark.
③ She felt disappointed because of she got a bad score on the exam.
④ Mira went bowling because she felt tired.
⑤ She did not come to school because of ill.

8. 다음 문장에 대한 설명으로 옳지 <u>않은</u> 것은?

> I think that it is a rabbit.

① that은 생략할 수 없다.
② that은 '~하는 것'으로 해석한다.
③ that 뒤에는 문장이 연결되어야 한다.
④ I가 She로 바뀌면 think가 'thinks'가 된다.
⑤ 생각을 표현할 때 사용할 수 있는 문장이다.

9. 다음 주어진 문장의 밑줄 친 that과 쓰임이 같은 것은?

> When you go autumn camping, remember <u>that</u> you must always be careful with fire.

① What can I do about <u>that</u>?
② We believe <u>that</u> is not good.
③ I guess <u>that</u> she's Amy's sister.
④ Do you see <u>that</u> man over there?
⑤ Do you remember <u>that</u> book on the table?

10. 다음 중 어법상 <u>틀린</u> 문장의 개수는?

> ⓐ Let's see a movie if you aren't busy.
> ⓑ I'm sure if he will come soon.
> ⓒ The food should be ready before the customers arrive.
> ⓓ Because of English is difficult, I should study it very hard.

① 1개   ② 2개   ③ 3개
④ 4개   ⑤ 5개

11. 다음 빈칸에 and, but, or 중 알맞은 말을 골라 쓰시오.

❶ Minji eats little, _____ she is fatter than me.
❷ Hurry up, _____ you will miss the train.
❸ Come to my graduation ceremony, _____ I'll be happy.

1. 다음 보기와 같이 의미에 맞게 문장을 영작하시오.

> 보기 I like to cook but I don't like to wash the dishes. (나는 요리하는 것은 좋아하지만, 설거지는 싫어한다.)

❶ He rides a bike, but _____.
(그는 자전거를 타지만, 그의 여동생은 타지 않는다.)

❷ They are friends, but _____.
(그들은 친구이지만, 같은 반은 아니다.)

❸ She plays the piano, but _____.
(그녀는 피아노는 치지만 노래를 부르지는 않는다.)

2. 다음 그림을 보고, 보기와 같이 주어진 표현을 사용하여 문장을 완성하시오.

> 보기
>
> (play soccer, be excited)
>
> When I play soccer, I am excited.

❶
(listen to music, feel calm)
When _____.

❷
(play the violin, feel happy)
When _____.

3. 다음 주어진 우리말과 같은 뜻이 되도록 문장을 완성하시오.

❶ 만약 내일 날이 맑다면, 나는 하이킹을 갈 것이다.

⇒ _____ _____ _____ _____

_____, _____ _____ _____

_____.

❷ 네가 너의 일을 마치면, 나는 너를 만날 것이다.

⇒ When _____ _____ _____ _____,

_____ _____ _____ _____.

4. 다음 대화를 통해 알 수 있는 원인과 결과를 보기처럼 한 문장으로 쓰시오.

> 보기
>
> Mina: Can I use your laptop?
> Justin: No, I'm afraid you can't. It's broken.
> ⇒ Mina can't use the laptop because it's broken.

❶ Mina: Can I open the window?
Justin: No, I'm afraid you can't. It's cold outside.

⇒ _____

❷ Mina: Can I swim in the lake?
Justin: No, I'm afraid you can't. It's very deep.

⇒ _____

5. 다음 두 문장을 because를 사용하여 한 문장으로 고쳐 쓰시오.

❶ I was late. / I woke up late.

⇒ _____ .

❷ We didn't go out. / The weather was cold.

⇒ _____ .

6. 다음 우리말과 뜻이 같도록 괄호 안의 말을 이용하여 문장을 완성하시오.

❶ 나는 점심을 먹은 후, 산책을 한다. (have lunch)

⇒ _____ , I take a walk.

❷ 네가 일을 시작하기 전에 나에게 알려줘. (begin to work)

⇒ _____ , please let me

know.

❸ 그는 그곳에 있는 동안, 돈을 많이 벌었다. (be there)

⇒ _____ , he made a lot of

money.

7. 다음 그림을 보고 주어진 질문에 알맞은 답을 쓰시오. (조건: a score와 the science test를 반드시 사용할 것)

A: Why is he so happy?

B: _____ he _____ .

(그가 과학 시험에서 좋은 점수를 얻었기 때문이야.)

8. 다음 두 문장을 알맞은 접속사를 넣어 한 문장으로 완성하시오.

❶ We'll win the game. We believe it.

⇒ We believe _____ .

❷ She can't understand it. She is too young.

⇒ She can't understand it _____

_____ .

9. 다음 문장의 틀린 부분을 바르게 고쳐 문장을 다시 쓰시오.

❶ Study hard, and you will fail the exam.

⇒ _____

❷ Jessica has many dogs but cats.

⇒ _____

❸ My English teacher spoke loudly, but everyone could hear her well.

⇒ _____

❹ Did you go to the movies and stay at home?

⇒ _____

❺ Press the button, or the door will open.

⇒ _____

memo

Chapter 13
전치사

13.1. 시간의 전치사

>>> 전치사란? 명사(구)나 대명사 앞에 쓰여서 시간, 장소, 방법, 이유 등을 나타낸다.

1 in, on, at

at	몇 시, 몇 분, 정오, 밤(시각, 시점) 등 매우 짧은 시간 **at** five o'clock 5시에, **at** noon 정오에, **at** night 밤에, **at** dawn 새벽에
on	날짜, 요일, 특정한 날 **on** the tenth of April 4월 10일에, **on** Monday 월요일에, **on** New Year's Day 새해 첫날에
in	at 보다 비교적 긴 시간, 월, 계절, 년도, 아침, 오후, 저녁 **in** April 4월에, **in** 1942 1942년에, **in** summer 여름에, **in** the 20th century 20세기에

* 시간이나 요일의 명사 앞에 this, that, next, last 등이 붙으면 전치사를 쓰지 않는다.

* 하루의 때를 나타낼 때는 in을 쓰지만, 특정 요일의 때는 on을 쓴다. ex) on Sunday morning 일요일 아침에

2 기타 시간의 전치사

in	시간의 경과, 미래시제에 쓰임. (~이 지나면[있으면], ~후에) She will come back **in** a few hours. 그녀는 몇 시간 후에 돌아올 것이다.
within	일정한 시간, 기간 이내를 나타냄. (~이내에) I will finish my project **within** a week. 나는 내 프로젝트를 일주일 이내에 끝낼 것이다.
around	시간의 대략을 나타냄. (~ 무렵에, ~ 경에) She arrived **around** 6 p.m. 그녀는 6시 무렵에 도착했다.
after	동작의 완료를 나타내며 과거시제에 쓰임. (~ 이후에) Minho came back **after** five days. 민호는 5일 후에 돌아왔다.
before	동작이 일어나기 전에 행동을 나타냄. (~ 전에) Wash your hands **before** dinner. 저녁 식사 전에 손을 씻어라.
for	기간을 나타내며 일반적 숫자 앞에 쓰임 (~동안) I am going to stay here **for** a week. 나는 이곳에 일주일 동안 머물 것이다.
during	상태의 계속을 나타내며 특정의 사건·기간 앞에 쓰임 (~중에) I fell asleep **during** the lesson. 나는 수업 중에 잠이 들었다.
until	어느 때까지의 동작의 계속을 나타내며 주로 동사 wait, work, study와 함께 쓰임. (~까지) Suji studied for the exam **until** 12 o'clock. 수지는 12시까지 시험 공부를 했다.
by	어느 때까지의 동작의 완료를 나타내며 주로 동사 finish와 함께 쓰임. (~까지) I will be here **by** nine. 나는 이곳에 9시까지 올 것이다.

A. 다음 문장의 빈칸에 in, on, at 중에서 알맞은 전치사를 골라 쓰시오.

① We go to church _____ the morning.

② We go to church _____ Sundays.

③ He is going to arrive _____ five this morning.

④ They will probably arrive _____ Friday evening.

⑤ He usually comes home late _____ the evening.

⑥ I'll get in touch with you when I arrive there _____ June.

⑦ She was born _____ 2002.

⑧ She was born _____ July 14, 2010.

⑨ We are living _____ the 21st Century.

⑩ We have much rain _____ summer.

⑪ The store opens _____ noon.

⑫ School begins _____ September.

⑬ The last class ends _____ 3:15 p.m.

⑭ The leaves change colors _____ fall.

⑮ Suji gets up _____ six _____ the morning.

⑯ _____ the second Friday _____ October, I went to Finland.

⑰ Koreans fly kites _____ special holidays.

B. 주어진 전치사를 각각 써넣어 문장을 완성하시오.

① for/during   She got a stomachache _____ the final exam.

　　　　　　　　　My wife and I have lived here _____ 5 years.

② for/around   The sun rises _____ 5 in summer.

　　　　　　　　　He studied _____ 2 hours.

③ by/until   I'll finish my homework _____ Sunday.

　　　　　　　　　Jim has to wait _____ next month for the result.

④ before/after   You should wash your hands _____ P.E. class.

　　　　　　　　　You should wash your hands _____ dinner.

13.2. 장소/방향의 전치사

1 in, at, on

in	도시, 국가 등 비교적 넓은 장소, 건물이나 사물의 내부를 말할 때
	in the box 상자 안에, **in** the room 방 안에, **in** Paris 파리에, **in** the building 건물 안에
at	비교적 좁은 장소나 하나의 지점을 말할 때
	at home 집에, **at** a party 파티에, **at** school 학교에, **at** the bus stop 버스 정류장에
on	어떤 표현에 접촉한 상태를 말할 때
	on the wall 벽에, **on** the first floor 1층에, **on** the street 거리에, **on** the table 탁자 위에

2 선(line)을 기준으로 사용되는 전치사

```
                         over(바로 위에)                      (위쪽으로)
                            |                                  up
above(비스듬히 위에) ↖       ○  on(놓여 있는 것 위에)            ↑


below(비스듬히 아래에) ↙      ○  beneath(접촉한 것 밑에)          ↓
                            |                                 down
                         under(바로 밑에)                    (아래쪽으로)
```

3 평면상(경계선)을 기준으로 사용되는 전치사

▦← round(넓은 주변), 공전, 자전 따위에 쓰임

■ ← in(넓은 장소- 경계선의 안쪽)
　★← at(좁은 지점 - 안이든 밖이든 한 지점을 가리킴)

◈ ← around(하나의 정지, 그 외의 동작)
← into(~안쪽으로)
▦ ← about(막연한 주변, 여기 저기)

↘ out of(운동 <안에서 밖으로>)

4 운동, 방향의 전치사

```
            ↑ across(~을 횡단하여)        ↑ through(~을 관통해서)
            ← along(~을 쭉 따라서)
```

A. 다음 문장의 빈칸에 in, on, at 중에서 알맞은 전치사를 골라 쓰시오.

① Don't sit _____ this chair.

② The visitors wrote their names _____ the paper.

③ I live _____ the 10th floor.

④ There were few cars _____ the road today.

⑤ A little rabbit got lost _____ a forest.

⑥ The game of soccer started _____ England.

⑦ I saw him _____ the welcoming ceremony.

⑧ There's a bookstore _____ 8th Street.

⑨ I worked as a volunteer _____ the fire station.

⑩ Jim and Elena were _____ their way home.

⑪ There is a fly _____ the ceiling.

⑫ We saw off our friends _____ the airport.

⑬ I was born in 2003 _____ Peru.

⑭ Look up the meaning of this word _____ the dictionary.

B. 다음 그림을 보고 빈칸에 알맞은 말을 쓰시오.

① There is a ball _____ the chair.

There is a cat _____ the basket.

② There is a cat _____ the basket.

There is a ball _____ the chair.

There is a book _____ the chair.

③ There is a cat _____ the chair.

There is a ball _____ the chair.

There are some books _____ the basket.

13.3. 여러 가지 전치사

1 구전치사

》》》 구전치사는 두 단어 이상이 함께 쓰여 구를 이루는 전치사를 말한다.

in front of	~앞에	The dog is standing **in front of** me. 그 개는 내 앞에 서 있다.
next to	~옆에	The pretty girl sat **next to** him. 그 예쁜 소녀는 그의 옆에 앉았다.
across from	~맞은 편에	There is a bakery **across from** my school. 나의 학교 맞은편에 빵집이 있다.
between A and B	A와 B 사이에	The store is **between** the bank **and** the library. 그 가게는 은행과 도서관 사이에 있다.
from A to B	A부터 B까지	I work **from** 9 a.m. **to** 5 p.m. 나는 오전 9시부터 오후 5시까지 일한다.

2 기타 전치사

by	~을 타고(교통수단), (일반적인 수단)을 통해	I go to school **by** bus. 나는 버스를 타고 학교에 간다. * 수단으로 by를 사용하는 경우, 수단 앞에는 관사를 사용하지 않는다. * 단, 걸어서 학교를 가는 경우는 on foot을 사용한다. cf. I go to school **on foot**. He got well **by** taking a rest. 그는 휴식을 취함으로써 나아졌다.
with	~을 가지고(도구), ~와 함께	He washes his car **with** a brush. 그는 솔을 가지고 세차를 한다. I will watch a movie **with** Suji. 나는 수지와 영화를 볼 것이다.
without	~없이	She can't read a book **without** glasses. 그녀는 안경 없이 읽을 수 없다. People can't live **without** water. 사람들은 물 없이 살 수 없다.
like	~처럼, ~와 같이	My cat looks **like** a tiger. 나의 고양이는 호랑이처럼 보인다. I want to be a teacher **like** my mom. 나는 나의 엄마 같은 선생님이 되고 싶다.
as	~처럼, (자격)…로(서)	People were all dressed **as** clowns. 사람들은 모두 광대처럼 옷을 입었다. I respect him **as** a doctor. 나는 그를 의사로서 존경한다.

A. 다음 그림을 참고하여 빈칸에 A-E 중 알맞은 것을 쓰시오.

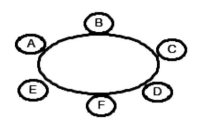

① A is between _____ and _____.　② D is across from _____.

③ B is next to _____ or _____.　④ F is between _____ and _____.

⑤ F is across from _____.

B. 다음 주어진 말을 이용하여 우리말과 뜻이 같도록 문장을 완성하시오.

① 우리집에서 학교까지 자동차로 1시간이 걸린다. (my house, take)

_____ _____ _____ _____ _____ _____ _____

_____ _____ _____.

② 동해는 한국과 일본 사이에 있다. (The East Sea, Korea, Japan)

_____ _____ _____ _____ _____ _____ _____ _____.

③ 수지는 우리 집 맞은 편에 산다. (live, house)

_____ _____ _____ _____ _____.

④ 나의 아빠는 그 나무 옆에 주차를 했다. (park, the tree)

_____ _____ _____ _____ _____ _____ _____.

C. 다음 괄호 안에 주어진 전치사 중 알맞은 것은 고르시오.

① My dad goes to work (with, by) subway.

② Emily wrote a diary (with, by) her brown pen.

③ You can use that glass (as, without) a vase.

④ Yura looks (like, as) her mom.

⑤ People can gargle (by, with) salt water.

1. 다음 빈칸에 알맞은 것은?

> He gets up _____ six in the morning.

① at   ② on   ③ in
④ into   ⑤ with

[2-4] 다음 빈칸에 공통으로 알맞은 것은?

2.

> - My aunt lives _____ San Francisco.
> - The wallet is _____ my bag.

① at   ② in   ③ on
④ in   ⑤ under

3.

> - School starts _____ Monday.
> - There is a cockroach _____ the wall.

① at   ② in   ③ on
④ in   ⑤ under

4.

> - I will go to the airport _____ taxi.
> - Will you pay _____ credit card?

① at   ② in   ③ on
④ in   ⑤ by

5. 다음 밑줄 친 부분 중 어법상 틀린 것은?

> My mom ① always ② prepares ③ breakfast
> ④ at 6 o'clock ⑤ at the morning.

6. 다음 빈칸에 들어갈 알맞은 전치사를 쓰시오.

> ❶ I bought some cookies _____ my nephew.
> ❷ Sally went there _____ car.

7. 다음 우리말과 같은 뜻이 되도록 빈칸에 알맞은 전치사를 쓰시오.

> 그는 한달 동안 그의 할머니 댁에서 머물렀다.
> = He stayed at his grandmother's _____ a month.

[8-10] 다음 빈칸에 알맞은 것은?

8.

> Jisu plays computer games _____ Sundays.

① at   ② on   ③ in
④ into   ⑤ with

9.

> Our winter vacation starts _____ December.

① at   ② on   ③ in
④ into   ⑤ with

10.

Hello, everyone. Pleased to meet you. My name is Minho Song. I live _____ Busan.

① at   ② from   ③ in
④ with   ⑤ on

단원평가 실전대비

1. 다음 빈칸에 빈칸에 공통으로 알맞은 것은?

- Minho always drives his car _____ top speed.
- My mother has breakfast _____ 7:00.

① to   ② at   ③ in
④ on   ⑤ for

2. 다음 글에서 밑줄 친 ⓐ~ⓓ 중 잘못된 것의 개수는?

This is my second visit to my uncle's house in Paris. My first visit was ⓐon 2008. ⓑAt Sunday, I went to the History Museum. I could learn about the history of France. ⓒOn Monday, I went to a concert. It was great! I came back to my uncle's house ⓓon 6 o'clock.

① 없음   ② 1개   ③ 2개
④ 3개   ⑤ 4개

3. 다음 중 빈칸에 들어갈 단어가 나머지와 다른 것은?

① The exam is _____ my birthday.
② I spoke to Jenny _____ Tuesday.
③ It's four o'clock _____ the afternoon.
④ I went to a library _____ March 25, 2017.
⑤ Come and have a party _____ Christmas day.

4. 다음 중 의미가 어색한 것은?

① It snowed a lot in December, 2017.
② My first visit to Australia was in 2007.
③ Audrey Hepburn was born in May 4, 1929.
④ My grandparents usually have lunch at 11:30.
⑤ Some students were absent from school on Friday.

5. 다음 그림의 내용과 일치하지 않는 것은?

① Bob is standing next to Julia.
② Chris is standing next to Susan.
③ Carl is sitting in front of Susan.
④ Susan is standing between Chris and Carl.
⑤ Julia is standing between Bob and Susan.

6. 다음 중 어법상 옳은 것은?

① I usually get up early at the morning.
② It rains a lot on August.
③ They ate dinner on seven thirty.
④ He left Hungary on Christmas.
⑤ My sister and he will get married in the last Sunday of May.

7. 다음 빈칸에 들어갈 전치사를 보기에서 골라 쓰시오.

> 보기 at   in   on

❶ I go fishing _____ summer.

❷ I start to work _____ 8 o'clock.

❸ Let's have a birthday party _____ Sunday.

8. 다음 중 어법상 옳지 않은 것은?

① It's usually warm in April.
② Sam often helps her mom on Saturday.
③ We sometimes swim in the pool.
④ He often goes to school by the bus.
⑤ I am always happy in the morning.

[9–10] 다음 빈칸에 공통으로 들어갈 알맞은 말을 쓰시오.

9.

> - There is a clock _____ the wall.
> - The office is _____ the fourth floor.
> - They don't work _____ Sundays.

10.

> - How many students are there _____ the classroom?
> - It's 6 o'clock _____ the evening.
> - They go on a picnic _____ June.

11. 다음 밑줄 친 부분을 어법상 바르게 고치시오.

❶ <u>During</u> ten years, she learned English.

❷ The office is open from 9 a.m. <u>in</u> 6 p.m.

12. 다음 대화의 빈칸에 들어갈 말이 바르게 짝지어진 것은?

> A: What will you do _____ your summer vacation?
> B: I will visit London _____ England.

① for – at   ② during – in
③ during – on   ④ for – in
⑤ by – in

13. 다음 주어진 문장의 밑줄 친 부분과 쓰임이 같은 것은?

> It looks <u>like</u> a small beanbag.

① I <u>like</u> classical music.
② Do you <u>like</u> playing soccer?
③ She swims <u>like</u> a fish.
④ I <u>like</u> to have a big bowl of salad.
⑤ She <u>likes</u> to see dramas.

14. 다음 빈칸에 알맞은 것은?

> Sam poured water _____ a glass.

① into   ② down   ③ in
④ to   ⑤ up

15. 다음 대화의 빈칸에 우리말과 같은 뜻이 되도록 알맞은 전치사를 쓰시오.

> A: Excuse me. Where is the Sisa building?
> B: Let me see…. It's _____ the bank and the flower shop. (은행과 꽃가게 사이에 있어요.)

16. 다음 대화의 빈칸에 들어갈 알맞은 전치사를 쓰시오.

> A: What's the weather _____ in Busan?
> B: It's cloudy and chilly.

17. 다음 글의 빈칸에 들어갈 전치사를 순서대로 쓰시오.

> During the week I get up early _____ the morning and go to bed late _____ night.

[18-20] 다음 그림을 보고 빈칸에 알맞은 말을 쓰시오.

18.

> A: Where is the flower?
> B: It's _____ _____ _____ the bed.

19.

> A: Where is the bed?
> B: It's _____ _____ the desk.

20.

> A: Where is the newspaper?
> B: It's _____ the table.

1. 다음 빈칸 ⓐ~ⓓ에 들어갈 표현이 바르게 연결된 것은?

> - It snows ⓐ_____ December.
> - They have lunch ⓑ_____ 12:30.
> - She doesn't like to go out ⓒ_____ night.
> - Sam was born ⓓ_____ January 11, 2002.

	ⓐ	ⓑ	ⓒ	ⓓ
①	in	on	on	at
②	on	in	at	in
③	in	at	in	on
④	on	in	in	at
⑤	in	at	at	on

2. 다음 중 빈칸에 들어갈 말이 나머지와 <u>다른</u> 것은?

① School begins _____ March in Korea.
② Tom will plan a party _____ Saturday.
③ Minho worked in the library _____ 2015.
④ I couldn't play computer games _____ the evening.
⑤ I usually enjoy drinking a cup of hot chocolate _____ winter.

3. 다음 중 어법상 옳지 <u>않은</u> 것은?

① The movie starts at 12:30.
② He got up early in the morning.
③ Don't play the piano at midnight.
④ I went to a concert in July.
⑤ We are going to travel in London in Christmas.

4. 다음 지도의 내용과 일치하는 것은?

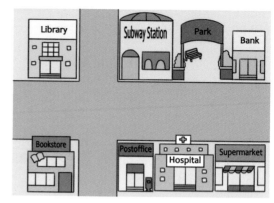

① The supermarket is next to the post office.
② The hospital is across from the supermarket.
③ The park is between the bank and the supermarket.
④ The library is next to bookstore.
⑤ The subway station is across from the post office.

5. 다음 중 밑줄 친 부분이 시간을 나타내는 전치사가 <u>아닌</u> 것은?

① I always get up <u>at</u> seven o'clock.
② We go skating and skiing <u>in</u> winter.
③ He was surprised <u>at</u> the news.
④ She watches TV <u>after</u> dinner.
⑤ I don't go to school <u>on</u> Sundays.

6. 다음 보기에서 알맞은 말을 골라 빈칸을 채우시오.

> 보기 at in on under over

❶ My brother lives _____ Chile.
❷ There is a fly _____ the wall.
❸ The river flows _____ the bridge.
❹ She bought a map _____ the station.
❺ You can see a big cloud _____ the mountain.

7. 다음 중 밑줄 친 부분이 잘못된 것은?

① Don't put your book <u>under</u> the table.
② Elena sat <u>between</u> Sally <u>and</u> Linda.
③ The picture is <u>on</u> the wall.
④ Put this apple <u>on</u> your bag.
⑤ There is a kitten <u>behind</u> the tree.

8. 다음 주어진 문장의 밑줄 친 for와 같은 뜻으로 쓰인 것은?

> I studied English <u>for</u> three hours.

① I am waiting <u>for</u> my friends here.
② My uncle stayed in the hospital <u>for</u> a month.
③ Dad made a chair <u>for</u> me.
④ When are we going to leave <u>for</u> the beach?
⑤ She prepares lunch <u>for</u> our family.

9. 다음 주어진 두 문장의 뜻이 같도록 빈칸에 알맞을 말을 쓰시오.

❶ The museum is near our school.
= The museum is not far _____ our school.

❷ He likes the girl who has brown hair.
= He likes the girl _____ brown hair.

10. 주어진 우리말과 같은 뜻이 되도록 빈칸에 공통으로 들어갈 알맞은 전치사를 쓰시오.

> - 아니 땐 굴뚝에 연기나랴.
> = There is no smoke _____ fire.
> - 우리는 물 없이는 살 수 없다.
> = We can't live _____ water.

11. 다음 밑줄 친 부분을 어법상 바르게 고치시오.

❶ <u>During</u> four years, I learned Spanish.

⇒ _____

❷ The hospital is open from 9 a.m. <u>for</u> 5 p.m.

⇒ _____

❸ There are no clouds <u>at</u> the sky.

⇒ _____

12. 다음 글의 빈칸에 공통으로 들어갈 알맞은 것은?

> - Freeze them _____ about 4 hours.
> - Our music club members play music _____ sick children.

① to   ② on   ③ for
④ with   ⑤ after

13. 다음 글의 밑줄 친 ⓐ~ⓔ 중 옳은 것은?

> This is my second visit to my cousin's house in L.A. My first visit was ⓐ<u>in</u> 2014. ⓑ<u>In</u> Monday, I went to the Universal Studio. I enjoyed many joyful rides. ⓒ<u>At</u> Tuesday, I went to a concert. It was great! I came back to my cousin's house ⓓ<u>on</u> 6 o'clock. We had a supper that night. Today, I visited my grandparents' house with my cousin. We came back home ⓔ<u>on</u> 8:30. We had a great time.

① ⓐ   ② ⓑ   ③ ⓒ
④ ⓓ   ⑤ ⓔ

1. 다음 그림과 일치하도록 빈칸에 알맞은 말을 보기에서 골라 쓰시오.

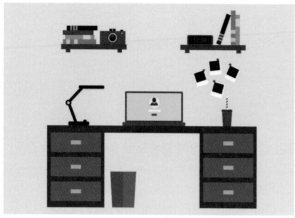

보기 on   next to   under

❶ There are photos _____ the wall.

❷ The is a lamp _____ the laptop.

❸ There is a trash bin _____ the desk.

2. 다음 문장에 공통으로 들어갈 전치사를 쓰시오.

❶ We will move to London _____ April.
   There are many student _____ the classroom.

❷ What do you do _____ Sunday morning?
   Melissa is sitting _____ a bench.

❸ The game starts _____ midnight.
   I have many friends _____ school.

3. 다음 우리말과 같게 빈칸에 알맞은 말을 넣으시오.

❶ 내 가방이 의자 위에 있다.
   ⇒ My bag is _____ the chair.

❷ Susan은 그 문 옆에 있다.
   ⇒ Susan is _____ the door.

❸ 겨울에는 눈이 온다.
   ⇒ We have snows _____ winter.

❹ 그녀는 지금 학교에 있다.
   ⇒ She is _____ school now.

❺ 꽃집과 빵집 사이에 학교가 있다.
   ⇒ There is a school _____ the flower
   shop _____ the bakery.

4. 다음 문장에서 틀린 부분을 모두 바르게 고쳐 문장을 다시 쓰시오.

❶ There is a hat hanging at the wall.
   ⇒ _____

❷ I have dinner in 8 o'clock on the evening.
   ⇒ _____

❸ John lived at Shanghai at 2016.
   ⇒ _____

❹ Bobby studied English at the test during four hours.
   ⇒ _____

부 록

동사의 불규칙 변화형

동사의 불규칙 변화형 (chapter 2. 일반동사)

■ A-B-C형 (동사원형-과거형-과거분사형 모양이 모두 다름)

동사원형	과거형	과거분사형	뜻
am	was	been	~이다, 있다
are	were	been	~이다, 있다
is	was	been	~이다, 있다
arise	arose	arisen	(나쁜 상황이) 생기다, 발생하다
awake	awoke	awoken	깨다, 일어나다, 깨우다
begin	began	begun	시작하다
bite	bit	bitten	물다
blow	blew	blown	불다
bear	bore	born	참다
break	broke	broken	깨지다
choose	chose	chosen	선택하다
do	did	done	하다
draw	drew	drawn	그리다
drive	drove	driven	운전하다
drink	drank	drunk	마시다
eat	ate	eaten	먹다
fall	fell	fallen	떨어지다
fly	flew	flown	날다
forgive	forgave	forgiven	용서하다
forget	forgot	forgotten	잊다
freeze	froze	frozen	얼다
give	gave	given	주다
go	went	gone	가다
get	got	gotten	얻다
grow	grew	grown	자라다
hide	hid	hidden	숨다
know	knew	known	알다
lie	lay	lain	눕다
ride	rode	ridden	(오토바이, 말, 자전거를) 타다

rise	rose	risen	오르다, 올라가다
ring	rang	rung	(벨이) 울리다
see	saw	seen	보다
shake	shook	shaken	흔들다
speak	spoke	spoken	말하다
steal	stole	stolen	훔치다
sing	sang	sung	노래하다
sink	sank	sunk	가라앉다
swell	swelled	swollen	붓다, 부풀다, 부어오르다
swear	swore	sworn	맹세하다, 욕하다
swim	swam	swum	수영하다
take	took	taken	(서비스, 물건 등을) 가지다
throw	threw	thrown	던지다
tear	tore	torn	찢다
wake	woke	woken	깨다, 일어나다, 깨우다
wear	wore	worn	입다
write	wrote	written	쓰다

■ **A-B-B형** (과거형과 과거분사형 모양이 같음)

동사원형	과거형	과거분사형	뜻
bend	bent	bent	구부리다
bind	bound	bound	묶다
bring	brought	brought	가져오다, 데려오다
build	built	built	(건물을) 짓다, 세우다
buy	bought	bought	사다
catch	caught	caught	잡다
dig	dug	dug	(땅을) 파다
feed	fed	fed	먹이를 주다, 먹이다
feel	felt	felt	느끼다
find	found	found	찾다, 발견하다
grind	ground	ground	갈다
hang	hung	hung	매달다
have	had	had	가지다

hear	heard	heard	듣다
hold	held	held	쥐다, 잡다, 개최하다
keep	kept	kept	지키다, 보존하다
lay	laid	laid	놓다, 두다, 눕히다
lead	led	led	이끌다, 인도하다
leave	left	left	떠나다
lend	lent	lent	빌려주다
lose	lost	lost	잃다, 지다
make	made	made	만들다
mean	meant	meant	뜻하다, 의미하다
meet	met	met	만나다
pay	paid	paid	지불하다
say	said	said	말하다
sell	sold	sold	팔다
send	sent	sent	보내다
shine	shone	shone	빛나다
shoot	shot	shot	쏘다
sit	sat	sat	앉다
sleep	slept	slept	자다
smell	smelt	smelt	냄새를 맡다, 냄새나다
spend	spent	spent	소비하다
stand	stood	stood	일어서다
stick	stuck	stuck	달라붙다
sting	stung	stung	찌르다
strike	struck	struck/stricken	때리다, 치다
swing	swung	swung	흔들리다
teach	taught	taught	가르치다
tell	told	told	말하다
think	thought	thought	생각하다
understand	understood	understood	이해하다
win	won	won	이기다
wind	wound	wound	감다

■ A−B−A형 (동사원형과 과거분사형 모양이 같음)

동사원형	과거형	과거분사형	뜻
become	became	become	∼이 되다
come	came	come	오다
run	ran	run	달리다

■ A−A−B형 (동사원형과 과거형 모양이 같음))

동사원형	과거형	과거분사형	뜻
beat	beat	beaten	때리다

■ A−A−B형 (동사원형과 과거형 모양이 같음)

동사원형	과거형	과거분사형	뜻
burst	burst	burst	터지다
broadcast	broadcast	broadcast	방송하다
cast	cast	cast	던지다
cost	cost	cost	비용이 들다
cut	cut	cut	자르다
hit	hit	hit	치다, 때리다
hurt	hurt	hurt	상하게 하다, 상처주다
let	let	let	∼하게 내버려두다
put	put	put	놓다, 두다
read[ri:d]	read[red]	read[red]	읽다
set	set	set	놓다
shut	shut	shut	닫다
spread	spread	spread	펴다

주의해야 할 동사 변화형

1 lie - lay - lain ▶ 눕다
  lie - lied - lied ▶ 거짓말하다
  lay - laid - laid ▶ 놓다, 두다, 눕히다

2 find - found - found ▶ 찾다, 발견하다
  found - founded - founded ▶ 설립하다

3 sow - sowed - sown ▶ 씨를 뿌리다
  sew - sewed - sewn ▶ 바느질하다
  saw - sawed - sawn ▶ 톱질하다

memo

memo

memo

저자 김보미

Ateneo 고등학교(필리핀)
Ateneo 대학(필리핀), 국제학 전공
한국외국어대학교 국제대학원 인도/아세안 사회학 전공
전) EBS 중학 프리미엄 영어강사
전) 다락원, 넥서스, 글로벌 21, 에듀스파, cts 기독교방송, 뇌새김, 윈글리쉬 등 다수 온라인 강의 진행
전) YBM(종로), 파고다(강남) 영어시험(OPIc, Toeic Speaking, TOEIC)강의
전) 삼성, LG, 롯데 등 대기업 영어 출강 및 성균관대, 중앙대, 한양대 등 다수 대학 강의 진행
현) 수박씨닷컴 중등영어 강사
현) 아이수박씨닷컴 초등영어 강사
현) 메가스터디 고등영어내신 강사
현) ebs 어학 회화 온라인 강의 진행

시험지에서 가져온~
중학영문법

초판인쇄	2017년 3월 13일
초판발행	2017년 4월 3일
저자	김보미
펴낸이	엄태상
책임 편집	이효리, 장은혜, 김효은, 정유항
디자인	진지화
마케팅	이상호, 오원택, 이승욱, 전한나, 왕성석
펴낸곳	랭기지플러스
주소	서울시 종로구 자하문로 300 시사빌딩
주문 및 교재 문의	1588-1582
팩스	(02)3671-0500
홈페이지	www.sisabooks.com
이메일	sisabooks@naver.com
등록일자	2000년 8월 17일
등록번호	1-2718호

ISBN 978-89-5518-431-0 (53740)

[서술형 1] 다음 상황에 맞게 상자 속의 주어진 단어들 중 옳은 것만을 사용하여 각 문장을 완성하시오. (중복 사용 가능) (6점)

for, the, wait, your, on, off, help, turn, be, take, phone, in

1) He always cuts in line.

⇒ You should _____ . (3점)

2) Some people use their phones in the movie theater.

⇒ You should _____ . (3점)

[서술형 2] 괄호 안의 단어를 이용하여 빈칸을 완성하시오. (3점)

It was my grandmother's birthday.

I 1) _____ her a gift. (give) (1점) My brother 2) _____ her picture. (take) (1점)

cookies. (make) (1점) My father 3) _____ her a picture.

11. 빈칸 ⓐ~ⓒ에 들어갈 단어를 순서대로 나열한 것은? (5점)

Put your hands together. Raise your arms ⓐ _____ your head.

Try ⓑ _____ hold it ⓒ _____ 30 seconds.

	ⓐ	ⓑ	ⓒ
①	on	and	about
②	above	to	for
③	on	and	by
④	above	to	with
⑤	over	and	for

12. 다음 그림과 일치하는 올바른 표현은? (5점)

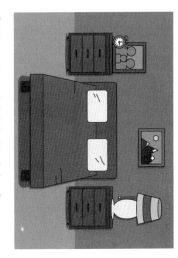

① There is a clock behind the frame.
② There are paintings on the wall.
③ There are two beds in the room.
④ There is a lamp next to the drawer.
⑤ There are two pillows on the bed.

13. 보기 와 제시대명사의 쓰임이 다른 것을 고르시오. (6점)

보기
He himself cleaned his desk.

① My grandmother lived in the house herself.
② I myself made the skirt.
③ He fixed the car himself.
④ She introduced herself to the class.
⑤ We ourselves decorated this room.

[14-15] 빈칸에 들어갈 말로 알맞은 것을 고르시오.

14. (4점)

A: How _____ does it take from here to your school?

B: Maybe thirty minutes.

① much ② many ③ big
④ often ⑤ long

15. (4점)

- What do you do _____ you have free time?
- Turn off your cell phone _____ you watch a movie at theater.

① when ② since ③ for
④ where ⑤ because

16. 빈칸에 make 동사를 쓸 수 없는 문장은? (6점)

① This book _____ Sora sleepy.
② Justin _____ me a happy girl.
③ My best friend tries to _____ me laugh.
④ I _____ my daughter to clean her car on weekends.
⑤ Yuna's teacher _____ her students clean the classroom.

17. 빈칸에 알맞은 표현은? (5점)

- I have two cars. One is at home and _____ is in my office building.
- I will visit three countries this year. One is India, another is Japan, and _____ is Egypt.

① the other - the other
② another - another
③ the other - another
④ another - the other
⑤ the other - the others

18. 다음 대화 중 가장 어색한 것을 고르면? (4점)

① A: You look tired. What happened?
   B: I stayed up all night.
② A: Let's go to the art hall.
   B: That sounds great.
③ A: Sora, are you okay?
   B: No, I'm feeling good today.
④ A: How do I look? Is it okay?
   B: Oh, it looks good on you.
⑤ A: I feel cold these days.
   B: You should go see a doctor.

모의고사 1회

- 총 문항수: 객관식 18문항, 서술형 2문항
- 총점: 100점

1. 다음 중 밑줄 친 be동사의 의미가 나머지와 다른 하나는? (5점)

① My dad is tall.
② Hi, this is my friend, Carl.
③ Come here. My car is over there.
④ Look at her. She is really pretty.
⑤ I have a dog. It is 5 years old.

2. 다음 중 there의 의미가 보기 와 다른 것은? (5점)

| 보기 | Are there many children in the park? |

① There is nothing in the cabinet.
② Is there a book on the desk?
③ There is a dog in the garden.
④ Let's meet at 7 o'clock there.
⑤ How many books are there in the library?

3. 다음 인물에 대해 답할 수 없는 것은? (5점)

Hi, my name is Pharrell Williams. I am from America. I live with my family in L.A. I am thirteen years old. I like singing and rapping. I'm very pleased to meet you.

① How old is he?
② Where is he from?
③ Where does he live?
④ What does his father do?
⑤ What does he like to doing?

4. 빈칸에 Do가 들어갈 수 없는 것은? (5점)

① _____ they like soccer?
② _____ Yuna eat breakfast every day?
③ _____ Jim and Minsu run fast?
④ _____ Mr. and Mrs. Brown like winter?
⑤ _____ you and your sister clean the room?

5. 다음 중 about의 의미가 나머지와 다른 하나는? (6점)

① The TV program is about the IT industry in India.
② Let's write a story about my dream.
③ The train is about 100 meters long.
④ I am reading a book about planets.
⑤ I thought about his talk for a long time.

6. 보기 에서 밑줄 친 may와 같은 뜻으로 사용된 것은? (6점)

| 보기 | This book may be very interesting for you. |

ⓐ You may need a car. It is very far.
ⓑ The baby may be hungry. She is crying.
ⓒ You may use my pen. I don't need it anymore.
ⓓ I am sorry to hear the news. May she rest in peace.

① ⓐ, ⓑ   ② ⓐ, ⓒ   ③ ⓐ, ⓓ
④ ⓑ, ⓒ   ⑤ ⓑ, ⓓ

[7~9] 다음 중 어법상 어색한 문장은?

7. (5점)

① Do not be mad.
② Come back home early.
③ Please study math and science hard.
④ Does the dishes, please.
⑤ Never enter the room with your shoes.

8. (4점)

① He read newspaper yesterday.
② She went shopping last weekend.
③ Romeo and Juliet studied together.
④ They visited their grandparents.
⑤ He eated a bowl of salad in the restaurant.

9. (5점)

① His eyes were big and blue.
② Every boy take pictures of her.
③ Her new bag looks very expensive.
④ My Korean teacher had lunch with me.
⑤ Both Mina and Kevin go to school by bus.

10. 밑줄 친 that 중 쓰임이 다른 하나는? (6점)

① I think that it will snow soon.
② He believes that Minji is diligent.
③ They know that Jiho is innocent.
④ She said that Jim had a cold.
⑤ I don't know that girl on the bench.

10. 짝지어진 두 문장의 의미가 다른 것은? (6점)
① You ate more apples than I.
= I ate as many apples as you.
② We played better than they.
= They didn't play as well as us.
③ You got up earlier than I.
= I didn't get up as early as you.
④ My house is smaller than yours.
= Your house isn't as small as mine.
⑤ I've been here longer than you.
= You haven't been here as long as I.

[서술형 2] 우리말과 같은 뜻이 되도록 주어진 단어들을 이용하여 문장을 완성하시오. (12점)

1) 그는 한국에서 가장 인기 있는 가수이다. (popular, singer) (4점)
→ _____ in Korea.

2) 나의 형은 우리 가족 중 키가 가장 작다. (brother, short) (4점)
→ _____ in my family.

3) 세상에서 가장 예쁜 여자는 누구인가? (who, pretty) (4점)
→ _____ in the world?

[서술형 3] ⓐ와 ⓑ에 들어갈 말을 보기에서 골라 차례대로 쓰시오. (4점)

보기 much / must not / many / must

There isn't ⓐ _____ water in Socotra. (2점)
So during your tour, you ⓑ _____ save water. (2점)

[서술형 4] 주어진 단어를 사용하여 문장을 완성하시오. (3점)

보기 (the bear / snacks / give)

A: Don't _____.
B: Okay, I won't.

11. 다음 밑줄 친 단어의 의미가 다른 하나를 고르시오. (5점)
① This is a hard choice.
② The ice cream is hard.
③ This is hard for me.
④ The homework is so hard.
⑤ I think English is not hard.

---

12. 다음 ⓐ~ⓔ 중 가리키는 대상이 나머지와 다른 것은? (6점)

At night, John and I heard a strange noise. ⓐIt was dark. We looked outside and saw a big shadow. We thought that ⓑit was a ghost. We were scared. Then, ⓒit turned around. ⓓIt wasn't a ghost! Whew! ⓔIt was John's dad.

① ⓐ   ② ⓑ   ③ ⓒ
④ ⓓ   ⑤ ⓔ

13. 다음 밑줄 친 단어의 쓰임이 다른 것은? (4점)
① From May, we can enjoy sunny days almost every day.
② No one wants to work with dirty, smelly people.
③ It was a rainy day, so he took an umbrella with him.
④ The beauty of the sunshine is amazing.
⑤ No one could answer this tricky question.

14. 다음 중 어법상 올바르게 쓰인 것은? (5점)
① You are too small to wore this shirt.
② She is too surprised to say anything.
③ Andy was too heavily to stand on the box.
④ This coffee is so hot that I couldn't drink it.
⑤ They are too young that they can drive a car.

15. 다음 보기의 밑줄 친 부분과 쓰임이 같은 것은? (5점)

보기 Students saved money to go to the concert.

① He will try to be quiet in class.
② I'd like to make a lot of friends.
③ Janice is going to listen to songs in English.
④ I have to finish my homework by this week.
⑤ Sumi got up early not to be late for school.

[서술형 5] 그림을 보고 주어진 표현을 이용하여 문장을 완성하시오. (4점)

make his bed / clean the window

1) Mom made Eric _____. (2점)
2) Mom ordered Eric _____. (2점)

모의고사 3회

날짜 _____ 이름 _____ 점수 [ ]

- 총 문항수: 객관식 15문항, 서술형 5문항
- 총점: 100점

1. 밑줄 친 부분이 올바른 것은? (5점)
   ① Is Tom David's twin brother?
   ② There is two pencils on the desk.
   ③ There is three people in my family.
   ④ There is many big parks in our town.
   ⑤ Is Sophie and Sally in the same family?

2. 대화가 가장 자연스러운 것은? (5점)
   ① A: Where do you live?
      B: I'm from Scotland.
   ② A: What grade are you in?
      B: I'm in the seventh grade.
   ③ A: When is it?
      B: It's at Tom's Pizza House.
   ④ A: When do you practice?
      B: I practice in a club room.
   ⑤ A: What's your favorite subject?
      B: I like autumn.

3. 다음 글에서 답을 찾을 수 없는 질문은? (5점)

   My name is Joy Kim. I'm from London, England. I like football and music. I like K-pop very much. I have a big family. There are six of us: Grandma, Dad, Mom, two brothers, and me. We have two dogs, too. My dogs names are Spotty and Ruby.

   ① Where is Joy from?
   ② What does Joy like?
   ③ How many dogs does Joy have?
   ④ Who is Joy's favorite K-pop star?
   ⑤ How many people are there in Joy's family?

4. 다음 중 어법상 바른 것은? (5점)
   ① Ann doesn't visit London during last summer.
   ② Did he enjoy his birthday party yesterday?
   ③ Students readed a lot of books in class.
   ④ I were hungry because I did lots of work.
   ⑤ He didn't said anything when he met her.

5. 다음 중 어법상 어색한 것은? (정답 2개) (5점)
   ① How fast he runs!
   ② What a lucky guy!
   ③ How pretty cups they are!
   ④ What a beautiful flowers is this!
   ⑤ How exciting the game is!

6. 다음 중 올바른 문장은? (5점)
   ① We have to calling him.
   ② You have not to come here.
   ③ He didn't make a cake for you.
   ④ Did Jane cleans the classroom?
   ⑤ The children has to do their homework.

7. 다음 빈칸에 들어가기에 알맞지 않은 것은? (4점)

   I _____ Jake a box.

   ① showed   ② gave   ③ sent
   ④ bought   ⑤ returned

8. 다음 중 어법상 어색한 것은? (5점)
   ① I think that he is smart.
   ② I am going to throw a party.
   ③ I think that Joe has too many pens.
   ④ I thought that Joe had too many balls.
   ⑤ I am going to wash the car the day before.

[서술형 1] 그림을 보고 many나 much 둘 중 하나를 사용하여 영어로 문장을 완성하시오. (3점)

There _____ .
(책들이 많이 있습니다.)

9. 다음 두 문장의 의미가 같도록 빈칸에 알맞은 것은? (4점)

   The chair is in front of the desk.
   = The desk is _____ the chair.

   ① beside   ② back   ③ before
   ④ behind   ⑤ around

11. 밑줄 친 부분이 어법상 좋은 것은? (5점)
① Soccer is the excitingest game.
② Today was the hotest day of the year.
③ This book I more thicker than that book.
④ Today's weather is nicer than yesterday.
⑤ The blue bag is heavyer than the red one.

[서술형 3] have to와 괄호 안에 주어진 표현이 모두 들어간 영어 문장을 완성하시오. (6점)

1) The cat is hungry. (2점)
→ It _____.
(eat something)

2) The boy has a math test. (2점)
→ He _____.
(study math)

3) The boy has a bad cold. (2점)
→ He _____.
(see a doctor)

[12~13] 다음 중 밑줄 친 부분의 의미가 나머지 넷과 다른 하나는?

12. (4점)
① I'm going to read those books.
② He's going to have lunch at noon.
③ She's going to bring an umbrella.
④ I'm going to draw a picture of you.
⑤ They're going to the swimming pool.

13. (5점)
① She went to the bakery to buy some bread.
② I need something to drink.
③ He turned on the TV to watch the show.
④ He took the bus to go to school.
⑤ I'm going to take the subway to save money.

[서술형 4] 다음 4형식 문장을 3형식 문장으로 전환할 때 빈칸에 알맞은 말을 쓰시오. (3점)
Can you buy me a computer?
= Can you buy _____ _____?

[서술형 5] 다음 상황에서 Yuna가 Howard에게 할 조언을 완성하시오.
(must를 반드시 사용할 것) (4점)
Yuna and Howard are in a museum now. There are many pieces of art. Howard is taking pictures with flash inside the museum, and Yuna wants him not to take pictures any more. Then what should she say?
Yuna: "Howard, you _____
inside the museum."

14. 보기 의 빈칸에 들어갈 부가의문문과 같은 것은? (4점)

보기 People usually buy gifts for others, _____?

① They have lots of books, _____?
② They don't give up, _____?
③ They will tell you the truth, _____?
④ People won't forget the meeting, _____?
⑤ People are having breakfast, _____?

15. 다음 중 어법상 올바른 문장의 개수는? (5점)
(a) Should I turn off the light?
(b) You should waste not water.
(c) My best friend is a shy girl.
(d) How wonderful the shoes are!
(e) The weather was fine, wasn't it?
(f) The soccer ball is biger than the baseball.
① 1개 ② 2개 ③ 3개
④ 4개 ⑤ 5개

[서술형 6] 다음 문장을 감탄문으로 고쳐 쓰시오. (9점)
1) The mother is very beautiful. (총 5단어) (3점)
→ _____!
2) This is a very old tree. (총 6단어) (3점)
→ _____!
3) It was a very wonderful festival. (총 6단어) (3점)
→ _____!

16. Which one is the WRONG sentence? (4점)
① There is a bed in my room.
② Is there a ball under the table?
③ There are two pencils on the desk.
④ Are there any pencils on the table?
⑤ There is a computer and a TV in the classroom.

17. 밑줄 친 부분이 좋은 것은? (3점)
① Knifes and forks are easy to use
② Look, the mouses are in the basket.
③ We should brush our teeth three times a day.
④ I looked it up in three different dictionarys.
⑤ There are lots of sheeps over there.

모의고사 2회

날짜 _____ 이름 _____ 점수 ☐

- ■ 총 문항수: 객관식 17문항, 서술형 6문항
- ■ 총점: 100점

1. 빈칸에 공통으로 들어갈 말로 알맞은 것은? (3점)

> - Tom always drives his car _____ top speed.
> - My grandmother has breakfast _____ 7:00.

① to   ② at   ③ in
④ on   ⑤ for

[서술형 1] have to와 to부정사를 활용하여 아래의 뜻에 맞게 영작하시오. (5점)

> 어제 경호는 아침에 운동하기 위해 일찍 일어나야 했다.
>
> → Kyung-ho _____
>   yesterday.

2. 다음 밑줄 친 when의 쓰임이 나머지 넷과 다른 하나는? (4점)

① When the man came to town, I felt scary.
② When is your birthday?
③ I buy some candies when I go shopping.
④ What do you do when you have free time?
⑤ When the bell rang, he picked up the phone.

[3~5] 다음 문장들 중 어법상 자연스러운 문장은?

3. (4점)

① She cannot digest this soup easily, can he?
② Your friends forgot your birthday, didn't they?
③ You aren't a bad person, do you?
④ When you eat rice, you use a spoon, didn't you?
⑤ Jane is excited, isn't Jane?

4. (4점)

① Mike was at the party last night, was not he?
② Sumi didn't buy a new bag, didn't she?
③ Your brother found the key, didn't you?
④ He goes to school by bus, does he?
⑤ You can speak Chinese, can't you?

5. 다음 빈칸에 알맞은 것은? (3점)

> There are pilot whales in _____ Indian Ocean.

① a   ② the   ③ an
④ to   ⑤ 아무것도 들어갈 필요가 없음

6. 다음 빈칸에 들어갈 말로 적당하지 않은 것은? (3점)

> A: I want to have many friends. What should I do?
> B: _____

① You should not keep your words.
② You should listen to your friends.
③ You should cheer up your friends.
④ You should not fight with your friends.
⑤ You should be kind to your friends.

7. 다음 중 어법상 잘못된 것을 고르면? (4점)

① I can't go outside because it rains.
② I can't go outside because of the rain.
③ She is happy because of him.
④ She is not happy because her bad score.
⑤ He moved to Busan because he got a new job.

8. 다음 문장의 의미가 자연스럽지 않은 것은? (4점)

① Everybody likes her because she is brave.
② Jane didn't eat breakfast because she was hungry.
③ Emily has to buy a bag because she lost her bag yesterday.
④ They didn't go swimming because the water wasn't clean.
⑤ I like Mark Twain because his stories are very interesting.

9. 다음 중 의미나 어법상 바른 문장은? (5점)

① A cat is as faster as a dog.
② He did very worse on the test.
③ I know nothing farthest about it.
④ The latest bus to go home is coming.
⑤ This cat is not so cute as my puppy.

10. 밑줄 친 부분에 들어갈 올바른 단어로 짝지어진 것은? (4점)

> The movie looks _____

> ⓐ well   ⓑ nice   ⓒ softly   ⓓ sadly   ⓔ young
> ⓕ strange   ⓖ interesting   ⓗ delicious

① ⓐ, ⓑ, ⓕ   ② ⓑ, ⓕ, ⓖ
③ ⓐ, ⓑ, ⓕ, ⓖ   ④ ⓐ, ⓔ, ⓕ, ⓖ
⑤ ⓑ, ⓒ, ⓔ, ⓕ

[서술형 2] 아래 문장을 어법에 맞게 완전한 문장으로 영작하시오. (5점)

> Peter의 성적은 Bob의 성적보다 더 좋다. (반드시 비교급을 사용할 것)
>
> → _____

9. 다음 지도의 병원에 도착하려면, 빈칸에 들어갈 말을 차례로 나열한 것은? (5점)

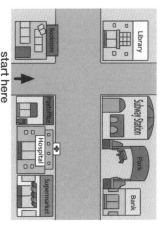

start here

W: Excuse me. _____ can I get to the hospital?
M: Go straight and turn _____ and you can see the
hospital _____ the post office and the supermarket
on your right side.
W: Oh, I see. Thank you.

① Where - right - between   ② How - left - behind
③ Where - left - behind   ④ How - right - between
⑤ How - left - across

10. 다음 중 A와 B의 대화가 어색한 것은? (5점)

① A: What did you do last Sunday?
   B: I took a trip with my family.

② A: Did you enjoy it?
   B: Yes, it was interesting.

③ A: What did you eat for lunch?
   B: I ate a bowl of bibimbap.

④ A: You look sleepy. What's wrong?
   B: I didn't sleep enough last night.

⑤ A: Is there a flower shop near here?
   B: Yes, there's no one here.

11. 다음 중 밑줄 친 부분이 올바른 것은? (4점)

① I bought a present of her.
② He made a nice desk to me.
③ Joseph sent a letter to me yesterday.
④ Please show an interesting story for me.
⑤ Scott gives a special experience for you.

12. 다음 두 문장이 같은 뜻이 되도록 주어진 단어를 나열했을 때 4번째 오는 단어를 고르면? (4점)

Don't sleep in class.
= sleep/in/should/you/not/class

① sleep   ② should   ③ not
④ you   ⑤ in

13. 다음 중 동사의 변화가 잘못된 것은? (4점)

① begin - begun - begun   ② break - broke - broken
③ catch - caught - caught   ④ feed - fed - fed
⑤ lose - lost - lost

14. 다음 중 어법상 잘못된 표현은? (4점)

① She looked so sad.
② My dad looked at me happily.
③ What are you looking at?
④ She looked like a superstar.
⑤ It sounds wonderfully tonight.

15. 각 표지판에 대한 설명이 가장 잘못된 것은? (4점)

①  You should not take pictures.
②  You should not smoke here.
③ You should park here.
④ You should not bring your dog.
⑤ You should not use your cellphone.

16. 다음 중 어법상 맞는 것은? (5점)

① I have many homework to do.
② I need much glasses of water.
③ There is many books in the room
④ There are much water in the tank.
⑤ There were many stars in the sky.

[서술형 3] 그림을 참고하여 A에게 제안하는 문장을 Why로 시작하는 말을 사용하여 쓰시오.

1)
   A: I'm very tired.
   B: _____? (5점)
   A: OK. I will.

2)
   A: I'm bored.
   B: _____? (5점)
   A: OK. I will.

17. 다음 중 밑줄 친 must의 의미가 나머지 넷과 다른 것은? (5점)

① Jim must get up now.
② Bob must arrive here by 5.
③ That boy must be very smart.
④ We must save energy for everybody.
⑤ Students must be quiet in the classroom.

모의고사 4회

날짜 _____ 이름 _____ 점수 [ ]

- 총 문항수: 객관식 17문항, 서술형 3문항
- 총점: 100점

1. B의 대답에 대한 A의 질문으로 어색한 것은? (4점)

A: _____
B: I enjoy playing baseball at school in my free time.

① What do you do?
② What is your hobby?
③ When do you play baseball?
④ What are you interested in?
⑤ Where do you enjoy baseball?

2. 다음 중 어법에 맞는 표현은 몇 개인가? (6점)

> This is my friend. Her's name is Julia Roberts. She and I are in the first graders in Washington middle school. She likes to watching French movies. She speaks France well.

① 없음   ② 1개   ③ 2개
④ 3개   ⑤ 4개

3. 다음 중 그림의 설명이 옳지 않은 것은? (5점)

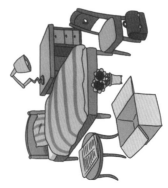

① There is one pillow on the bed.
② There is a bed next to the desk.
③ There is a newspaper on the chair.
④ There is nothing in the box.
⑤ There is a lamp on the desk.

[서술형 1] 괄호 안에 단어를 현재형으로 알맞게 고쳐 문장을 다시 쓰시오. (6점)

1) He (play) the piano.
2) She (live) in Canada.
3) He (watch) TV on weekends.

1) _____ (2점)
2) _____ (2점)
3) _____ (2점)

---

4. 밑줄 진 단어의 쓰임이 나머지와 다른 것은? (4점)

① This baby is <u>lovely</u>.
② My homeroom teacher is <u>friendly</u>.
③ We recycle cans and bottles <u>daily</u>.
④ We have a <u>weekly</u> meeting on Wednesdays.
⑤ Our <u>monthly</u> event is to go on a picnic.

5. 다음을 어순에 맞게 의문문으로 고친 것은? (4점)

> Jiho works for a bank.

① Jiho work for a bank?
② Do Jiho work for a bank?
③ Do Jiho works for a bank?
④ Does Jiho work for a bank?
⑤ Does Jiho works for a bank?

6. 다음 밑줄 친 부분이 어법상 틀린 것은? (5점)

① Tom is planning <u>not to skip</u> breakfast.
② He finished <u>running</u> to the finish line.
③ She hoped <u>to be</u> a movie star.
④ Do you mind <u>to open</u> the door?
⑤ They kept <u>writing</u> letters to his teacher.

[서술형 2] 다음 두 문장을 because를 이용해 문맥이 자연스럽도록 한 문장으로 바꾸어 쓰시오. (5점)

- She didn't go to school today.
- She was sick.

→ _____

7. 밑줄 친 부분에 들어갈 말이 나머지와 다른 하나는? (5점)

① _____ Edward have a sister?
② _____ your dad teach social science?
③ My dog _____ not like meat.
④ _____ they read books every day?
⑤ Her baby _____ not know about the color.

8. 다음 중 어색한 문장의 수는 모두 몇 개? (6점)

- Dance and get a prize.
- Get up and get ready for school.
- Be not late again.
- Enjoy interesting books and free drinks.
- Washes your hands.
- Don't be lose your ticket.

① 1개   ② 2개   ③ 3개
④ 4개   ⑤ 5개

문법과 내신을 동시에 잡는

시험지에서

가져온~

중학영문법

저자 김보미

Level 1

해설집

랭기지플러스

문법과 내신을 동시에 잡는

시험지에서 가져온~

중학영문법

Level 1

해설집

랭기지플러스

Chapter 1
인칭대명사와 be동사

1.1. 인칭대명사와 be동사   P.11

A.
1. She
2. He
3. It
4. You
5. We
6. He
7. It
8. She

B.
1. am
2. is
3. are
4. is
5. are
6. are
7. is
8. is

C.
1. is, ~(에) 있다
2. are, ~이다
3. is, ~이다
4. is, ~(에) 있다
5. are, ~이다

1.2. be동사의 부정문과 의문문   P.13

A.
1. is not[isn't]
2. is not[isn't]
3. is not[isn't]
4. Am I
5. Are they
6. Are you
7. am not

B.
1. Is Mrs. Kim a science teacher?
   Mrs. Kim is not[isn't] a science teacher.
2. Is she from Brazil?
   She is not[isn't] from Brazil.
3. Are they diligent?
   They are not[aren't] diligent.

C.
1. not
2. Is he
3. he is

1.3. 인칭대명사의 격 변화   P.15

A.
1. He
2. Its
3. me
4. my
5. yours
6. her, his
7. She, her
8. my, them

B.
1. hers
2. them
3. her
4. his
5. it
6. Sam's

C.

❶ 주격

❷ 소유격

❸ 소유대명사

❹ 목적격

❺ 주격

❻ 소유대명사

❼ 주격

---

1. ③　2. ③　3. ②　4. ③　5. ③　6. ②　7. ④
8. are not　9. ①　10. ❶ Are you　❷ Is her
father

1. Amy and I를 대신할 수 있는 대명사는 나를 포함한 다른 사람들이기 때문에 We(우리들)이다.

2. Seho and I는 We라고 바꾸는 것이 알맞다.

3. 질문에 알맞은 대답은 「Yes, 주어 + be동사」 또는 「No, 주어 + be동사 not」인데 뒤에 이어지는 말로 보아 B는 학생이 맞으므로 ②번(Yes, I am.)이 정답이다.

4. be동사의 부정문은 be동사의 뒤에 not을 붙여준다.

5. ③ am not은 축약형으로 만들 수 없다.

6. You와 We에 공통으로 알맞은 be동사는 are이다.

7. '당신은 Susan입니까?'라는 A의 질문에 B가 '나는 Susan Brown입니다'라고 밝히고 있으므로 I를 주어로 하는 긍정적인 대답이 알맞다.

8. be동사의 부정문은 be동사의 뒤에 not을 붙여준다.

9. John과 Jim은 3인칭 복수이므로 대명사로 표기할 때 They라고 하는 게 알맞다.

10. be동사의 의문문은 「Be동사 + 주어 ~?」이다.

---

1. ①　2. them　3. ❶ He, He is　❷ She, She is
4. ④　5. ④　6. ③　7. ③　8. ①　9. ❶ You
❷ I　❸ She　❹ It　❺ He　10. ②　11. ①, ⑤
12. ③　13. ④　14. ④　15. ③　16. ①　17. ②
18. ④　19. ⑤　20. my uncle

1. A: 나는 부산 출신입니다.
   B: 나도 부산 출신입니다.
   A와 B가 둘 다 부산 출신이라고 말하고 있기 때문에 1인칭 복수인 We를 써야 한다.

2. 복수인 these shoes를 대신할 수 있는 대명사는 them이 알맞다.

3. ❶ Adam은 남자의 이름이기 때문에 He라는 대명사를 쓰며 He는 be동사로 is를 쓴다.
   ❷ Elizabeth는 여자의 이름이기 때문에 She라는 대명사를 쓰며 She는 be동사로 is를 쓴다.

4. 주어인 He(그)를 묘사해 주는 말로 사물인 bags(가방들)는 알맞지 않다.

5. ④번의 be동사는 '~(에) 있다'라는 의미를 나타내고 나머지는 '~ 이다'의 의미를 나타낸다.

6. '그는 아프니?'라는 의문문에 알맞은 대답은 Yes, he is. 또는 No, he isn't.가 알맞다.

7. ③번의 's는 소유격을 나타내는 표현이며 나머지는 is의 축약형이다.

8. My grandma는 3인칭 단수이므로 is, We는 1인칭 복수이므로 are, His cousin은 3인칭 단수이므로 is, Her dogs는 3인칭 복수이므로 are을 be동사로 쓴다.

9. ❶ be동사 are에 알맞은 주어는 You이다.
   ❷ am에 알맞은 주어는 I이다.
   ❸ Jane은 여자 이름이기 때문에 She라는 주격 대명사가 알맞다.
   ❹ A book의 대명사는 It이다.
   ❺ James는 남자 이름이기에 He라는 주격 대명사가 알맞다.

10. ① '너는 뉴질랜드에서 왔니?'라는 질문에 알맞은 대답은 Yes, I am. 또는 No, I'm not.이다.
    ③ '수지의 친구들은 화났니?'라는 질문에 알맞은 대답은

Yes, they are. 또는 No, they aren't.이다.
④ '너는 일하고 있었니?'라고 과거의 일을 묻고 있으므로 Yes, I was. 또는 No, I won't.라고 대답해야 한다.
⑤ '이것은 너의 사진 앨범이니?'라는 질문에 알맞은 대답은 Yes, it is. 또는 No, it isn't.이다.

11. ② '그녀의'를 나타내는 소유격은 Her로 써야 한다.
③ Suji and Sejin은 3인칭 복수이므로 be동사는 are을 써야 한다.
④ It의 소유격은 Its가 알맞다.

12. ① These는 복수형이므로 be동사 are를 써야 한다.
② I에 알맞은 be동사는 am이다.
④ she에 알맞은 be동사는 Is이다.
⑤ Jina and Emily는 3인칭 복수이기 때문에 be동사 are을 써야 한다.

13. – Jane and her sister <u>are</u> upset.
– My parents <u>are</u> very tall.
– <u>Are</u> Suji and Sumi sisters?
– Is <u>your</u> brother a basketball player?

14. ⓓ는 주어가 3인칭 단수(your cat)이기 때문에 Is가 알맞다.

15. I에 맞는 be동사는 am이기 때문에 I am not in my room.(나는 내 방안에 있지 않다.)이 알맞다. They는 3인칭 복수이기 때문에 are을 써야 하고, Is는 3인칭 단수 주어와 함께 사용되기 때문에 the hamster가 알맞다.

16. ② You and I는 We라고 바꾸는 것이 알맞다.
③ Susan은 여자의 이름이므로 She라고 하는 것이 알맞다.
④ Joseph and you는 You라고 바꾸는 것이 알맞다.
⑤ Sara and John은 3인칭 복수이므로 They라고 하는 것이 알맞다.

17. ① 주어가 3인칭 단수이므로 are은 is로 바꾸는 것이 알맞다.
③ 주어가 3인칭 단수이므로 are은 is로 바꾼다.
④ I의 소유격은 My로 써야 한다.
⑤ He가 주어이므로 be동사는 is를 써야 한다.

18. ⓐ Jonathan and Suji 두 사람을 나타내는 대명사는 They이다. ⓑ Jonathan은 Suji의 오빠이므로 she의 소유격인 her를 써야 한다. ⓒ '그들의 친구들'이므로 알맞은 소유격은 Their이다. ⓔ '학교의' 이름이기에 소유격은 Its가 알맞다.

19. ① '너는 바쁘니?'에 대한 대답은 Yes, I am. 또는 No,

I'm not.이 알맞다.
② '그는 의사니?'에 대한 알맞은 대답은 Yes, he is. 또는 No, he isn't.이다.
③ '내가 맞지?'에 대한 알맞은 대답은 Yes, you are. 또는 No, you aren't.이다.
④ '그들은 친절하니?'에 대한 알맞은 대답은 Yes, they are. 또는 No, they aren't.이다.

20. 대답에서 be동사의 뒷부분은 질문에서 반복되어 나오기 때문에 생략이 가능하다.

단원평가　　고난도　　P.20

1. ②	2. ②	3. ④	4. ③	5. ③	6. ①	7. ③
8. ③	9. ③	10. ②				

1. ②번에는 is, 나머지는 are[Are]이 알맞다.

2. ① My sister and I는 be동사로 are을 쓰고, Your hamster는 is를 쓴다.
③ Everyone은 3인칭 단수이기 때문에 is를, My students는 3인칭 복수이기 때문에 are을 be동사로 쓴다.
④ I는 be동사로 am을, She는 is를 쓴다.
⑤ The bank는 3인칭 단수이므로 be동사로 is를, My brothers는 복수이므로 are을 쓴다.

3. ⓐ is, ⓑ am, ⓒ am, ⓔ is

4. ③번에서 be동사는 '~(에) 있다'의 의미이고 나머지는 '~이다'의 의미를 가진다.

5. be동사 다음에는 주어를 꾸며주는 명사나 형용사가 필요한데 ③번은 부사이므로 적절치 않다.

6. 나라: 엄마, 제 우산을 찾을 수 없어요.
엄마: 지수가 오늘 아침 너의 우산을 가져갔어.
나라: 지수가요? 왜 그 애는 항상 <u>내 것</u>을 사용하나요? <u>그의 것</u>은 어디 있어요?
엄마: 그 애는 자기 우산을 찾지 못했어.
나라: 그러면 <u>당신의 것</u>(엄마의 것)을 사용할 수 있을까요?
엄마: 그렇게 하렴.
ⓐ에는 '나의 것'을 의미하는 mine이 적절하고 ⓑ에는 '그의 것'을 의미하는 his가 ⓒ에는 '당신의 것'을 의미하는 yours가 알맞다.

Chapter 2

일반동사

7. be동사가 were이기 때문에 3인칭 단수인 Our teacher(우리의 선생님)는 주어 자리에 들어갈 수 없다.

8. 보기와 나머지 선택지의 her은 소유격을 나타내고 ③번의 her은 목적격 대명사를 나타낸다.

9. 질문: ⓐ,ⓑ와 ⓒ에 알맞은 표현은 무엇인가?
ⓐ는 주어가 3인칭 단수이기 때문에 is가 알맞다. 대화의 흐름상 ⓑ는 '너의 것'이라는 뜻의 yours가 알맞고 ⓒ는 '나의 것'을 나타내는 mine이 적절하다.

10. ① am과 not은 축약형으로 쓸 수 없다.
③ Cindy and I는 복수이므로 be동사로 are을 써야 한다.
④ Her aunts는 3인칭 복수이기 때문에 are을 be동사로 써야 한다.
⑤ Ivan and Tom은 3인칭 복수이기 때문에 aren't가 알맞다.

서술형 대비학습 P.22

1. ⓔ Her dogs are cute and smart.

2. are not[are't] at home, are at school

3. ❶ He is not[isn't] my brother.
❷ This is not[isn't] a cat.
❸ I am[I'm] not a student.
❹ She is not[isn't] a teacher.

4. ❶ Is your brother short and thin
❷ Is Chris busy today
❸ Is Mrs. Choi a dentist
❹ Are they at a zoo

5. ❷ am thirteen years old
❸ am from England
❹ is blue
❺ is listening to music

2.1. 일반동사의 의미와 형태 P.25

A.
❶ impresses
❷ reads
❸ goes
❹ flies
❺ shows
❻ cheers
❼ touches
❽ closes
❾ catches
❿ sits
⓫ misses
⓬ reaches
⓭ believes
⓮ lays
⓯ passes
⓰ mixes
⓱ rides
⓲ washes
⓳ crosses
⓴ throws
㉑ says

B.
❶ goes to school and studies very hard
❷ enjoys eating Kimchi
❸ drinks a lot of water every day
❹ worry about their health

C.

1. cries
2. speaks
3. close
4. drink
5. goes

2.2. 일반동사의 과거형   P.27

A.

1. shopped
2. wished
3. loved
4. jumped
5. arrived
6. hurried
7. swallowed
8. practiced
9. played
10. answered
11. carried
12. dropped
13. learned
14. spelled
15. kicked
16. missed
17. wanted
18. raised
19. planned
20. cried
21. obeyed

B.

1. had
2. did
3. bought
4. met
5. drew

6. passed

C.

1. helps
2. worked
3. stopped
4. had
5. studied
6. reads
7. lost
8. forgot

2.3. 일반동사의 부정문과 의문문   P.29

A.

1. We don't sing Christmas carols.
2. You didn't ride a bike yesterday.
3. Her brother doesn't eat curry and rice.
4. He didn't know my name.
5. Minho didn't invite her girlfriend to his birthday party.
6. Suji doesn't go to school by bus.
7. Jim didn't read comic books last week.
8. My father didn't go fishing a year ago.
9. Minho and Suji don't like skating.
10. I didn't lose my pet dog in the street.
11. My washing machine doesn't work well.
12. We didn't believe the story.

B.

1. Did she watch TV last night? / she did
2. Did Suji leave a message yesterday? / she didn't
3. Does Charlie jog with his friend every morning? / he does
4. Do they always wash their car on Sundays? / they do
5. Did she pass the exam? / she didn't

1. took　2. ❶ was　❷ visited　❸ didn't
❹ practice　❺ teaches　3. ④　4. ④　5. ①
6. ④　7. goes　8. ③　9. swam　10. ❶ went
❷ met　❸ reads

1. take의 과거는 took이다.

2. ① last night (지난밤)이란 과거를 나타내는 부사구가
있으므로 was가 정답이다.
② last summer(지난여름)이란 과거를 나타내는 부사
구가 있으므로 visited가 정답이다.
③ do라는 일반동사가 있으므로 일반동사의 부정문을
만들어주는 didn't를 선택한다.
④ doesn't 뒤에는 동사원형이 와야 한다.
⑤ 주어가 Mr. and Mrs. Smith로 복수이므로 teach
를 선택한다.

3. 과거 의문문은 「Did + 주어 + 동사원형 ～?」의 형태로
쓴다.

4. make의 과거형은 made이다.

5. 지난 금요일에 무엇을 했는지 묻고 있으므로 과거를 나
타내는 대답을 선택해야 한다.

6. 티비를 보았냐는 질문에 음악을 들었다고 대답하고 있
으므로 부정의 대답을 선택해야 한다. Did로 물을 때는
did로 대답해야 하므로 ④번이 정답이다.

7. 주어가 3인칭 단수이고 반복적인 일상을 나타내므로 go
를 3인칭 단수형인 goes로 바꾼다.

8. 어제의 날씨를 이야기하고 있으므로 be동사의 과거형인
was가 적절하다.

9. 강에서 수영을 했으므로 swim의 과거인 swam이 정답
이다.

10.❶ 과거를 나타내는 부사(yesterday)가 있으므로 went
를 써야 한다.
❷ 과거를 나타내는 부사(last week)가 있으므로 met
을 써야 한다.
❸ 매일 반복적으로 하는 일이므로 read의 3인칭 단수
현재형인 reads를 쓴다.

1. ②　2. ①　3. ④　4. ②　5. ④　6. ③　7. ④
8. did　9. ④　10. No, I don't. → No, I didn't.
/ watch → watched　11. ⑤　12. ⑤　13. ⑤
14. ④　15. ②　16. ①　17. ④　18. ④　19. ④
20. ②

1. 3인칭 일반동사의 부정문은 「주어 + does not[doesn't]
+ 동사원형」이므로 likes를 like로 고쳐야 한다.

2. are의 과거형은 were, am의 과거형은 was이다.

3. 질문: 수지는 무슨 요일에 영화를 보러 갔는가?
수지는 토요일에 영화를 보러 갔다(go to a movie).

4. 질문: 지난 화요일에 수지는 무엇을 했나?
지난 화요일에 수지는 축구를 했다(play soccer).

5. 동사가 과거형이므로 과거를 나타내는 부사(구)들을 사
용해야 한다. now(지금)는 현재형과 쓰인다.

6. ⓐ Last Sunday는 과거를 나타내는 3인칭 단수 주어
이므로 be동사 was를 써야 한다. ⓑ Some of our
players(우리의 선수들 중 몇몇은)는 복수 주어이므로
were을 써야 한다.

7. 본문에 we did not win이라는 문장으로 보아 '우리는'
경기에서 졌으므로 lose의 과거형 lost를 써야 한다.

8. do one's best(최선을 다하다)의 과거형이므로 did를
써야 한다.

9. ① Did he like her?
② Did it rain last night?
③ She didn't write a letter.
⑤ Did she get up early yesterday?

10.과거의 일을 물어봤기 때문에 No, I didn't.로 대답하는
것이 옳다. watch도 과거형인 watched로 고쳐야 한다.

11.⑤ '너는 햄버거를 먹었다.'는 과거시제이기 때문에 과거
형의 부정문인 「주어 + didn't + 동사원형」으로 고쳐야
한다.

12.⑤ were의 현재형은 are이다.

13.study의 과거형은 studied, go의 과거형은 went이다.

14. last Sunday는 지난 일요일이므로 과거형으로 쓰인 문장만 들어갈 수 있다.

15. 일반동사 과거형의 의문문은 「Did + 주어 + 동사원형?」으로 나타낸다.

16. Mrs. Brown은 3인칭 단수이므로 works를 써야 한다.

17. '너는 주말에 무엇을 하길 원하니?'라는 현재형의 질문에는 현재형으로 답하는 것이 옳다.

18. ① She works[worked] hard at the cafeteria.
    ② I like ice cream.
    ③ Miss Lee sells fruits in a market.
    ⑤ I went to school 3 days ago.

19. 주어가 3인칭 단수인 일반동사의 의문문은 「Does + 주어 + 동사원형?」으로 쓰며, B의 대답은 드라마가 아닌 스포츠를 좋아한다는 내용이므로 likes가 적절하다.

20. ① Did you meet Tom yesterday?
    ③ I don't play the violin tomorrow.
    ④ What did you do last Sunday?
    ⑤ They didn't get up early yesterday.

단원평가　　고난도　　P.34

1. ②　2. read　3. ④　4. ③　5. ⑤　6. ④
7. He likes to read books, but don't[→doesn't] like sports. / Are[→Do] you see the boys outside? / Going[→Go] out and play with them. / There is[→are] lots of exciting sports. / But he doesn't listens[→listen] to her and just read[→reads] books at home all the time.
8. ⑤　9. She waters the plants on Fridays.
10. ⑤

1. 시간의 흐름을 나타내는 표현을 잘 활용한다.
   ⓒ 오늘, 나는 바빴다. → ⓓ 나는 아침 식사 후에 설거지를 했다. → ⓐ 점심 식사 후, 나는 엄마와 함께 쇼핑을 하러 갔다. → ⓑ 저녁에는 나의 여동생의 숙제를 도와주었다.

2. read의 과거형은 read로 쓴다.

3. A의 질문은 Did you have some pizza yesterday?(너는 어제 피자를 먹었니?)이다.

4. Yesterday Sam goes to a dinner party at his friend's house. → Yesterday Sam went to a dinner party at his friend's house.
   There was a lot of people. → There were a lot of people.
   He has a good time there. → He had a good time there.

5. 빈칸에 들어갈 말은 순서대로 Are, is, Does, Does, Do 이다.

6. ① I am outgoing.
   ② I don't sing well.
   ③ He doesn't like basketball.
   ④ He always does his homework hard.
   ⑤ We are good friends.

7. He likes to read books, but don't like sports.
   → 주어가 3인칭 단수인 일반동사 부정문은 「doesn't + 동사원형」으로 쓴다.
   Are you see the boys outside?
   → 주어가 you인 일반동사의 의문문은 「Do + 주어 + 동사원형?」으로 쓴다.
   Going out and play with them.
   → 명령문은 동사원형으로 시작한다.
   There is lots of exciting sports.
   → exciting sports가 복수이기 때문에 be동사 are을 써야 한다.
   But he doesn't listens to her and just read books at home all the time.
   → doesn't 다음에 동사원형을 쓰며 read는 주어가 he 이기 때문에 reads로 써야 한다.

8. ⑤ spoken을 spoke으로 바꿔야 한다.

9. 표를 보면 Bella가 금요일마다 하는 일은 식물에 물을 주는 것이다. 따라서 She waters the plants on Fridays.로 쓸 수 있다.

10. b. He ate lunch.
    d. She swims very well.
    e. He didn't like math.

서술형 대비학습 P.36

1. ❶ Maria watches TV / she does not[doesn't] listen to music
   ❷ Maria plays the guitar / she does not[doesn't] sing

2. ❶ gave ❷ made ❸ took

3. ❶ John lives in Busan.
   ❷ Do they like horror movies?
   ❸ She does not[doesn't] practice English every day.

4. (예시)
   ❶ He plays the piano on weekends.
   ❷ He doesn't play the piano on weekends.
   ❸ Does he play the piano on weekends?

5. (예시)
   ❶ Sumi and I made cookies last night.
   ❷ Sumi and I didn't make cookies last night.
   ❸ Did Sumi and I make cookies last night?

6. ❶ cleaned his house ❷ didn't send an e-mail to Suji ❸ played soccer with his friends ❹ went shopping ❺ didn't study English

7. ❶ Did they close the door last night?
   ❷ Jonathan does not[doesn't] have breakfast.

8. cleans the house / watches soccer games / play with our dog, Dongki

9. went to the concert / had dinner / did his homework / went to bed

10. ❶ 너의 생일이 다가오고 있다. 너는 무엇을 하고 싶은가? (예시) I want to throw a birthday party.
    ❷ 지난 일요일에 무엇을 하였는가?
    (예시) I studied English last Saturday.

Chapter 3

조동사

3.1. 조동사의 성격 P.41

A.

❶ may not be
❷ be able to
❸ may
❹ take
❺ Can
❻ can
❼ may not
❽ will not
❾ May
❿ lend
⓫ must
⓬ will read
⓭ catch
⓮ can fly
⓯ must not

B.

❶ be able to
❷ have
❸ run
❹ must not
❺ Will
❻ be
❼ may not
❽ be

3.2. will, be going to P.43

A.

❶ Is he going to do his homework after dinner?
❷ She will take a computer lesson.

- ❸ My parents are going to arrive in Busan tomorrow.
- ❹ The train will not[won't] leave on time.

B.

- ❶ will go swimming
- ❷ is going to study English
- ❸ is going to wash the dishes
- ❹ are going to watch movies

C.

- ❶ this evening
- ❷ take
- ❸ tomorrow
- ❹ this
- ❺ drop

3.3. can, may   P.45

A.

- ❶ were able to find
- ❷ Are, able to fix
- ❸ was not[wasn't] able to remember
- ❹ Is, able to make
- ❺ is able to dry
- ❻ is able to bake

B.

- ❶ 허가
- ❷ 허가
- ❸ 추측
- ❹ 추측
- ❺ 허가
- ❻ 허가

3.4. must, have to, should   P.47

A.

- ❶ must cross

- ❷ must not smoke
- ❸ must wear
- ❹ must not use
- ❺ must not take

B.

- ❶ had to
- ❷ have to
- ❸ has to
- ❹ have to
- ❺ have to

C.

- ❶ She must be telling a lie again.
- ❷ Children should not eat junk food.
- ❸ They ought to take off their shoes.

단원평가   몸풀기   P.48

1. ② 2. can 3. ① 4. ⑤ 5. ③ 6. ❶ will[am going to] ❷ can[is able to] 7. ③
8. ③ 9. ② 10. ④

1. 조동사의 의문문은 「조동사 + 주어 + 동사원형?」의 형태로 쓴다.

2. Can으로 하는 질문에 긍정적으로 답하고 있으므로 can이 옳다.

3. ② Can you <u>help</u> me, please?
   ③ He <u>can</u> not play the piano.
   ④ I will <u>be</u> a mother next year.
   ⑤ It will <u>rain</u> tomorrow.

4. B의 빈칸 뒤에 이어지는 내용으로 보아 A의 질문에 대한 부정적인 대답이 필요하며, 주어가 3인칭 복수(cars)이므로 No, they won't.가 가장 적절하다.

5. can과 같은 의미의 표현은 be able to이며 주어가 3인칭 단수(Julia)이므로 is able to가 정답이다.

6. ❶ 미래를 나타내는 조동사는 will[be going to]이다.
   ❷ 능력을 나타내는 조동사는 can[be able to]이다.

10

7. 주어가 3인칭 단수이기 때문에 ③번의 경우는 wants to play로 써야 한다.

8. 조동사는 연속해서 쓸 수 없으므로 ③번이 빈칸에 알맞지 않다.

9. 휴대폰을 반드시 꺼야 하며, 책을 올바른 자리에 놓아야 하는 것은 도서관에서 지켜야 할 규칙이다.

10. must는 have to와 바꿔 쓸 수 있다.

단원평가 실전대비 P.49

1. ② 2. ⑤ 3. ④ 4. ② 5. ③ 6. ⑤ 7. ③
8. ⑤ 9. ⑤ 10. ② 11. ① 12. ④ 13. ②
14. ⑤ 15. ④ 16. ① 17. ③ 18. ③ 19. ④
20. ⑤ 21. ⑤

1. 첫 번째 빈칸에는 '시력이 좋지 않다. 나는 잘 볼 수가 없다.'이기에 can't가 올바르다. 두 번째 빈칸에는 '나는 다음 주 수요일에 영어시험이 있다. 나는 주말 동안 열심히 공부를 할 것이다.'이기에 미래를 나타내는 will이 적절하다.

2. 설거지를 해달라는 A의 부탁에 B는 학교에 늦었다고 대답하고 있으므로 거절하는 표현이 적절하다.

3. '태호가 전화를 안 받는다.'에 대한 응답으로 적절한 것은 '그는 집에 없을지도 모른다.'이므로 「추측의 조동사 may + not + 동사원형」의 형태로 쓰인 ④번이 정답이다.

4. ② Can으로 묻는 질문에 대한 부정의 대답은 「No, 주어 + can't.」로 한다.

5. ① Edison has to wear glasses.
   ② You must not be late for school again.
   ④ May I ask a personal question?
   ⑤ I must finish this report today.

6. 날씨가 좋기 때문에 우산을 가져갈 필요가 없으므로 '~할 필요가 없다'란 표현의 don't have to가 적절하다.

7. 조동사 뒤에는 동사원형이 온다.

8. 대화 속에서 엄마는 '날씨가 춥기 때문에 나가지 말아야 한다'와 '숙제를 먼저 해야 한다'는 약한 의무를 이야기하

고 있으므로 빈칸에 should not과 should가 차례로 알맞다.

9. ⑤ '쓰레기 통에 쓰레기를 버려서는 안 된다.'는 도서관에 적합한 규칙이 아니다.

10. 피노키오는 거짓말을 했기 때문에 '진실을 말해야 한다'라는 뜻의 ②번이 피노키오에게 해줄 조언으로 가장 적절하다.

11. 주어진 문장은 '그녀는 수영을 아주 잘 한다.'라는 뜻으로 능력을 나타내고 있기 때문에 can을 이용한 문장으로 바꿔 쓸 수 있다.

12. ④번은 허락을 요청하는 can이며 나머지는 능력을 나타내는 can이다.

13. – 선생님의 말을 잘 들어야 한다.
    – 항상 제 시간에 와라.
    – 수업 중에는 친구들과 이야기해서 안 된다.
    – 매일 교실을 청소해라.
    이런 규칙들을 지켜야 하는 장소는 학교이다.

14. 조동사 뒤에는 반드시 동사원형이 온다.

15. ④ 조동사의 부정문은 「주어 + 조동사 + not + 동사원형」이다.

16. '그는 안 좋아 보인다.'라는 문장 다음에 이어질 내용은 '아픈 것이 틀림없다'라는 ①번이 가장 적절하다.

17. ③ 미래를 나타내는 will과 과거를 나타내는 yesterday는 한 문장에서 사용될 수 없다.

18. ① James has to wear glasses.
    ② You must not turn on your cell phone.
    ④ May I go to the toilet?
    ⑤ I must meet her today.

19. 미래를 나타내는 조동사는 will이며, be going to와 바꿔 쓸 수 있다.

20. ⑤번은 허가를 나타내며 나머지는 추측을 나타낸다.

21. – 문이 더러웠다. 나는 그것을 닦아야 했다.
    – Jina는 몇 년 전에 바이올린을 연주할 수 있었다.
    두 문장 모두 과거를 나타내므로 had to와 could를 써야 한다.

1. ⑤　2. ③　3. ④　4. ③　5. ①, ③　6. ③
7. ②　8. ⑤　9. ②　10. ⑤

1. Susan은 일본어를 하지 못한다.

2. 질문: 영화관에서의 올바른 에티켓은 무엇인가?
   ① 크게 말하거나 먹어야 한다.
   ② 휴대폰을 켜야 한다.
   ③ 쓰레기통에 쓰레기를 버려야 한다.
   ④ 발로 앞에 앉은 사람의 의자를 차야 한다.
   ⑤ 영화가 시작하고 난 후에 들어가야 한다.

3. ④번은 허가를 나타내며 나머지는 추측을 나타낸다.

4. 대화의 마지막에 A가 "You must not park here.(이곳에 주차를 하면 안 된다.)"라고 했으므로 주차금지 표지판이 정답이다.

5. ①번은 부정의 추측, ③번은 허가를 나타내고 보기와 나머지는 선택지는 능력을 나타낸다.

6. ③ 사람들은 동물에게 잔인하게 하면 <u>안 된다</u>.
   ③번은 must not이 적절하며 나머지는 의무를 나타내는 must[have to]가 알맞다.

7. 나머지는 긍정과 부정으로 짝지어진 문장들이므로 ②번이 정답이다.

8. ⑤ '나는 수학에서 안 좋은 성적을 받았다.'에 대한 응답으로 '매니저에게 전화를 해야 한다.'는 적절하지 않다.

9. 보기와 ②번의 must는 의무를 나타내며 나머지는 강한 추측을 나타낸다.

10. '~할 필요가 없다'라는 뜻의 표현은 don't have to가 알맞다.

1. ❶ can ride a bike[can make pizza]
   ❷ can play the piano[can ride a bike]
   ❸ can't play the piano
   ❹ can't make pizza

2. ❶ Jack will be okay.
   ❷ Jack won't be okay.

3. ❶ She has to
   ❷ We don't have to

4. ❶ has to clean
   ❷ don't have to wear
   ❸ had to wake up

5. ❶ not smoke
   ❷ must not swim

6. ❶ will[be going to]
   ❷ Will
   ❸ must

7. ❶ is, going to
   ❷ have to

8. ❶ will be high school students
   ❷ can speak English well

9. writing, singer

10. ❶ can
    ❷ may
    ❸ may[can]
    ❹ must[has to, should]
    ❺ must

Chapter 4

동사의 시제

4.1. 현재시제와 과거시제　　　　P.59

A.

❶ watched
❷ gives
❸ boils
❹ makes
❺ flew

B.

❶ goes
❷ rode
❸ put
❹ arrives
❺ ended
❻ talks
❼ went
❽ was
❾ plays
❿ is

C.

❶ didn't
❷ don't
❸ don't
❹ didn't
❺ doesn't
❻ didn't

4.2. 진행시제 (현재진행, 과거진행)　　P.61

A.

❶ arriving　❷ beginning　❸ coming
❹ cutting　❺ crying　❻ dancing
❼ dying　❽ driving　❾ getting
❿ going　⓫ hitting　⓬ jogging
⓭ living　⓮ swimming　⓯ waking
⓰ writing　⓱ running　⓲ ringing

B.

❶ He is taking a walk in the forest.
He is not[isn't] taking a walk in the forest.
Is he taking a walk in the forest? / he is

❷ Suji was running after her dog.
Suji was not[wasn't] running after her dog.
Was she running after her dog? / she was

C.

❶ was
❷ cleaning
❸ were
❹ am
❺ listening

단원평가　몸풀기　　　　P.62

> 1. ①　2. ①, ②　3. ④　4. ④　5. ②　6. ⑤
> 7. ⑤　8. ④　9. ③　10. ①

1. 일반동사 과거형의 의문문은 「Did + 주어 + 동사원형?」이다.

2. ③ stopping ④ swimming ⑤ lying

3. 진행형의 부정문은 「주어 + be동사 not + v-ing」이다.

4. A와 B의 시제가 과거이므로 과거를 나타내는 부사를 넣어야 한다.

5. ① writing ③ listening ④ sitting ⑤ eating

6. last night은 '어젯밤'을 나타내므로 빈칸에는 과거형이 들어가야 한다.

7. 일반동사 과거형의 의문문은 「Did + 주어 + 동사원형?」이며 과거시제 질문은 과거시제로 답해야 한다. study의 과거형은 studied이다.

8. 주어진 문장에 이미 is가 있으므로 일반동사를 이어 쓸 수 없다.

9. 진행형의 의문문은 「Be동사 + 주어 + v–ing?」의 형태로 쓰며 주어가 3인칭 단수이므로 Is를 써야 한다.

10. 일반동사 현재형의 의문문은 「Do + 주어 + 동사원형?」의 형태로 쓰며 주어가 3인칭 단수이므로 Does를 써야 한다.

단원평가 실전대비 P.63

1. ⑤ 2. ② 3. ❶ played ❷ didn't ❸ rained
❹ were ❺ brought 4. ② 5. ② 6. ③ 7. ②
8. ① 9. ③ 10. ⑤ 11. ④ 12. ⑤ 13. ⑤
14. ④ 15. ⑤ 16. ① 17. ① 18. ② 19. ②
20. ①

1. – 매 화요일마다 규칙적으로 테니스를 하고 있기 때문에 현재형이 알맞다.
   – 지금(now) 하고 있는 동작을 표현할 때는 현재진행형이 알맞다.

2. ① Did he dance yesterday?
   ③ She went to Kimhae last weekend.
   ④ Who sent the picture?
   ⑤ Suji didn't do the dishes after dinner.

3. 어제(yesterday) 있었던 일들이기 때문에 모든 동사를 과거형으로 고쳐 써야 한다.

4. Angela는 화요일에 수영을 하므로 ②번이 알맞지 않다.

5. ② 해가 동쪽에서 뜨는 것은 일반적인 사실이므로 현재형으로 써야 한다.

6. ③ 파리가 프랑스의 수도인 것은 일반적인 사실이므로 현재형으로 써야 한다.

7. ⓑ Bomin is sitting on the floor.
   ⓓ Taehoon is running in the park.
   ⓔ Bobae is eating an ice cream.

8. ① 남자가 신발을 사고 있는 모습은 그림에서 찾을 수 없다.

9. ③ swiming → swimming

10. ⓐ Kate와 Anna는 영어를 공부하고 있으므로 주어를 3인칭 복수로 하는 부정의 대답이 알맞다.
    ⓑ Sam은 편지를 쓰고 있으므로 주어를 3인칭 단수로 하는 부정의 대답이 알맞다.

11. 일반동사 현재형의 의문문은 「Do + 주어 + 동사원형?」의 형태로 쓰는데 주어가 3인칭 단수이므로 does가 알맞고, 일반동사 과거형의 의문문은 「Did + 주어 + 동사원형?」의 형태로 쓴다.

12. ⑤ eat의 과거형은 ate이다.

13. ⑤번에는 Did가 들어가는 것이 올바르다.

14. ④ know는 현재진행형으로 만들 수 없는 동사이다.

15. 그는 지금(now) 기분이 좋기 때문에 과거형 felt가 아닌 현재형 feels를 써야 한다.

16. 지난 여름에 비가 많이 내렸기에 과거형인 rained를 쓴다.

17. 현재진행형이기 때문에 현재를 나타내는 시간부사 now(지금)가 알맞다.

18. ① Jimmy is reading a novel now.
    ③ Where did you go last weekend?
    ④ He had his birthday party yesterday.
    ⑤ A man was listening to music in the room.

19. 질문: 빈칸에 알맞은 말을 고르시오.
    '누워있는 중이다'는 be lying으로 나타낸다.

20. 과거에 일어났던 일들을 나열하고 있으므로 빈칸에는 동사의 과거형을 써야 한다.

단원평가 고난도 P.66

1. ④, ⑤ 2. ③ 3. ② 4. ④ 5. ③ 6. ④
7. ② 8. ④ 9. ③ 10. taught → is teaching,
study → studying 11. ③

1. ⓐ와 나머지: was, ④, ⑤: were

2. ① Tom watches TV. (과거의문문)
   → Did Tom watch TV?
   ② He got up at 6:30 in the morning. (의문문)
   → Did he get up at 6:30 in the morning?

14

④ Ben went to New York by plane. (부정문)
→ Ben did not <u>go</u> to New York by plane.
⑤ My sister ate lunch at 12. (현재진행형)
→ My sister <u>is eating</u> lunch at 12.

3. ② know는 현재진행형으로 만들 수 없는 동사이다.

4. ④ 지금 공부를 하고 있냐는 현재를 묻는 질문에 과거에 공부를 하고 있었다는 대답은 어색하다.

5. ① He <u>danced[was dancing]</u> last night.
② He can <u>play</u> the guitar.
④ We can't <u>do</u> anything to help him.
⑤ Are you <u>reading</u> a book?

6. 지난 주말에 여동생이 무엇을 했는지 묻고 있으므로 주어를 She로 하는 과거시제 문장으로 대답해야 한다.

7. ②번의 밑줄 친 going은 미래시제를 나타내는 be going to의 going이다.

8. ④번의 interesting은 진행형과 형태는 같지만 '~한, ~하는'이라는 뜻의 현재분사이다.

9. 민아: I <u>stopped</u> the car.
지원: Did you <u>pass</u> the exam last year?
현진: She <u>went</u> to school by bus yesterday.

10. now라는 부사를 보아 현재 진행되고 있는 일이므로 동사를 현재진행형으로 바꿔야 하며(taught → is teaching), 현재진행형 부정문은 「be동사 + not + v-ing」의 형태로 쓴다.(study → studying)

11. ③ <u>Did</u> she write a postcard last night?

1. ❶ Mr. Nah washes his car on weekends.
❷ He does taekwondo every day after school.
❸ Do you usually watch television every night?
❹ Mira does not study math on Mondays.

2. ❶ They are eating dinner together.
❷ She is smiling at her baby.
❸ I am drinking green tea with my mom.

3. ❶ made　❷ flew　❸ went　❹ fell

4. (예시)
❶ She played the piano yesterday.
❷ She didn't play the piano yesterday.

5. ❶ reading　❷ drinking　❸ running

6. ❶ is an animal doctor[takes care of animals]
❷ No, isn't
❸ is riding a bike (now)

7. ❶ am writing a letter
❷ is taking a picture

8. ❶ She is taking a shower.
❷ She is having breakfast.
❸ She is going to school.
❹ She is studying at school.
❺ She is playing with friends.
❻ She is having dinner.
❼ She is doing homework.
❽ She is watching TV.

9. was wearing, was cleaning, is wearing, is talking

10. ❶ Is it raining outside?
❷ They were my doctors.
❸ Why were you angry?

11. My son <u>was</u> cooking something last night. He was <u>baking</u> a cake for me.

Chapter 5
명사와 관사

5.1. 명사의 종류 P.73

A.
1. ③
2. ②
3. ①
4. ⑤
5. ③
6. ④
7. ⑤
8. ③

B.
1. Korea
2. peace
3. freedom
4. happiness
5. Jessica
6. a tree
7. sugar
8. bread
9. family
10. money

C.
1. Australia
2. flies
3. water
4. information
5. cheese

5.2. 명사의 복수형 P.75

A.
1. parties
2. videos
3. roofs
4. presents
5. buses
6. eggs
7. selves
8. posters
9. headaches
10. oxen
11. teeth
12. habits
13. women
14. deer
15. children
16. potatoes
17. brushes
18. maps

B.
1. monkeys, watches, zebras
2. teeth, keys, octopuses
3. apples, rabbits, oxen
4. houses, cats, families

C.
1. boxes
2. women
3. fish
4. watches
5. leaves
6. pens
7. geese
8. feet
9. students
10. photos

5.3. 명사의 수량표현 P.77

A.
1. a little
2. a few
3. a little
4. a few
5. a few
6. a little

B.

① glass
② glass
③ spoonful
④ pieces
⑤ cup
⑥ sheet
⑦ pair
⑧ cups
⑨ gloves
⑩ tons of coal

C.

① pair
② glasses
③ piece
④ piece
⑤ spoonfuls

5.4. 관사의 종류 P.79

A.

① a
② an
③ an
④ a
⑤ the
⑥ the
⑦ the
⑧ The, the
⑨ the
⑩ the
⑪ the
⑫ a

B.

① The sun
② a book[the book]

③ an apple[apples]
④ the cello
⑤ handsome
⑥ Tim
⑦ the piano
⑧ the Han River
⑨ a ball[his ball]
⑩ the Bible
⑪ Jane
⑫ a day

5.5. 관사의 생략 P.81

A.

① the
② The
③ x
④ x
⑤ a
⑥ x
⑦ a
⑧ x
⑨ a
⑩ the
⑪ an, a
⑫ x
⑬ the
⑭ the
⑮ x

5.6. There is / There are P.83

A.

① is
② are
③ Are
④ is

⑤ is

⑥ are

B.

① is → are

② Are → Is

③ Is → Are

④ is → are

⑤ are → is[a problem → problems]

⑥ is → are

C.

① There is not[isn't] a cat on the table.

② Is there a bag next to the bed?

③ Are there oranges in the refrigerator?

④ There was not[wasn't] a house in the woods.

⑤ Are there three cups on the table?

단원평가　몸풀기　P.84

1. ⑤　2. ⑤　3. ③　4. an　5. ①　6. ①　7. ①
8. ①　9. ⑤　10. ②

1. ⑤ baby의 복수형은 babies로 쓴다.

2. ⑤ 소유격 앞에는 관사를 붙이지 않는다.

3. 앞에서 언급된 것을 말할 때 정관사 the를 붙인다.

4. 직업 앞에도 관사를 붙이는데 engineer는 첫 소리가 모음이므로 an을 써야 한다.

5. 동사가 are이기 때문에 뒤에는 복수 명사가 와야 한다.

6. ① 뜨거운 음료의 경우 a cup of를 활용한다.

7. milk는 물질명사로 셀 수 없다.

8. ② two glasses of milk
   ③ three pairs of shoes
   ④ a piece of pizza
   ⑤ ten slices of cheese

9. 책상 위에 시계가 있냐고 묻는 A의 질문에 B는 상자 안에 있다고 했으므로 빈칸에는 부정의 대답이 와야 한

다. Is there ~?로 묻는 경우 부정 대답은 No, there isn't.로 한다.

10. Are there ~?로 묻는 질문은 there are로 대답한다.

단원평가　실전대비　P.85

1. ②　2. ②　3. ⑤　4. ④　5. ③　6. ②　7. ❶
an uniform → a uniform　❷ by a bus → by
bus　❸ have the dinner → have dinner　8.
③　9. ⑤　10. ②　11. t[T]he　12. ①　13.
③　14. ②　15. ❶ Yes there Is　❷ No there
aren't　16. ②　17. ⑤　18. ⑤　19. ⑤　20.
three glass → three glasses　21. ⑤

1. ②번의 there은 유도부사가 아닌 위치를 나타내는 부사이며 의미는 '거기에'이다.

2. ① There are many books in this room.
   ③ There are four seasons in Korea.
   ④ There are ticket machines in the stations.
   ⑤ Are there any famous places in your country?

3. ⓒ teeth → tooth, ⓓ tooth → teeth

4. ④ activity의 복수형은 activities이다.

5. ③번의 audio는 첫 소리가 모음이므로 앞에 an을 써야 한다.

6. ② a sheet of paper가 올바르다.

7. ❶ uniform은 소리가 반자음으로 시작되므로 관사 a를 써야 한다.
   ❷ 「by + 교통수단」 사이에 관사를 쓰지 않는다.
   ❸ 식사명 앞에는 관사를 쓰지 않는다.

8. '~가 있다'는 「There + be동사 + 명사」로 나타내는데, 명사가 복수이므로 「There are + 복수명사 ~」로 쓴다.

9. ① Sheep give us wool.
   ② Those boxes are very heavy.
   ③ Los Angeles is a busy city.
   ④ I want three bottles of water.

10. 악기 앞에는 the를 써야 한다.

11. 앞에 언급한 명사를 다시 반복할 때, 세상에서 유일한 것 앞에, 수식을 받아 대상이 분명한 명사 앞에는 the를 쓴다.

12. ①번은 is, 나머지는 are를 써야 한다.

13. ① They need five pieces of paper.
② We drank four cups of coffee.
④ I had two pieces of pizza for lunch.
⑤ Will you bring me a glass of water?

14. There are 다음에 복수 명사가 와야 한다.

15. ❶ 휴대폰이 의자 위에 있기 때문에 긍정의 대답을 쓴다.
❷ 책상 위에는 컵이 없기 때문에 부정의 대답을 쓴다.

16. '나는 소녀이고 학생이며 한국인이다.'라는 소개에 부합하는 것은 ②번이다.

17. ① 그림에는 몇 명의 사람들이 있다. → 그림에는 아무도 없다.
② 나무 뒤에 시청이 있다. → 시청 근처에는 나무가 없다.
③ 그림에는 박물관들이 있다. → 박물관은 한 개만 있다.
④ 박물관 앞에는 시계탑이 있다. → 그림에는 시계탑이 없다.
⑤ 식당 옆에 꽃가게가 있다.

18. ⑤ 식사 앞에는 관사를 붙이지 않는다.

19. ① 상자 안에 개 두 마리가 있다. → 상자 안에는 개 한 마리가 있다.
② 탁자 밑에 접시가 있다. → 탁자 밑에는 책 두 권이 있다.
③ 탁자 옆에 컵이 있다. → 컵은 탁자 위에 있다.
④ 상자 안에는 3개의 쿠키가 있다. → 상자 안에는 개가 있다.

20. 세 잔이기 때문에 three glasses라고 표현하는 것이 올바르다.

21. ⑤ meat는 셀 수 없는 명사이므로 앞에 many를 쓸 수 없다.

1. ② 2. ① 3. ⑤ 4. ③ 5. ④ 6. ④ 7. ⑤
8. ① 9. ⑤ 10. ② 11. ④ 12. ❶ much
water ❷ by bike

1. womans → women , babyes → babies, knifes → knives, tooth → teeth

2. ①번은 유도부사가 아닌 위치를 나타내는 부사이며 의미는 '거기에'이다.

3. 탁자 위에 있는 사물이 있냐는 질문에 대한 답으로 본인이 앞으로 할 행동을 이야기하는 ⑤번은 알맞지 않다.

4. album은 첫 소리가 모음으로 시작하므로 앞에 an을 쓰고, 소유격 앞에는 관사를 쓰지 않으며 앞에서 언급된 명사를 다시 언급할 때는 정관사를 쓴다.

5. 보기와 ④번의 a는 '~마다'의 의미이다.

6. There are 다음에는 복수 명사를 써야 한다.

7. ⑤ Give me two pieces of cake, please.

8. ⓔ와 ⓕ의 앞에 a/an을 붙일 수 있다.

9. ⑤ hour는 첫 소리 발음이 모음이므로 앞에 관사 an을 쓴다.

10. ⓐ She teaches math to us.
ⓒ I'll make three sandwiches.
ⓔ She feels happy these days.
ⓕ I have two dogs and three cats.

11. ④번: a, 나머지: the[The]

12. ❶ 셀 수 없는 명사의 많음을 표현할 때는 앞에 much를 쓴다.
❷ 「by + 교통수단」: ~을 타고

정답 및 해설 19

1. ❶ There is a big bed in my room.
    ❷ There are many mountains in this country.
    ❸ There are many beans in the rice.
    ❹ There is a small pink vase on the table.
    ❺ She exercises four times a week.

2. ❶ There are three books
    ❷ Yes there is

3. ❶ a → an
    ❷ week → a week
    ❸ a → an
    ❹ A → The
    ❺ a moon → the moon

4. Three times a week.

5. (예시)
    ❶ There is a bike next to the tree.
    ❷ There are some bottles in front of the trash can.

Chapter 6

대명사

6.1. 지시대명사   P.93

A.
❶ Those
❷ this
❸ Is that
❹ Is this
❺ Those are
❻ Those are
❼ This is
❽ Are these
❾ Those are

B.
❶ it
❷ They
❸ it
❹ they

6.2. 부정대명사 (1)   P.95

A.
❶ ones
❷ it
❸ one
❹ It
❺ it

B.
❶ one
❷ ones
❸ it
❹ ones
❺ one

C.

1. one
2. One
3. it
4. ones
5. It

D.

1. some
2. any
3. any
4. Some
5. any

6.3. 부정대명사 (2)   P.97

A.

1. the other
2. another
3. One
4. the others
5. another
6. the other
7. another, the other
8. other
9. others
10. another

B.

1. one
2. another
3. One, the other
4. One, another, the other
5. the others
6. the other
7. the others
8. One
9. One, the others

10. the other

6.4. 비인칭 주어 it   P.99

A.

1. 대
2. 비
3. 비
4. 대
5. 비
6. 대
7. 비
8. 비
9. 대
10. 비
11. 대
12. 비
13. 비
14. 비
15. 비

B.

1. x
2. It
3. It
4. It
5. it

6.5. 재귀대명사   P.101

A.

1. herself
2. herself
3. myself
4. himself
5. themselves
6. themselves
7. myself

⑧ ourselves

⑨ itself

⑩ herself

⑪ myself

⑫ himself

B.

❶ grow them ourselves

❷ closed, itself

❸ wash herself

❹ be proud of yourself

C.

❶ 강

❷ 강

❸ 재

❹ 재

단원평가 몸풀기 P.102

1. ① 2. ① 3. 해설참조 4. ③ 5. ④ 6. ❶ herself ❷ themselves 7. ④ 8. ① 9. ③ 10. ④

1. 전화상에서 '저는 ~입니다'는 This is ~로 표현한다.

2. 시각을 표현할 때 비인칭 주어 it을 활용한다.

3.

단수	재귀대명사	복수	재귀대명사
1인칭	myself	1인칭	ourselves
2인칭	yourself	2인칭	yourselves
3인칭	herself	3인칭	themselves
	himself		
	itself		

4. ③번은 대명사 It이고 나머지는 비인칭 주어 It이다.

5. ④번은 대명사 It이고 나머지는 비인칭 주어 It이다.

6. She의 재귀대명사는 herself, They의 대명사는 themselves이다.

7. 둘 중에 하나는 one, 다른 하나는 the other로 표현한다.

8. ① This는 단수 명사를 가리키는 지시대명사이기 때문에 단수 명사가 와야 한다. my backpacks → my backpack

9. 날짜를 표현할 때 비인칭 주어 It을 활용한다.

10. Are those ~?로 묻는 질문의 긍정 대답은 Yes, they are.이다.

단원평가 실전대비 P.103

1. ④ 2. ② 3. ③ 4. ③ 5. ① 6. ④ 7. ④
8. ③ 9. ① 10. ② 11. These are 12. ⑤
13. ❶ 비 ❷ 비 ❸ 지 14. ② 15. ⑤ 16. ②
17. ② 18. ③ 19. One, the other 20. ①
21. ④

1. 셋 중에 하나는 one으로 표현하고 나머지는 the others로 표현한다.

2. ②번은 대명사 It이고 나머지는 비인칭 주어 It이다.

3. by oneself는 '혼자서, 스스로'라는 의미로, 주어가 She이기 때문에 herself를 써야 한다.

4. enjoy oneself는 '즐기다'라는 의미로, 주어가 They이기 때문에 themselves를 써야 한다.

5. 나 자신이 스스로에게 자랑스러움을 느꼈기 때문에 재귀대명사 myself를 써야 한다.

6. ④번은 종류가 같은 것 중 하나이므로 one이 들어가야 한다.

7. '다른 것, 또 다른 것'을 나타낼 때는 another을 쓴다.

8. 셋 중에 하나는 one, 나머지는 the others로 표현한다.

9. one은 앞에서 언급된 tie를 대신하고 있다.

10. say to oneself는 '혼잣말하다'라는 의미로, 주어가 She이기 때문에 herself를 써야 한다.

11. This의 복수형은 These이다.

12. ⑤번의 재귀대명사는 재귀용법으로 쓰였고 나머지는 강조용법으로 쓰였다.

13. ❶ 날짜를 나타낼 때 비인칭 주어 it을 쓴다.
   ❷ 날씨를 나타낼 때 비인칭 주어 it을 쓴다.
   ❸ '그것은'이라고 해석되므로 지시대명사 it이다.

14. Is this ~?에 대한 부정 대답은 No, it isn't.로 표현한다.

15. ① The other <u>is</u> yours.
   ② <u>It</u> is chilly in autumn.
   ③ <u>These</u> babies are cute.
   ④ These cookies <u>are</u> very delicious.

16. 앞에서 언급된 것과 종류가 같은 하나는 one으로 표현할 수 있다.

17. ② 나 자신을 소개하는 것이므로 me 대신 myself를 써야 한다.

18. ③ 강조용법으로 사용된 재귀대명사는 생략 가능하다.

19. 둘 중에 하나는 one, 나머지 하나는 the other로 표현한다.

20. 주어진 대화와 ①번의 it은 지시대명사이며 나머지는 비인칭 주어이다.

21. '그녀 자신'이라는 뜻으로 쓰려면 목적격 her를 재귀대명사 herself로 바꿔야 한다.

5. ④번의 재귀대명사는 재귀용법으로, 나머지의 재귀대명사는 강조용법으로 쓰였다.

6. Taipei의 날씨는 흐리지만 춥지는 않다.

7. 여러 개 중에 하나는 one, 나머지는 others로 표현한다.

8. by oneself는 '혼자서, 혼자의 힘으로', in itself는 '자체, 본래로, 스스로'라는 의미를 가진다.

9. 두 개 중 하나는 one으로 표현하고 나머지는 the other로 표현한다. 세 개 중 하나는 one, 또 다른 하나는 another, 나머지는 the other로 표현한다.

10. ④ 부정문 또는 의문문에서는 any를 사용한다.

11. ④ 앞에 언급된 명사를 다시 언급할 때는 it으로 표현한다.

12. ③번은 앞에 언급된 것과 같은 종류의 것이므로 one을 써야 하며 나머지 빈칸에는 it[It]을 써야 한다.

단원평가 고난도 P.106

1. ③ 2. ② 3. ③ 4. sunny → cloudy, windy → rainy 5. ④ 6. ③ 7. ③ 8. ③
9. ① 10. ④ 11. ④ 12. ③

1. ③번은 재귀대명사가 들어갈 수 없는 위치에 쓰였다.

2. 선생님이 그녀 스스로의 소개를 했으므로 재귀대명사 herself, 선생님이 우리들을 알고 싶어하기 때문에 목적격 인칭대명사 us가 빈칸에 들어가야 한다.

3. ⓐ, ⓔ, ⓕ, ⓗ의 it은 지시대명사이며, ⓑ, ⓒ, ⓓ, ⓖ의 it은 비인칭 주어이다.

4. 날씨는 화창했다가(sunny), 구름이 끼고 바람이 불기 시작해서(cloudy and windy), 비가 내렸다(rainy).

1. It's sunny (in Jeonju).

2. It's cloudy (in Paris).

3. It's snowy (in Moscow).

4. It's rainy (in Manila).

5. it isn't

6. ❶ This is a toy car.
   ❷ These are not dolls.
   ❸ Is that your house?

7. ❶ I finished homework by myself.
   ❷ She is looking at herself

8. ❶ 점점 어두워지고 있다.
   ❷ 오늘 아주 춥다.
   ❸ 울산부터 서울까지 얼마나 먼가요?

9. It's September 6th. / It's Wednesday. / What time is it?

10. One, the other

11. ❶ Are there ❷ Those girls are

12. It's September fourth.

13. the other is green

Chapter 7

의문사

7.1.   who, what, which   P.113

A.

❶ Who

❷ What

❸ Which

❹ What

❺ What

❻ What

❼ Which

❽ What

❾ Who

❿ What

⓫ Who

⓬ What

⓭ Who

⓮ What

⓯ Which

⓰ What

⓱ What

⓲ Who

B.

(예시)

❶ My favorite color is blue.

❷ I played tennis with my sister last weekend.

7.2.   when, where, why   P.115.

A.

❶ Why

❷ When

❸ Why

❹ Where

❺ When

❻ Where

❼ Where

❽ Where

❾ When

❿ Where

⓫ What time

⓬ Why

⓭ Where

⓮ When

⓯ Why

⓰ Why

B.

❶ ④

❷ ①

❸ ③

❹ ②

7.3. how

P.117

A.

❶ How

❷ How many

❸ How much

❹ How tall

❺ How

❻ How long

❼ How long

❽ How far

❾ How old

❿ How often

B.

❶ How much is it?

❷ How long did you study?

❸ How far is it?

❹ How often does she go jogging?

❺ How old is he?

단원평가   몸풀기

P.118

1. ① 2. ② 3. ② 4. When 5. ④ 6. ④
7. ③ 8. ⑤ 9. ⑤ 10. ④

1. 그 여자가 누구인지를 물어보기 때문에 Who가 알맞다.

2. 도서관에 있는 소녀가 누구인지를 물어보고 있으므로 그 소녀가 누구인지 알려주는 선택지가 정답이다.

3. B가 늦은 이유를 대답하고 있으므로 이유를 물어보는 Why가 알맞다.

4. What time은 When으로 바꿔 쓸 수 있다.

5. 키가 얼마나 큰지 물어볼 때는 How tall을 쓴다.

6. B가 금액을 대답하고 있으므로 How much로 시작하는 의문문이 알맞다.

7. How often은 '얼마나 자주'라는 뜻으로 빈도수를 물어보는 의문사이다.

8. B가 국적을 대답하고 있으므로 Where are you from?(너는 어디 출신이니?)이 알맞다.

9. '~하는 게 어때?'는 How about ~?으로 묻는다.

10. B가 위치를 대답하고 있으므로 Where이 빈칸에 알맞다.

단원평가   실전대비

P.119

1. ① 2. ① 3. ④ 4. ④ 5. ⑤ 6. ③ 7. ①
8. ④ 9. ① 10. ③ 11. ⑤ 12. ② 13. ②
14. ④ 15. ② 16. ② 17. ④ 18. ⑤ 19. ③
20. ⑤

1. '나는 야구를 좋아해.'라고 대답하고 있으므로 '어떤 운동을 좋아하는지' 물어보는 질문이 알맞다.

2. 사람이 누구인지를 물어보기 때문에 Who가 알맞다.

3. How about you?는 '너는 어때?'라고 물어보는 표현으로 보통 앞에 나온 질문을 짧게 다시 물어볼 때 쓰인다. B가 필리핀에서 왔다고 대답하고 있으므로 출신이 어디인지 묻는 ④번이 적절하다.

4. ④ 그가 어디에 있는지를 물어보는 질문에 그가 아프다고 대답하고 있으므로 어색한 대화이다.

5. ⑤ 영어를 공부하는 방법을 물어보는 질문에 한국 친구들과 이야기를 나눈다는 대답은 어색하다.

6. ③번은 When(언제)으로 묻는 질문에 '장소'를 답하고 있으므로 어색하다.

7. B가 모두 장소를 대답하고 있으므로 빈칸에는 위치를 묻는 Where로 시작하는 질문이 가장 적절하다.

8. B가 위치를 대답하고 있으므로 '위치'를 묻는 질문이 아닌 것을 찾아야 한다. ④번은 '너는 박물관에 어떻게 가

니?'라고 방법을 묻고 있다.

9. 질문: Jessica의 가족은 몇 명인가?
Jessica의 가족은 5명(Dad, mom, my older brother John, my little brother Joshua and me)이다.

10. ③번에는 What이 들어가야 하며 나머지는 How를 써야 한다.

11. ⑤ 선물이 무엇인지는 광고문에서 언급되지 않았다.

12. Which는 둘 중 하나를 묻는 의문사이므로 스포츠와 음악 중 더 선호하는 것으로 대답해야 한다.

13. '너는 무엇이 되고 싶니?'라는 질문에는 의문사 What을 쓰며, '왜 영화감독이 되고 싶니?'라는 질문에는 의문사 Why가 필요하다.

14. 거리를 물어볼 때는 How far를 사용하고 어떻게 가는지 방법을 물어볼 때는 How를 사용한다.

15. ⓐ When ⓒ How ⓓ Who ⓔ What

16. ②번에는 Who가 들어가는 것이 알맞다. (누가 너희 엄마니?)

17. ④번은 공원에 있는 남자들이 누군지 묻는 질문에 그들은 친절하다고 답하고 있으므로 어색하다.

18. ⑤번은 거리를 묻고 있으므로 How far를 써야 한다.

19. ③번은 What 대신 When이 적절하다.

20. 다니고 있는 학교를 대답하고 있으므로 어떤 학교를 다니냐는 질문이 가장 적절하다.

단원평가 　고난도　　　　　P.122

1. ① 2. ② 3. ⑤ 4. ① 5. ② 6. ③ 7. ②,
⑤ 8. ② 9. ⑤ 10. ⑤ 11. ⑤ 12. ⑤ 13.
②

1. ① 구체적인 시각을 물어보는 경우는 when으로 바꿀 수 없다.

2. ⓐ old ⓑ much ⓒ many ⓓ often ⓔ long

3. ① How is he doing? 그는 어떻게 지내니?

② How do you go to work? 너는 직장에 어떻게 가니?
③ How was your holiday? 네 휴일은 어땠니?
④ How much is that laptop? 저 노트북은 얼마니?
⑤ Who invited Jimmy to the party? 누가 Jimmy를 파티에 초대했니?

4. 방과 후에 무엇을 하는지 물을 때는 What을, 수업이 몇 시에 끝나는지 물을 때는 What time을, 언제 숙제를 하는지 물을 때는 When을 사용해서 질문한다.

5. 연주의 주체, 콘서트의 시간, 콘서트 장소에 대한 의문문이 되어야 하므로 순서대로 Who, When, Where이 알맞다.

6. 어디에서 네 남동생을 볼 수 있냐는 질문에 '그는 수영을 매우 잘한다.'라는 대답은 적절하지 않다.

7. 주어진 글에는 Jessica의 가족 수와 성(family name)이 언급되어 있다.
① Jessica의 직업은 무엇이니?
② Jessica의 가족은 몇 명이니?
③ Jessica는 어디에 살고 싶어하니?
④ Jessica는 무엇을 잘하니?
⑤ Jessica의 성은 무엇이니?

8. ⓐ A: 너희 어머니의 성함이 무엇이니?
　　B: 의사이셔.
ⓑ A: 네 이모는 어떻게 생기셨니?
　　B: 매우 친절하셔.
ⓒ A: 그의 성격은 어떠니?
　　B: 그는 매우 다정해.
ⓓ A: 짧은 머리를 한 그 여자 아이는 누구니?
　　B: 그녀는 아직 공부를 해.
ⓔ A: 그 검은 치마를 입은 여자는 누구니?
　　B: 그녀는 내 미술 선생님이야.

9. ① Where을 When으로 바꿔야 자연스럽다.
② When을 Where로 바꿔야 자연스럽다.
③ 가격을 묻고 있으므로 가격에 관한 대답을 해야 한다.
④ 동아리에 가입하는 방법을 묻고 있으므로 그에 알맞은 대답을 해야 한다.

10. 커피를 더 좋아한다는 대답에 알맞은 질문은 Which로 시작하는 선택의문문이다.

11. 걸어서 간다는 방법에 대한 의문사는 How(어떻게)가 적절하다.

12. 파티가 얼마나 오랫동안 이어질 지는 초대장에 나타나지 않았다.

13. ②번의 What은 목적어로 '무엇을'이라는 뜻으로, 나머지 선택지의 What은 '무엇이'라는 뜻으로 쓰였다.

서술형 대비학습 P.125

1. ❶ He studies math
   ❷ They swim on Tuesday

2. ❶ I cook.
   ❷ Usually spaghetti.
   ❸ Yes. I'm good at it.
   ❹ Three times a week.

3. ❶ What ❷ When ❸ What ❹ How ❺ come

4. ❶ is from Shanghai
   ❷ goes to Edmonds Middle School
   ❸ lives in Washington

5. She usually has dinner at 6:30.

6. ❶ How old is she?
   ❷ What is her job?[What does she do?]
   ❸ Why is she here?

7. ⓐ 왜 그 책을 사지 않았니?
   ⓑ 도서관에서 그것을[그 책을] 빌리는 건 어때?

8. When, How many, six classes, What, English

9. She has nine pets.

Chapter 8

문장의 종류

8.1. 부가의문문 P.129

A.
❶ she
❷ don't
❸ doesn't
❹ does
❺ shall
❻ do
❼ isn't
❽ will
❾ doesn't
❿ isn't
⓫ will
⓬ can
⓭ wasn't
⓮ shall

B.
❶ aren't you, I am
❷ will they, they won't
❸ can't she, she can't
❹ doesn't he, he does
❺ wasn't he, he was
❻ won't we, we will
❼ does he, he doesn't
❽ didn't it, it didn't

8.2. 부정의문문과 선택의문문 P.131

A.
❶ Won't
❷ Don't
❸ Doesn't

B.

① No, I don't want to go to a mountain.

② Yes, I am going to see a movie.

③ No, I didn't have dinner.

C.

① Do you like summer or winter?

② Will you go to the mountain or the river?

8.3. 감탄문

P.133

A.

① How

② What

③ What

④ How

⑤ What

⑥ What

⑦ How

⑧ How

⑨ What

⑩ What

⑪ How

⑫ What

⑬ What

⑭ What

B.

① smart Jane is

② honest the boy is

③ interesting my first trip was

④ an adorable doll it is

⑤ colorful pants she wears

⑥ an old house it is

⑦ a beautiful flower this is

⑧ young that singer is

⑨ a small calendar he has

⑩ a long tail that dog has

8.4. 명령문

P.135

A.

① come

② Don't

③ don't

④ Be

⑤ Don't

⑥ not

⑦ Never

B.

① Change the rule.

② Please speak clearly.

③ Turn off the computer.

④ Don't[Never] be scared of the dog.

⑤ Don't[Never] make a noise.

C.

① Let's not

② Let's not

③ Let's

④ Let's

⑤ Let's

단원평가 　 몸풀기

P.136

> 1. ①　2. ③　3. ③　4. ⑤　5. ③　6. ③　7. ⑤
>
> 8. ④　9. ③　10. ③

1. ① 부정 명령문은 「Don't + 동사원형」이므로 Don't be late for school.이 알맞다.

2. 부정 명령문은 「Don't + 동사원형」의 형태로 쓰는데 shy는 형용사이므로 Don't be shy.로 써야 한다.

3. A는 수요일에 영화를 보러가자고 제안하고 있고, B는 목요일에 시험이 있다고 대답하고 있으므로 거절하는 표현이 가장 적절하다.

4. ⑤ 날씨가 덥다는 사람에게 뜨거운 것을 먹으라는 내용

의 대화는 어색하다.

5. 부가의문문의 형태에 상관없이 축구를 좋아하는 것이 맞으므로 긍정의 대답을 한다.

6. 주절이 긍정의 be동사 과거 문장이므로 wasn't와 주어의 대명사를 이용해 부가의문문을 만든다.

7. what 감탄문은 「What (a/an) 형용사 + 명사 (+ 주어 + 동사)!」로, how 감탄문은 「How + 형용사/부사 + 주어 + 동사!」의 형태로 쓴다.

8. 부정의문문은 부정형으로 의문문을 시작한다. You are happy.(너는 행복하다) → Aren't you happy?(너는 행복하지 않니?)

9. ① Can't she sing?
   ② Doesn't she drive a car?
   ④ Don't you like soda?
   ⑤ Aren't you sleepy?

10. 부정의문문은 질문에 상관없이 긍정이면 긍정의 대답을, 부정이면 부정의 대답을 쓴다.

단원평가 실전대비 P.137

1. ④ 2. ① 3. ⑤ 4. ② 5. do, don't
6. Yes, I do 7. ①, ④ 8. ② 9. ③ 10. ①
11. ⑤ 12. ④ 13. ① 14. Which, or 15.
Don't[Never] 16. ❶ is it ❷ don't they 17. ③
18. ③ 19. ③ 20. ③

1. 부정명령문은 must not으로 바꿔서 표현할 수 있다.

2. ② Don't be careful.
   ③ Turn on the light.
   ④ Be kind to your friends.
   ⑤ Don't talk with your friend.

3. 부정의문문은 의문문의 형태에 상관없이 긍정이면 긍정의 대답을, 부정이면 부정의 대답을 해야 한다.

4. ① is she ③ did they ④ wasn't she ⑤ can't you

5. 일반동사의 부정의문문은 질문의 형태에 상관없이 대답이 긍정이면 「Yes, 주어 + do/does.」, 부정이면 「No, 주어 + don't/doesn't.」로 한다.

6. 일반동사의 부정의문문에 긍정으로 답할 때는 질문의 형태에 상관없이 「Yes, 주어 + do/does.」를 쓴다.

7. ② Plant tulips!
   ③ Don't be late for school!
   ⑤ Jane, watch out!

8. 긍정이면 「Yes, 주어 + can.」, 부정이면 「No, 주어 + can't.」로 대답한다.

9. 부가의문문이 don't you?이므로 주절에 일반동사가 와야 한다.

10. 형용사의 명령문은 형용사 앞에 Be를 쓰고, 일반동사의 부정명령문은 동사 앞에 Don't[Never]를 쓴다.

11. ⑤ How scary the movie was!

12. 주어가 You인 일반동사의 긍정 문장이므로 don't you, 주어가 3인칭 단수 사물인 be동사의 긍정 문장이므로 isn't it을 부가의문문으로 쓸 수 있다.

13. ①번은 How, 나머지는 What이 들어가야 한다.

14. 선택의문문은 which와 or를 사용하여 만들 수 있다.

15. 모두 영화관에서 하지 말아야 할 행동들이므로 앞에 Don't[Never]를 써서 부정명령문을 만들어야 한다.

16. ❶ 주어가 3인칭 단수 사물이고 be동사의 부정 문장이므로 is it을 쓴다.
    ❷ 주어가 3인칭 복수이고 일반 동사의 긍정 문장이므로 don't they를 쓴다.

17. 일반동사의 부정명령문은 Don't[Never]로 시작한다.

18. ① You can keep a secret, can't you?
    ② She is a teacher, isn't she?
    ④ He doesn't like it, does he?
    ⑤ Sue can't cook well, can she?

19. 주어가 3인칭 단수 남자이고 be동사의 긍정 문장이므로 isn't he, 주어가 You인 일반동사의 긍정 문장이므로 don't you를 부가의문문으로 써야 한다.

20. A: Jim은 음악을 좋아해, 그렇지 않니?
    B: 응, 맞아. 그는 모든 종류의 음악을 할 수 있어.

---

1. ④　2. ②　3. ①　4. ③　5. ①　6. ②　7. ③
8. **❶** Do not　**❷** Be　9. ②　10. ②　11. ⑤
12. ②　13. How kind he is!　14. **❶** Yes,
can　**❷** No, am not　**❸** No, didn't

---

1. That's surprising.(그거 놀랍다.)과 비슷한 의미의 문장
은 I can't believe it!(믿을 수 없어!)이다.
   ① 조심해! = 조심해!
   ② 속도를 줄여! = 빨리 달리지 마!
   ③ 그건 맞지 않아. = 그건 틀렸어.
   ⑤ 너는 그곳에 가야 해. = 너는 그곳에 가야 해.

2. 주어진 단어를 이용하여 문장을 완성하면 Cover your
nose and don't take the elevator.이므로 문장에서
★에 들어가는 단어는 don't이다.

3. 우리가 종이를 낭비하는 것에 대한 환경보호 실천방안으
로 '나무들을 베자.'는 알맞지 않다.
   ② 우리는 많은 음식을 낭비한다.
   ⇒ 접시에 있는 음식을 다 먹자.
   ③ 우리는 종종 비닐봉투를 사용한다.
   ⇒ 종이 봉투를 사용하자.
   ④ 자동차들이 너무 많다.
   ⇒ 자전거를 타자.
   ⑤ 우리는 너무 많은 쓰레기를 만든다.
   ⇒ 분리수거를 하려 노력하자.

4. what 감탄문은 「What + (a/an) 형용사 + 명사 (+ 주어
+ 동사)!」로 how 감탄문은 「How + 형용사/부사 + 주어
+ 동사!」로 쓴다.

5. ① The box is Minho's, isn't it?이 올바른 문장이다.

6. ②번은 '그녀는 몇 살이니?'라는 뜻이며 나머지는 '그녀
는 나이가 매우 많다.'라는 의미이다.

7. ① He is so handsome. ⇒ How handsome he is!
   ② It's a very sunny day. ⇒ What a sunny day
   it is!
   ④ This is a really nice present. ⇒ What a nice
   present this is!
   ⑤ These are great jeans! ⇒ What great jeans
   these are!

8. **❶** 일반동사의 부정명령문은 「Do not[Don't] + 동사원

형」으로 쓴다.
   ❷ 형용사 또는 명사의 명령문은 「Be + 형용사/명사」
   로 쓴다.

9. 명령문의 부가의문문은 will you?로 쓴다.

10. 지니는 내일 학교를 가야 하기 때문에 빈칸에는 '늦게까
지 깨어있지 말라.' 또는 '일찍 자라.' 등의 표현들이 알맞
다.
   ① 일찍 잠자리에 들거라.
   ② 늦게까지 깨어 있어라, 지니.
   ③ 너무 늦게까지 깨어있지 말아라.
   ④ 꼭 일찍 잠자리에 들어라.
   ⑤ 내일을 위해 잠을 충분히 자거라.

11. 친구의 휴대 전화의 벨이 계속 울려 방해를 받고 괴로워
하고 있는 상황이므로, 친구에게 '휴대 전화를 꺼 달라'라
고 말하는 명령문이 알맞다.
   ① 공부를 더 열심히 해라.
   ② 점심을 먹으러 가자.
   ③ 휴대 전화를 켜줘.
   ④ 일어나서 나가라.
   ⑤ 휴대 전화를 꺼줘.

12. 긍정명령문은 동사원형으로 시작하고 부정명령문은
「Don't + 동사원형 ~」으로 쓴다.

13. what 감탄문은 「What + (a/an) 형용사 + 명사 (+ 주어
+ 동사)!」로 how 감탄문은 「How + 형용사/부사 + 주어
+ 동사!」로 쓴다.

14. 부정의문문의 대답은 질문의 형태에 상관없이 긍정이면
긍정의 대답을, 부정이면 부정의 대답을 한다.

1. ❶ Don't eat all the food on your plate.
   ❷ Put your arms on the table.
   ❸ Don't eat too fast.

2. ❶ Don't be late.
   ❷ Don't make a noise.[Be quiet.]
   ❸ Don't use the cell phone (during the class).
   ❹ Don't forget to bring your homework.

3. ❶ run ❷ quiet ❸ Don't ❹ swim

4. ❶ didn't they ❷ doesn't she ❸ can't he

5. ❶ beautiful this flower is, a beautiful flower this is
   ❷ wonderful these toys are, wonderful toys these are

6. ❶ You like to listen to music, don't you?
   ❷ You are a good dancer, aren't you?[You aren't a good dancer, are you?]
   ❸ Susan can sing very well, can't she?[Susan can't sing very well, can she?]
   ❹ You did your homework, didn't you?

7. ❶ aren't you
   ❷ aren't you
   ❸ will you
   ❹ will you
   ❺ can you
   ❻ didn't he
   ❼ shall we

8. How[What] about, Let's eat out

Chapter 9

문장의 형태

9.1. 문장의 형식 P.147

A.
   ❶ I wanted to see a movie.
   ❷ This gift shop is very popular.
   ❸ My favorite season is summer.
   ❹ He has no money.
   ❺ The man in the park looks handsome.
   ❻ Mary found the book boring.

B.
   ❶ I always get up early.
   ❷ John goes to Hawaii every summer.
   ❸ The girl with a skirt stands next to me.
   ❹ My parents drink soda.
   ❺ He walked to school yesterday.
   ❻ This soup smells great.

C.
   ❶ We pay electric bill.
   ❷ I bought some new shoes.
   ❸ You must wear your seat belt.
   ❹ Susan met her old friend last weekend.
   ❺ He knows my name and number.
   ❻ Boys play soccer in the yard.

D.
   ❶ I am a student.
   ❷ The class is boring.
   ❸ The news made us shocked.
   ❹ My mom made me clean the room.
   ❺ I found Jolie famous.
   ❻ She became a model.

E.

① <u>She</u> <u>arrives</u> at the museum. 1형식
   주어   동사

② <u>Ted</u> <u>collects</u> <u>a lot of stamps</u> as a hobby. 3형식
   주어   동사   목적어

③ <u>Her explanation</u> <u>sounds</u> <u>easy</u>. 2형식
      주어   동사 보어

④ <u>He</u> <u>saw</u> <u>John</u> <u>ride a bike</u> in the park. 5형식
  주어동사 목적어   보어

9.2. 감각동사 + 형용사   P.149

A.

① healthy
② looks like
③ interesting
④ terrible
⑤ looks like
⑥ sweet
⑦ beautiful

B.

① look heavy
② smells strong
③ feels soft
④ looks interesting
⑤ tastes fresh

C.

① smart
② different
③ feels like
④ look
⑤ sleepy

9.3. 수여동사 + 직접목적어 + 간접목적어 P.151

A.

① the story to him
② a favor of you
③ a concert ticket for me
④ ramen for me

B.

① I gave my friend two postcards.
② Grace taught children English at the community center.
③ My father bought my mother a diamond ring.

C.

① Give him some more milk
② make me some sandwiches
③ pass it to me

9.4. 동사 + 목적어 + 목적격보어   P.153

A.

① happy
② warm
③ to open
④ wag
⑤ sit
⑥ let
⑦ interesting

B.

① 나는 불렀다 / 그를 / 바보로
② 그녀의 어머니는 만들었다 / 그녀를 / 유명한 음악가로
③ 나는 믿는다 / 그녀를 / 아주 친절하다고
④ 우리는 칠했다 / 문을 / 다른 색깔로

C.

① call him a coward
② made her sleepy
③ the door open
④ saw you dance with him

1. ⑤　2. ⑤　3. ③　4. ④　5. ①　6. ③　7. ①
8. ❶ happy　❷ happiness　9. ②　10. ②

1. 감각동사 다음에는 형용사를 써야 한다.

2. ⑤ 감각동사 다음에는 형용사를 써야 하는데 loudly는 부사이므로 어법상 옳지 않다.

3. 감각동사 다음에는 형용사를 써야 하므로 선택지에서 형용사를 찾아야 한다. ③번을 제외한 나머지는 모두 부사이다.

4. 4형식 문장에서 3형식으로 전환 시 간접목적어 앞에 for를 쓰는 동사는 buy[bought]이다.

5. 주어진 문장의 빈칸은 뒤에 간접목적어와 직접목적어가 이어서 나오므로 4형식 수여동사가 들어갈 자리이다. ①번은 수여동사가 아니다.

6. 간접목적어 자리에는 명사 또는 인칭대명사의 목적격을 쓴다.

7. 선생님의 생김새를 묻고 있는 질문에 대한 답을 찾아야 한다.

8. ❶ 감각동사 다음에는 형용사를 써야 하므로 happy가 알맞다.
❷ 4형식 문장에서 직접목적어 자리에는 명사를 써야 하므로 happiness가 알맞다.

9. 빈칸 뒤에 목적어와 동사원형의 목적격보어가 이어지므로 사역동사가 빈칸에 들어간다.

10. want는 5형식 문장으로 쓰일 때 목적격보어 자리에 to부정사를 써야 한다.

1. ④　2. ①　3. ⑤　4. ①　5. ④　6. ④　7. ③
8. ③, ④　9. ②　10. ①　11. ②　12. ④　13. ②
14. ⑤　15. ①, ⑤　16. ④　17. ①　18. ③　19. ①
20. ①, ④

1. 학교 첫날에 대한 감정을 물어보고 있으므로 빈칸에는 감정을 나타내는 형용사가 적절하다. I feel kind.(나는 친절함을 느껴.)는 질문에 대한 대답으로 어색하다.

2. ① 감각동사 다음에는 형용사를 쓸 수 있으므로 It tastes sweet.이 올바른 문장이다.

3. 감각동사 다음에는 형용사만 쓸 수 있다. 보기 중 형용사로만 짝지어진 것은 ⑤번 뿐이다.

4. 「감각동사 + like + 명사」: '~처럼 보인다/냄새가 난다/느껴진다/맛이 난다/들린다'

5. ④ The music sounds sleepy.

6. 빈칸 뒤에 간접목적어와 직접목적어가 있으므로 빈칸에는 수여동사가 들어가야 한다. ④번은 수여동사가 아니다.

7. 4형식 문장은 「주어 + 동사 + 간접목적어 + 직접목적어」의 형태로 쓴다.

8. ③ Minho sent an e-mail to his friends.
④ John's mother made dinner for his son.

9. ① She had a serious look on his face.
= She looks serious.
③ Because he failed the test, his voice was sad.
= He failed the test. So his voice sounded sad.
④ Sam bought Anne a present.
= Sam bought a present for Anne.
⑤ Mom made me a pretty doll.
= Mom made a pretty doll for me.

10. ①번은 3형식, 나머지는 4형식 문장이다.

11. ② The man showed nice shoes to Amy.

12. 4형식을 3형식으로 전환할 때 간접목적어 앞에 ask는 of, show는 to, buy는 for를 쓴다.

13. ② A contest makes me nervous.

14. 주어진 문장과 ⑤번은 3형식, 나머지는 4형식이다.

15. 4형식을 3형식으로 전환할 때 tell, send는 전치사 to를 사용한다.

16. 첫 빈칸은 부사 자리이므로 happily가 올바르다. 두 번째 빈칸은 감각동사 뒤이므로 형용사 자리이다. 마지막

은 '~처럼 보인다'라는 의미로 look like an angel을 써야 한다.

17. ① 4형식을 3형식으로 전환할 때 동사 make는 전치사 for를 사용한다. 나머지 동사들은 전치사 to를 사용한다.

18. ③번은 4형식 문장이고, 나머지는 5형식 문장이다.

19. make는 5형식으로 쓰일 때 목적격보어 자리에 동사원형이 온다.

20. 지각동사의 목적격보어 자리에는 동사원형 또는 분사가 온다.

식이다. ①, ⑤: 5형식, ③, ④: 3형식

8. tell은 목적격보어로 「to + 동사원형」을 쓰며 부정은 to 앞에 not을 쓴다.

9. ③번의 두 문장의 feel은 '~하게 느끼다'로 의미가 같다.
① : ~이다/~에 있다, ② : ~이 되다/어울리다, ④ : 기르다/~해지다, ⑤ : ~되다/돌다

10. ③ They let us go outside to play soccer.

단원평가   고난도   P.158

1. ③   2. ③   3. ⑤   4. ④   5. ①   6. ❶ ⑤   ❷
④   ❸ ①   ❹ ②   ❺ ③   7. ②   8. not to touch
9. ③   10. ③

1. 지나: The coffee smells good.
   효섭: Her perfume smells nice.
   진석: The music sounds beautiful.

2. a, b, c, e: look / d, f: look like

3. ① She made me this cake.
   ⇒ She made this cake for me.
   ② You can ask him this question.
   ⇒ You can ask this question of him.
   ③ Ms. Brown can teach us science.
   ⇒ Ms. Brown can teach science to us.
   ④ Dad will send mom some flowers.
   ⇒ Dad will send some flowers to mom.

4. ④번은 동사가 있는 완전한 문장이므로 빈칸에 be동사가 필요 없다.

5. ② My grandfather passes a pen to me.
   ③ She bought a new computer for me.
   ④ Grandma made me a birthday cake.
   ⑤ He taught his children Korean.

6. ❶ ⑤: 5형식, ❷ ④: 4형식, ❸ ①: 1형식, ❹ ②: 2형식, ❺ ③: 3형식

7. 주어진 문장과 ②번은 make가 수여동사로 쓰여진 4형

서술형 대비학습   P.160

1. ❶ tired ❷ sounds like ❸ tasted

2. gives lots of stress to

3. ❶ sent his mom a card
   ❷ made a cake for her mom

4. ❶ let ❷ had[made]

5. ❶ Suji sent her some cookies.
   ❷ John's dad showed John many photos.
   ❸ Please get me some water[get some water for me].

6. ❶ Bring me two cups of coffee.
   ❷ They ask me many questions of me.

7. ❶ to John ❷ for his wife

8. ❶ smoothly → smooth
   ❷ share → to share
   ❸ to study → study

9. ❶ walking a dog ❷ barking loudly at night

10. ❶ 미나는 책을 쉽게 찾았다.
    ❷ 미나는 책이 쉽다는 것을 알았다.

11. ❶ Jenny gave useful information to me.
    ❷ Jim's uncle sent a gift to him.
    ❸ My uncle bought a bike for me.
    ❹ Ms. Kim teaches math to us.

12. ❶ He wrote his teacher a card.
    ❷ Father cooked us dinner.
    ❸ Helen bought him skates.

13. ❶ to be quiet in the classroom
    ❷ to take care of his sister

Chapter 10

형용사

10.1. 형용사의 역할 P.165

A.

1. 서술
2. 서술
3. 한정
4. 서술
5. 한정
6. 한정
7. 서술
8. 서술

B.

1. something spicy
2. these two lovely birds
3. new novel is interesting
4. an important meeting today

C.

1. much
2. much
3. much
4. much
5. a few
6. a few

10.2. 부사의 역할 P.167

A.

1. carefully
2. well
3. quickly
4. fast
5. newly
6. truly
7. easily
8. happily
9. greatly
10. wonderfully

B.

1. 형
2. 형
3. 부
4. 부
5. 형

C.

1. 동사
2. 형용사
3. 부사
4. 동사
5. 문장

10.3. 빈도부사 P.169

A.

1. She is always honest.
2. Minho always makes fun of me.
3. My dad usually comes home late in the evening.
4. I usually sleep for about 8 hours every night.
5. She can't often sleep well.
6. I never break my promise.
7. I seldom drink coffee at night.
8. I will never miss the chance.
9. He often feels tired in the morning.
10. I sometimes hang out with my friends after school.

10.4. 비교급/최상급 변화 P.171

A.

1. smaller – smallest
2. larger – largest
3. busier – busiest
4. bigger – biggest
5. better – best
6. more – most
7. easier – easiest
8. better– best
9. hotter – hottest
10. more – most
11. less – least
12. worse – worst
13. more useful – most useful
14. more popular – most popular
15. more interesting – most interesting
16. happier – happiest
17. more beautiful – most beautiful
18. more precious – most precious
19. fatter – fattest
20. heavier – heaviest

B.

1. colder
2. shorter
3. more beautiful
4. more expensive
5. biggest
6. highest
7. farthest
8. more talkative

10.5. 비교표현 (원급, 비교급)   P.173

A.

1. tall
2. cold
3. big

4. not as
5. as

B.

1. Hailey, Jim
2. bigger
3. Brain's (pencil)
4. more interesting

C.

1. shorter, shorter
2. The more, the fatter
3. cooler and cooler
4. better and better

10.6. 비교표현 (최상급)   P.175

A.

1. busiest
2. boys
3. of
4. more important
5. friends
6. in
7. the most beautiful
8. the most delicious
9. the most popular
10. anyone

B.

1. as famous as[more famous than]
2. more useful
3. more difficult
4. the most precious
5. better than

> 1. ①   2. ①   3. ①   4. ②   5. kind boy   6. ④
> 7. ①   8. ①   9. ①   10. ④

1. 빈도부사는 일반동사 앞에 위치한다.

2. fast는 형용사와 부사의 형태가 같다.

3. ①번의 형용사는 서술적 용법이고 나머지는 한정적 용법이다.

4. 최상급이 들어가야 하는 자리이므로 비교급인 ②번은 알맞지 않다.

5. 형용사 kind는 서술적 용법과 한정적 용법으로 모두 쓸수 있다.

6. a lot of는 many 또는 much로 바꿔 쓸 수 있는데 bread는 셀 수 없는 명사이므로 much가 알맞다.

7. 빈도부사는 조동사의 뒤에 위치하므로(He will never come back.) 세 번째로 오는 것은 never이다.

8. 유나는 학교에 전혀 걸어서 가지 않으므로 이를 나타내는 빈도부사는 never가 알맞다.

9. ② Does she <u>sometimes</u> watch TV?
   ③ He is <u>often</u> late for school.
   ④ They <u>always</u> go to church.
   ⑤ I can <u>never</u> stay up late.

10. ① Soccer is the <u>most exciting</u> game.
    ② Today was the <u>hottest</u> day of the year.
    ③ This book is <u>thicker</u> than that book.
    ⑤ The blue bag is <u>heavier</u> than the red one.

> 1. ①, ⑤   2. ④   3. ④   4. ③   5. ⑤   6. ④
> 7. Sam is seventeen years old.   8. ③   9. ⑤
> 10. ③   11. ④   12. ②   13. ②   14. ②   15. ⑤
> 16. ②   17. ④   18. ⑤   19. ②   20. ②

1. 형용사 cold를 꾸며줄 부사가 필요하다.

2. 형용사가 2개 이상인 경우는 「지시형용사 + 수량형용사 (수, 양, 정도) + 성질형용사(성질, 상태, 모양)」의 순서로 쓴다.

3. 비교급을 강조할 때 부사 much, far, even, still, a lot 을 쓴다.

4. ① Andrew는 Linda보다 키가 더 크다.
   ② Linda는 Andrew보다 나이가 더 어리다.
   ④ Linda는 Jim보다 몸무게가 더 많이 나간다.
   ⑤ Jim은 셋 중에 나이가 가장 어리다.

5. ⑤ –ous로 끝나는 형용사는 앞에 more, most를 붙여 비교급과 최상급을 만든다.

6. ④ 학생들은 배드민턴보다 테니스를 더 좋아한다.

7. Susan은 14살이며 Jack은 Susan보다 한 살이 더 많고 Sam은 Jack보다 2살이 더 많기 때문에 Sam의 나이는 17살이다.

8. ③ Jack is the <u>strongest</u> boy in our class.

9. ① Do you <u>always</u> wear pants?
   ② I <u>don't[never]</u> catch a cold in winter.
   ③ He <u>usually</u> comes home late in the evening.
   ④ We <u>sometimes</u> play badminton together.

10. ③번의 부사는 형용사를 꾸며주고 나머지 선택지의 부사들은 동사를 꾸며준다.

11. ④ I practiced singing very <u>hard</u>.

12. ① I am never late for school.
    나는 절대 학교에 늦지 않는다.
    ③ I usually play computer games at night.
    나는 보통 밤에 컴퓨터 게임을 한다.
    ④ He is always kind to me.
    그는 항상 내게 친절하다.
    ⑤ Anna often eats breakfast.
    Anna는 종종 아침을 먹는다.

13. ② 부사는 명사를 꾸며줄 수 없으므로 She is a <u>good</u> dancer.로 고쳐야 한다.

14. ② She is <u>more powerful</u> than Iron Man.

15. ⑤ Bob's homework is not as much as Jim's.
    Bob의 숙제는 Jim의 숙제만큼 많지 않다.
    ≠ Bob has more homework than Jim has. Bob 은 Jim보다 더 많은 숙제를 가지고 있다.

16. '나의 여동생은 남동생보다 더 무겁다.'라는 문장은 ② '나의 남동생은 여동생보다 더 가볍다.'와 같은 의미이다.

17. ④ hardly의 의미는 '거의(좀처럼) ~하지 않는'이다.

18. 셀 수 있는 명사(people)와 셀 수 없는 명사(fun)를 다 꾸며줄 수 있는 표현은 a lot of이다.

19. ②번은 any, 나머지는 some이 들어가야 한다.

20. She is smarter than I. 그녀는 나보다 더 똑똑하다. = I am not as smart as her. 나는 그녀만큼 똑똑하지 않다.

단원평가 고난도 P.180

> 1. ❶ always ❷ often ❸ never 2. ③ 3. ④
> 4. ② 5. ① 6. ② 7. ❶ Much ❷ sweeter
> 8. ② 9. ③

1. 수학공부는 매일 하기 때문에 always, 집 청소는 주 3일 하기 때문에 often, 지각은 한 번도 안 하기 때문에 never로 표현할 수 있다.

2. ③ We played better than they. 우리는 그들보다 더 경기를 잘했다.
   ≠ They played as well as us. 그들은 우리만큼 경기를 잘했다.

3. ④ Her class usually finished at three o'clock.을 보면 수업이 대체로 3시에 끝난다는 것을 알 수 있다.

4. A. I usually get up at 7:00.
   D. I never exercise.
   G. I am never late.

5. large의 비교급은 larger, heavy의 비교급은 heavier, big의 비교급은 bigger이다.

6. 7명의 학생들이 치킨을 좋아하기 때문에 반 이상이 치킨을 좋아한다는 ②번은 적절하지 않다.

7. ❶ 비교급을 강조할 때는 부사 much를 쓴다.
   ❷ 비교급 문장이므로 sweeter를 쓴다.

8. hard는 형용사로 '딱딱한, 어려운', 부사로는 '열심히'라는 의미를 가진다.

9. ① present 아빠는 나에게 선물로 멋진 전화를 사 주셨다.
② waist 그는 허리 둘레에 끈을 묶었다.
③ 오프라 윈프리의 토크쇼는 내가 가장 좋아하는 프로그램이다.
④ useful 나는 이 세탁기가 매우 유용하다고 생각한다.
⑤ excited 모두가 내일 소풍의 대해 매우 신나있다.

서술형 대비학습 P.182

1. (예시)
   ❶ I sometimes go to the library after school.
   ❷ I always go to the movies on Sunday.
   ❸ I usually listen to K-pop in my free time.

2. ❶ the cheapest
   ❷ the biggest
   ❸ the most expensive
   ❹ smaller than

3. ❶ always ❷ never ❸ usually

4. ❶ the tallest ❷ the heaviest

5. ❶ The heaviest man in the world is Mr. Uribe.
   ❷ The longest river in the world is the Amazon River.

Chapter 11
to부정사와 동명사

11.1. to부정사의 명사적 용법　　P.185

A.
1. to drink a glass of juice
2. to wear a coat
3. to take a rest
4. to eat a slice of pizza

B.
1. will learn how to make pizza
2. how to eat sushi
3. what to buy for the party

C.
1. To cook[Cooking] Japanese food
2. how to take good pictures
3. what to eat

D.
1. James likes to drive on Sundays.
2. I hope to have a hamburger for lunch.
3. Julia likes to watch fashion shows on TV.

11.2. to부정사의 형용사적 용법　　P.187

A.
1. to believe
2. something warm
3. games to enjoy
4. to help
5. nothing fresh to eat

B.
1. I have a lot of homework to do.
2. There are many places to visit in Korea.
3. Give me something cold to drink, please.
4. Gyeongju was a nice place to visit.
5. Grandpa has funny stories to tell you.
6. Suji got the dentist's bill to pay.

11.3. to부정사의 부사적 용법　　P.189

A.
1. ①
2. ④
3. ⑤
4. ③
5. ②

B.
1. 목적, 그들은 산책을 하러 공원에 갔다.
2. 목적, 나는 버스를 잡기 위해 서둘러야 한다.
3. 원인, 밤에 전화해서 미안합니다.
4. 결과, 그는 아들이 성공하는 것을 볼 때까지 살았다.
5. 형용사/부사 수식, 이 책은 읽기 어렵다.
6. 원인, 나는 그 소식을 듣고 화가 났다.
7. 형용사/부사 수식, 일본어는 배우기 쉽다.

11.4. 동명사의 역할　　P.191

A.
1. Getting[To get]
2. writing[to write]
3. Playing[To play]
4. teaching[to teach]
5. watching

B.
1. to write
2. smoking
3. crying
4. playing
5. opening

⑥ to ski

⑦ to plant

⑧ to drink

⑨ to buy

⑩ helping

⑪ finishing

⑫ to get

⑬ making

⑭ to take

단원평가 몸풀기 P.192

1. listening 2. ④ 3. ③ 4. ② 5. how to swim 6. ② 7. ④ 8. ② 9. ❶ to buy ❷ to buy ❸ to buy ❹ to buy 10. to do

1. 문장의 주격보어와 enjoy의 목적어로 쓰일 수 있는 것은 동명사이다.

2. like는 목적어로 to부정사와 동명사를 모두 쓸 수 있다.

3. like와 want는 모두 to부정사를 목적어로 쓸 수 있다.

4. want는 목적어로 to부정사를 쓴다.

5. 「how to + 동사원형」은 '~하는 방법, 어떻게 ~할지'라는 의미를 가진다.

6. need는 목적어로 to부정사를 쓴다.

7. 「how to + 동사원형」은 '~하는 방법, 어떻게 ~할지'라는 의미를 가진다.

8. 제안하는 표현인 How about 뒤에는 동명사를 쓴다.

9. want 뒤에는 「to + 동사원형」의 형태인 to부정사를 써야 한다.

10. 「to + 동사원형」이 명사를 뒤에서 꾸며 주면 '~할'로 해석할 수 있다.

단원평가 실전대비 P.193

1. ① 2. ② 3. ④ 4. where to go 5. ④
6. ❶ Learing ❷ playing ❸ dancing 7. ④
8. ② 9. ❶ what to eat ❷ when to start 10.
❶ when leaving → when to leave
❷ anything to wear warm → anything warm to wear 11. ③ 12. ❶ cold to drink ❷ to help 13. ④ 14. ② 15. ④ 16. ④ 17. ④ 18. To eat fast food often 19. ③ 20. ② 21. ②

1. 보기와 ①번: to부정사의 명사적 용법
   ②번: be going to, ③번: to부정사의 형용사적 용법
   ④, ⑤번: to부정사의 부사적 용법

2. 「in order to + 동사원형」은 「to + 동사원형」 또는 「so as to + 동사원형」으로 바꿔 쓸 수 있다.

3. ① I hope to see you soon.
   ② To ride a bike is fun.
   ③ To do your best is very important.
   ⑤ His hobby is to go to the park.

4. 「where to + 동사원형」: '어디로[에서] ~할지'

5. ④ I like to go[going] to the movies.

6. ❶ 문장의 주어로 쓰인 to부정사는 동명사로 바꾸어 쓸 수 있다.
   ❷ start는 to부정사와 동명사를 모두 목적어로 쓸 수 있다.
   ❸ 전치사 다음에는 동명사를 써야 한다.

7. want는 to부정사를 목적어로 쓴다.

8. ② want는 to부정사만 목적어로 쓸 수 있다.

9. 「의문사 to + 동사원형」은 「의문사 + 주어 + should + 동사원형」으로 바꿔 쓸 수 있다.

10. ❶ 「의문사 + to 동사원형」
    ❷ 「-thing으로 끝나는 대명사 + 형용사 + to부정사」

11. 주어진 문장과 ③번의 to부정사는 명사적 용법으로 주격보어로 쓰였다. ①, ⑤번: 주어, ②, ④번: 목적어

12. ❶ –thing으로 끝나는 대명사는 형용사가 뒤에서 수식하며, 그 뒤에 to부정사를 쓴다.
❷ to부정사의 형용사적 용법은 명사를 뒤에서 꾸며준다.

13. 주어가 긴 경우 주어를 뒤로 보내고 가주어 It을 문장의 앞에 쓴다.

14. 「too + 형용사/부사 + to 동사원형」: '너무 …해서 ~할 수 없다'

15. 「too + 형용사/부사 + to 동사원형」은 「so + 형용사/부사 + that + 주어 can't ~」로 바꿔 쓸 수 있다. 주절의 시제가 과거이므로 couldn't를 선택해야 한다.

16. 「Don't forget to + 동사원형」: '(미래에) ~할 것을 잊지 마라'

17. mind는 동명사를 목적어로 취하는 동사이다.

18. to부정사는 주어 자리에 쓸 수 있으며 '~하는 것은'이라고 해석한다.

19. hope는 to부정사를 목적어로 취하는 동사이다.

20. enjoy는 동명사를 목적어로 취하는 동사이다.

21. 「too + 형용사/부사 + to 동사원형」: '너무 …해서 ~할 수 없다'
「형용사/부사 + enough + to부정사」: '~할 정도로 충분히 …한'

단원평가 고난도 P.196

1. ③ 2. ③ 3. ⑤ 4. ② 5. ③ 6. ❶ going ❷ playing ❸ Reading[To read]
7. ❶ chair to sit on ❷ pen to write with
8. ⑤ 9. ② 10. ❶ on ❷ in ❸ with 11. ②
12. ③

---

1. 명사적 용법으로 목적어 자리에 있는 to부정사를 찾아야 한다.
ⓐ I'm happy <u>to be</u> here tonight. – 부사적 용법: 감정의 원인
ⓑ I got up early <u>to climb</u> a mountain. – 부사적 용법: 목적
ⓓ Would you like something <u>to drink</u>? – 형용사

적 용법

2. ③번은 명사적 용법으로 쓰였다. 나머지는 부사적 용법으로 쓰였다.

3. look forward to의 to는 전치사이므로 뒤에 명사 또는 동명사를 써야 한다.

4. 보기와 ②번의 to부정사는 형용사적 용법으로 쓰였다.

5. '너무 …해서 ~할 수 없다'는 「too + 형용사/부사 + to 동사원형」 또는 「so + 형용사/부사 + that + 주어 can't ~」 구문으로 표현할 수 있다.

6. ❶ about은 전치사이므로 동명사를 목적어로 쓴다. 따라서 going이 알맞다. (go to see a movie 영화를 보러 가다)
❷ enjoy는 목적어로 동명사를 쓰므로 playing이 알맞다. (play soccer 축구를 하다)
❸ 문장의 주어 자리에는 동명사 또는 to부정사를 쓸 수 있다. (read comic books 만화책을 읽다)

7. '앉아야 할 의자'는 chair to sit on, '쓸 펜'은 pen to write with로 표현할 수 있다.

8. 동명사와 to부정사를 둘 다 목적어로 취할 수 있는 동사는 start, begin, like, love, continue 등이 있다. enjoy는 동명사만 목적어로 쓸 수 있다.

9. to부정사의 부정은 「not[never] + to부정사」로 표현한다.

10. ❶ '쓸 종이' = paper to write on
❷ '살 집' = a house to live in
❸ '같이 살 룸메이트' = a roommate to live with

11. 체육관에 가는 이유로 가장 알맞은 것은 ② '탁구를 치기 위해서'이다.

12. '너무 ~해서 …할 수 없다'의 뜻은 「too + 형용사/부사 + to부정사」로 나타낸다.

1. (예시)
   ❶ I want to go to see a movie.
   ❷ I want to go to China.
   ❸ I want to throw a birthday party.

2. **❶** to learn English
   ❷ to be at home alone
   ❸ to arrive on time

3. **❶** started to cry[crying]
   ❷ stopped reading a newspaper
   ❸ Thank you for inviting

4. **❶** love watch → love to watch[love watching]
   ❷ homework finishing → homework to finish

5. **❶** I want a book to read.
   ❷ My hometown is a good place to visit.

Chapter 12

접속사

12.1. 등위 접속사 and, but, or, so   P.201

A.
❶ and
❷ or
❸ so
❹ and
❺ so
❻ or
❼ or
❽ or

B.
❶ or → and
❷ but → and
❸ but → so
❹ and → or
❺ and → or

C.
❶ or, and
❷ and, or

12.2. 종속 접속사 (때)   P.203

A.
❶ ③
❷ ①
❸ ②

B.
❶ When she was going to the museum
❷ after it snowed
❸ while he was eating
❹ until I die

⑤ when he was ten years old

⑥ before the train starts

12.3. 종속 접속사 (이유/조건)　　　P.205

A.
① because

② If

③ if

④ because

⑤ see

⑥ because of

B.
① b

② d

③ c

④ a

⑤ e

12.4. 종속 접속사 that　　　P.207

A.
① 목적어

② 보어

③ 주어

④ 보어

⑤ 목적어

⑥ 주어

⑦ 목적어

⑧ 주어

⑨ 보어

⑩ 목적어

B.
① think that it will snow soon

② hope that the Korean team will win the game

③ remember that I met him at the party

④ believe that she will become a good doctor

⑤ know that he lies every day

단원평가　　몸풀기　　　P.208

> 1. ①　2. When I have a cold, I drink a cup of
> lemon tea.[I drink a cup of lemon tea when I
> have a cold.]　3. ③　4. ④　5. ③　6. ④
> 7. Because　8. ②　9. Eric eats breakfast at 7
> a.m., but Mark doesn't eat breakfast.　10. ②

1. when은 '~할 때'를 의미한다.

2. When I have a cold, I drink a cup of lemon tea.
   또는 I drink a cup of lemon tea when I have a
   cold.(나는 감기에 걸릴 때, 레몬 차를 한 잔 마신다.)의
   형태로 쓸 수 있다.

3. 접속사 that은 목적어절을 이끌 수 있다.

4. 주절은 '미나는 웃고 있는 중이다'라는 뜻이기 때문에 웃
   는 이유로 ④ '시험을 잘 봤다'가 가장 적절하다.

5. 목적어절을 이끄는 that은 생략 가능하다.

6. 빈칸 앞뒤 문장이 대조를 이루고 있으므로 접속사 but을
   써야 한다.
   – Jim은 화가 났지만, Sally는 화가 나지 않았다.
   – 나는 첼로를 잘 연주하지 못하지만, 노래는 잘 부를
   수 있다.

7. 이유를 묻고 있으므로 Because가 알맞다.
   A: 왜 화가 났니?
   B: 운전면허 시험에 또 떨어졌기 때문이야.

8. 빈칸 앞뒤 문장이 대조를 이루고 있으므로 접속사 but을
   사용하여 두 문장을 연결해야 한다.

9. 주어진 두 문장이 대조를 이루고 있으므로 두 문장 사이
   에 접속사 but을 쓴다.

10. '~할 때'를 나타내는 접속사와 '언제'를 나타내는 의문사
    는 when이다.
    – 제가 당신의 이름을 부를 때 들어오세요.
    – 언제 한국으로 돌아왔니?

> 1. ② 2. ③ 3. ④ 4. ② 5. ② 6. ① 7. ⑤
> 8. ② 9. ① 10. ⑤ 11. ④ 12. ① 13. ②
> 14. ② 15. ① 16. ④ 17. ④ 18. ⑤ 19. ④
> 20. ⑤

1. 결과와 나열을 나타내는 접속사가 필요하다. (나는 학교 밴드의 기타리스트여서 내 기타는 나에게 중요하다. 나는 세 개의 기타가 있고, 가장 작은 것이 내가 가장 좋아하는 기타이다.)

2. 접속사 다음에는 「주어 + 동사」를 쓰며 when이 이끄는 접속사절에서는 현재시제가 미래시제를 대신한다. 따라서 being over를 is로 고쳐야 한다.

3. 건기임에도 비가 많이 오기 때문에 대조를 나타내는 but이 필요하다.

4. 보기와 나머지 빈칸에는 when이 필요하며 ②번에는 but이 적절하다.
   보기: 반 고흐는 병원에 있을 때 슬픈 늙은 남자를 그렸다.
   ① 그녀는 나를 기다리고 있을 때 책을 읽었다.
   ② 나는 겨울을 좋아하지 않지만 스키를 타러 가는 것은 좋아한다.
   ③ 그는 내가 침대에 있을 때 나에게 전화했다.
   ④ 내가 도서관에 있을 때, 이모는 우리집을 방문했다.
   ⑤ 그는 책을 읽고 있을 때 잠이 들었다.

5. ② I lived with my grandma when I was young.

6. ①번은 '언제'를 의미하는 의문사 when이고 나머지는 '~할 때'를 의미하는 접속사 when이다.

7. '~할 때'를 나타내는 접속사 when을 사용해 문장을 만들어야 하며 주절의 시제와 부사절의 시제를 일치시켜야 한다.

8. '나는 행복하다'라는 문장이 주어졌기 때문에 행복한 감정과 어울리지 않는 문장을 찾아야 한다.
   ① 맛있는 음식을 먹을 때
   ② 엄마가 많이 아프실 때
   ③ 매우 재미있는 책을 읽을 때
   ④ 시험에서 좋은 점수를 받을 때
   ⑤ 가족들과 재밌는 게임을 할 때

9. think는 목적어로 that절을 쓸 수 있다.

10. ⑤번의 빈칸 앞은 '매우 춥다', 빈칸 뒤는 '나는 나가지 않았다'이므로 결과를 나타내는 접속사 so가 빈칸에 알맞다.

11. ④ A는 민수가 오늘 학교에 오지 않은 이유를 물어보고 있는데 B는 민수가 공부를 매우 열심히 하기 때문이라고 대답하고 있으므로 대화 내용이 어색하다.

12. ①번의 that은 지시대명사이고 나머지는 접속사이다.

13. ②번의 빈칸 앞뒤 문장은 인과관계를 나타내므로 because를 써야 한다. 나머지는 목적어절을 이끄는 that을 써야 한다.

14. when절에서는 현재시제가 미래시제를 대신한다.

15. 목적어절을 이끄는 that은 생략 가능하다.

16. '나는 밖에 나갈 수 없었다'에 이어질 수 있는 가장 자연스러운 접속사절을 찾아야 한다.
    ① 내가 그곳에 가지 않기 때문에
    ② 그가 지금 출발하지 않으면
    ③ 날이 매우 어두워지기 전에
    ④ 숙제가 많았기 때문에
    ⑤ 내가 집에 돌아올 때

17. ④ She is not happy because of her bad score.

18. ⑤번의 that은 지시대명사로 사용되었기 때문에 생략할 수 없다.

19. ❶ ③ 그녀는 시험에서 좋은 성적을 얻었기 때문에 행복하다.
    ❷ ⑤ 그는 그 영화가 너무 슬퍼서 울고 있다.
    ❸ ② 그는 다리가 부러져서 병원에 있다.
    ❹ ① 그녀는 곰을 봤기 때문에 도망가고 있었다.

20. 주어진 대화에 들어갈 알맞은 접속사는 because이다.
    ①, ②, ④: so, ③: although(그럼에도 불구하고), ⑤ because

> 1. ④ 2. ② 3. ④ 4. ⑤ 5. ② 6. ② 7. ②
> 8. ① 9. ③ 10. ② 11. ❶ but ❷ or ❸ and

1. 결과를 나타내는 접속사가 필요하다.
   어제 날씨가 따뜻해서, 우리는 산책하러 나갔다.

2. when his friends were looking for him에서 다섯 번째로 오는 단어는 looking이다.

3. 주어진 문장에 들어갈 접속사는 so이다. ①, ②, ③, ⑤번은 빈칸에 so를 쓸 수 있으며 ④번은 when이 가장 적절하다.
   지난 주말, 나의 식물이 매우 건조해 보였다. 그래서 나는 그것에 물을 주었지만 상태가 더 나빠졌다.
   ① 나는 치통이 있어서 진찰을 받으러 갈 것이다.
   ② 나는 아픈 사람들을 돕고 싶어서 의사가 되고 싶다.
   ③ 오늘 비가 많이 와. 그러니까 레인 부츠를 신는 게 어때?
   ④ 내가 열 살 때 놀라운 일이 일어났다.
   ⑤ 단지 몇몇 스케이트 선수들만이 경주에 참가해서 경주는 어제 일찍 끝났다.

4. ⑤번은 의미 전달이 안되는 어법상 옳지 않은 문장이다.

5. ②번의 when은 의문사이고 보기와 나머지의 when은 접속사이다.

6. (B) He is fat because he eats much.
   (D) He couldn't sleep well last night because he was so afraid.
   (E) She didn't enjoy lunch because she had a lot of problems.

7. ① I stayed home because it was cold.
   ③ She felt disappointed because she got a bad score on the exam.
   ④ Mira didn't go bowling because she felt tired.
   ⑤ She did not come to school because of illness.

8. ① 목적어절을 이끄는 that은 생략 가능하다.

9. 주어진 문장과 ③번: 접속사, ①, ②번: 지시대명사, ④, ⑤번: 지시형용사

10. ⓑ I'm sure that he comes soon.
    ⓓ Because English is difficult, I should study it very hard.

11. ❶ 민지는 조금 먹지만 나보다 더 뚱뚱하다.
    ❷ 서둘러라, 그렇지 않으면 기차를 놓칠 것이다.
    ❸ 내 졸업식에 와, 그러면 난 행복할 거야.

1. ❶ his sister doesn't (ride a bike)
   ❷ aren't in the same class
   ❸ doesn't sing

2. ❶ I listen to music, I feel calm
   ❷ I play the violin, I feel happy

3. ❶ If it is sunny[fine] tomorrow, I will go hiking
   ❷ you finish your work, I will meet you

4. ❶ Mina can't open the window because it's cold outside.
   ❷ Mina can't swim here because it's very deep.

5. ❶ I was late because I woke up late
   ❷ We didn't go out because the weather was cold

6. ❶ After I have lunch
   ❷ Before you begin to work
   ❸ While he was there

7. Because, he got a good score in the science test.

8. ❶ that we'll win the game
   ❷ because she is too young

9. ❶ Study hard, or you will fail the exam.
   ❷ Jessica has many dogs and cats.
   ❸ My English teacher spoke loudly, so everyone could hear her well.
   ❹ Did you go to the movies or stay at home?
   ❺ Press the button, and the door will open.

Chapter 13

전치사

13.1. 시간의 전치사 P.219

A.
1. in
2. on
3. at
4. on
5. in
6. in
7. in
8. on
9. in
10. in
11. at
12. in
13. at
14. in
15. at, in
16. On, in
17. on

B.
1. during, for
2. around, for
3. by, until
4. after, before

13.2. 장소/방향의 전치사 P.221

A.
1. on
2. on
3. on
4. on
5. in
6. in
7. at
8. on
9. at
10. on
11. on
12. at
13. in
14. in

B.
1. on, in
2. in, under, on
3. on, under, in

13.3. 여러 가지 전치사 P.223

A.
1. B, E
2. A
3. A, C
4. E, D
5. B

B.
1. It takes an hour from my house to school by car
2. The East Sea is between Korea and Japan
3. Suji lives across from my house
4. My dad parked next to the tree

C.
1. by
2. with
3. as
4. like
5. with

1. ① 2. ② 3. ③ 4. ⑤ 5. ⑤ 6. ❶ for ❷ by 7. for 8. ② 9. ③ 10. ③

1. 시각 앞에는 at을 쓴다.

2. in은 도시나 나라 앞에 또는 '~안에'라는 의미로 쓰인다.

3. on은 요일 앞이나 '~위에'라는 의미로 쓰인다.

4. by는 교통수단 앞이나 '~을 통해'라는 의미로 쓰인다.

5. ⑤ in the morning이 알맞다.

6. ❶ '~동안'의 뜻으로 기간 앞에 쓰이는 전치사는 for이다. ❷ 교통수단 앞에 by를 써서 '~를 타고'라는 의미를 나타낸다.

7. 숫자로 된 기간 앞에는 for를 쓴다.

8. 요일 앞에는 on을 쓴다.

9. 월 앞에는 in을 쓴다.

10. 도시나 비교적 넓은 장소 앞에는 in을 쓴다.

1. ② 2. ④ 3. ③ 4. ③ 5. ④ 6. ④ 7. ❶ in ❷ at ❸ on 8. ④ 9. on 10. in 11. ❶ For ❷ to 12. ② 13. ③ 14. ① 15. between 16. like 17. in, at 18. in front of 19. next to 20. on

1. at top speed: '최고 속도로', 시각 앞에는 at을 쓴다.

2. ⓐ in ⓑ On ⓓ at

3. ③번에는 in, 나머지는 on을 쓴다.

4. ③ Audrey Hepburn was born on May 4, 1929.

5. ④ Susan is standing between Julia and Chris.

6. ① I usually get up early in the morning.
② It rains a lot in August.

③ They ate dinner at seven thirty.
⑤ My sister and he will get married on the last Sunday of May.

7. 계절 앞에는 in, 시각 앞에는 at, 요일 앞에는 on을 쓴다.

8. ④ 교통수단 앞에는 관사를 붙이지 않는다.

9. on the wall: 벽에, on the fourth floor: 4층에, on Sundays: 일요일마다

10. in the classroom: 교실에, in the evening: 저녁에, in June: 6월에

11. 정확한 기간 앞에는 for를 쓰고, '~부터 ~까지'는 from ~ to ~로 표현한다.

12. '~동안'은 during, 나라 앞에는 in을 쓴다.

13. 보기와 ③번의 like는 전치사로 쓰였고 나머지 선택지의 like는 동사로 쓰였다.

14. '~안으로'는 into로 표현한다. pour A into B: A를 B에 붓다'

15. '~사이에'는 between으로 표현한다.

16. What's the weather like?는 날씨를 물어보는 표현이다.

17. in the morning: 아침에, at night: 밤에

18. 꽃은 침대 앞에 있으므로 in front of(~앞에)를 쓴다.

19. 침대는 책상 옆에 있으므로 next to(~ 옆에)를 쓴다.

20. 신문은 탁자 위에 있으므로 on(~위에)을 쓴다.

1. ⑤ 2. ② 3. ⑤ 4. ⑤ 5. ③ 6. ❶ in ❷ on ❸ under ❹ at ❺ over 7. ④ 8. ② 9. ❶ from ❷ with 10. without 11. ❶ For ❷ to ❸ in 12. ③ 13. ①

1. 월 앞에는 in, 시각 앞에는 at, 정확한 시점 앞에는 at, 날짜 앞에는 on을 쓴다.

2. ②번은 요일 앞이므로 on, 나머지는 in을 쓴다.

3. ⑤ 특정한 날 앞에는 on이 알맞다.

4. ① The supermarket is next to the hospital.
② The hospital is across from the park.
③ The park is between the subway station and the bank.
④ The library is across from the bookstore.

5. ③ be surprised at ~은 '~에 놀라다'라는 뜻의 표현이다.

6. ❶ 나라 앞에는 in을 쓴다.
❷ on the wall: 벽에
❸ under the bridge: 다리 아래에
❹ at the station: 역에서
❺ over the mountain: 산 위에

7. ④ Put this apple in your bag.

8. 주어진 문장과 ②번의 for는 '~동안'의 뜻으로 기간을 나타낸다. ①, ③, ⑤번: ~을 위해, ④번: ~로

9. far from: ~에서 멀리 떨어진, with + 신체사항: 신체사항을 가진

10. without은 '~없이'라는 뜻이다.

11. ❶ 숫자로 표현된 기간이므로 for와 함께 쓴다.
❷ 'A부터 B까지'는 from A to B로 나타낸다.
❸ 넓은 장소를 나타낼 때는 in이 알맞다.

12. for는 시간 앞에서는 '~동안', 사람 앞에서는 '~위해'라는 의미를 가진다.

13. ⓑ In → On, ⓒ At → On, ⓓ on → at, ⓔ on → at

1. ❶ on
❷ next to
❸ under

2. ❶ in
❷ on
❸ at

3. ❶ on
❷ next to
❸ in
❹ at
❺ between, and

4. ❶ There is a hat hanging on the wall.
❷ I have dinner at 8 o'clock in the evening.
❸ John lived in Shanghai in 2016.
❹ Bobby studied English for the test for four hours.

모의고사 1회

1. ③ 2. ④ 3. ④ 4. ② 5. ③ 6. ① 7. ④
8. ⑤ 9. ② 10. ⑤ 11. ② 12. ⑤ 13. ④
14. ⑤ 15. ① 16. ④ 17. ① 18. ③

[서술형 1] 1) wait for your turn
          2) turn off your phone
[서술형 2] 1) gave 2) made 3) took

1. ③번은 '~에 있다'를 의미하는 be동사이고 나머지는 '~
   이다'를 의미한다.

2. ④번의 there은 '거기에'라는 의미의 부사이고 보기와 나
   머지 선택지의 there은 문장을 이끄는 유도부사이다.

3. 아버지의 직업에 대한 언급은 글에서 찾을 수 없다.

4. ②번은 주어가 3인칭 단수이기 때문에 Does가 들어가
   고 나머지는 Do가 들어간다.

5. ③번의 about은 '대략, 약'의 의미이고 나머지 선택지의
   about은 '~에 대해서'라는 의미이다.

6. 보기, ⓐ, ⓑ의 may는 추측을 나타내고 ⓒ의 may는 허
   가, ⓓ의 may는 기원을 나타낸다.

7. ④ 명령문은 동사원형으로 시작하므로 Does를 Do로 바
   꿔야 한다.

8. ⑤ eat의 과거는 ate이다.

9. ② Every가 꾸며주는 명사는 단수이므로 take의 3인칭
   단수형인 takes를 써야 한다.

10. ⑤번의 that은 지시형용사이며 나머지 선택지의 that은
    접속사이다.

11. ⓐ '~위로'의 의미의 above, ⓑ '~하기를 노력하다, 애
    쓰다'의 의미를 가진 'try to 동사원형' ⓒ '~동안의'의
    의미를 가진 for가 빈칸에 적절하다.

12. ⑤ 침대 위에 두 개의 베개가 있다.

13. ④번의 재귀대명사는 재귀용법으로, 보기와 나머지 선택
    지의 재귀대명사는 강조용법으로 쓰였다.

14. 걸리는 시간을 물어보고 있기 때문에 '얼마나 오래'의 의

미를 가진 how long이 알맞다.

15. '~할 때'의 의미를 가진 접속사 when이 빈칸에 가장 적
    절하다.

16. ③ make는 목적격보어로 to부정사를 쓸 수 없다.

17. 둘 중에 하나는 one, 나머지 하나는 the other을 쓴다.
    셋 중에 하나는 one, 또 다른 하나는 another, 나머지
    하나는 the other을 쓴다.

18. 괜찮냐는 A에 질문에, B는 No라고 대답했으므로 부정
    의 내용이 이어져야 한다.

모의고사 2회

1. ② 2. ② 3. ② 4. ⑤ 5. ② 6. ① 7. ④
8. ② 9. ⑤ 10. ② 11. ④ 12. ⑤ 13. ②
14. ① 15. ④ 16. ⑤ 17. ③

[서술형 1] had to wake up early to exercise in
          the morning
[서술형 2] Peter's grade is better than Bob's
          (grade).
[서술형 3] 1) has to eat something
          2) has to study math
          3) has to see a doctor
[서술형 4] a computer for me
[서술형 5] must not take pictures with flash
[서술형 6] 1) How beautiful the mother is!
          2) What an old tree this is!
          3) What a wonderful festival it was!

1. at top speed: 전속력으로, at + 시간

2. ②번의 When은 의문사로 '언제'의 의미를, 나머지의
   when은 부사절 접속사로 '~할 때'의 의미를 나타낸다.

3. ① can he → can she ③ do you → are you ④
   didn't you → don't you ⑤ isn't Jane → isn't she

4. ① was not he → wasn't he ② didn't she →
   did she ③ didn't you→ didn't he ④ does he →
   doesn't he

5. 강, 바다, 산맥 이름 앞에는 정관사 the를 붙인다.

6. 많은 친구를 사귀기 위한 조언으로 ① '너는 약속을 지켜서는 안 돼.'는 적절하지 않다.

7. ④ because → because of
because + 주어 + 동사 / because of + 명사(구)

8. ② 'Jane은 배고프기 때문에 아침을 먹지 않았다.'는 의미가 어색하다.

9. ① faster → fast
② very → even, much, far, still, a lot
③ farthest(가장 멀리) → further(더, 더욱)
④ latest(최신의) → last(마지막)

10. ⓐ, ⓒ, ⓓ는 부사이기 때문에 감각동사와 함께 쓰일 수 없다. ⓔ, ⓗ는 영화를 꾸며주는 말로 적절하지 않기 때문에 정답이 아니다.

11. ① excitingest → most exciting
② hotest → hottest
③ more thicker → thicker
⑤ heavyer → heavier

12. ⑤번은 '~로 가고 있는 중이다'의 현재진행형이고 나머지는 미래를 나타내는 be going to(~할 것이다)이다.

13. ②번의 to부정사는 형용사적 용법이다. 나머지는 to부정사의 부사적 용법이다.

14. 보기의 부가의문문은 don't they이며 ①번에 들어갈 부가의문문과 동일하다.
② do they ③ won't they ④ will they ⑤ aren't they

15. (a), (c), (d), (e)가 올바른 문장이다.
(b) You should not waste water.
(f) The soccer ball is bigger than the baseball.

16. 질문: 어느 것이 틀린 문장인가?
⑤ There are a computer and a TV in the classroom.

17. ① knifes → knives
② mouses → mice
④ dictionarys → dictionaries
⑤ sheeps → sheep

모의고사 3회

1. ① 2. ② 3. ④ 4. ② 5. ③, ④ 6. ③
7. ⑤ 8. ⑤ 9. ④ 10. ① 11. ② 12. ①
13. ④ 14. ② 15. ⑤

[서술형 1] are many books
[서술형 2] 1) He is the most popular singer
2) My brother is the shortest
3) Who is the prettiest woman
[서술형 3] 1) much 2) must
[서술형 4] give the bear snacks
[서술형 5] 1) make his bed
2) to clean the window

1. ①번을 제외한 나머지는 주어가 복수이기 때문에 are이 올바르다.

2. ②번에서는 A는 학년을 묻고 있고 B는 이에 대해 적절한 대답을 하고 있다.

3. Joy가 K-Pop을 좋아한다는 내용은 있지만 가장 좋아하는 가수에 대한 언급은 없다.

4. ① Ann didn't visit London during last summer.
③ Students read a lot of books in class.
④ I was hungry because I did lots of work.
⑤ He didn't say anything when he met her.

5. ③ What pretty cups they are!
④ What beautiful flowers these are!

6. ① We have to call him.
② You don't have to come here.
④ Did Jane clean the classroom?
⑤ The children have to do their homework.

7. 4형식 문장에 들어가는 수여동사는 show, give, send, buy 등이 있다.

8. I am going to wash the car는 앞으로의 계획을 나타내기 때문에 과거를 나타내는 부사(구)와 함께 쓰일 수 없다.

9. in front of(앞에)의 반대 표현은 behind(뒤에)이다.

10. You ate more apples than I.(너는 나보다 더 많은 사

과를 먹었다.) ≠ I ate as many apples as you.(나는 너만큼 많은 사과를 먹었다.)

11. ②번은 '딱딱한'을 의미하고 나머지는 '어려운'을 의미한다.

12. ⓐ는 명암을 나타낼 때 사용한 비인칭 주어이며 나머지는 John의 아빠를 가리킨다.

13. ④번은 명사이며 나머지는 형용사이다.

14. ① You are too small to wear this shirt.
    ③ Andy was too heavy to stand on the box.
    ④ This coffee is so hot that I can't drink it.
    ⑤ They are so young that they can drive a car.

15. 보기의 to부정사는 목적을 나타내는 부사적 용법이며 ⑤번이 같은 쓰임으로 쓰였다. 나머지는 명사적 용법으로 사용되었다.

모의고사 4회

1. ① 2. ③ 3. ③ 4. ③ 5. ④ 6. ④ 7. ④
8. ③ 9. ④ 10. ⑤ 11. ③ 12. ① 13. ①
14. ⑤ 15. ③ 16. ⑤ 17. ③

[서술형 1] 1) He plays the piano.
         2) She lives in Canada.
         3) He watches TV on weekends.
[서술형 2] She didn't go to school today because she was sick.
[서술형 3] 1) Why don't you go to bed?
         2) Why don't you play soccer?

1. ① 너는 무슨 일을 하니?
   ② 너의 취미는 무엇이니?
   ③ 너는 언제 야구를 하니?
   ④ 너는 무엇에 관심이 있니?
   ⑤ 너는 어디에서 야구를 즐겨 하니?

2. Her's → Her, graders → grade, watching → watch, France → French

3. ③ 의자 위에 신문이 있다. → 신문은 탁자 위에 있다.

4. ③번은 부사이며 나머지는 형용사이다.

5. 3인칭 단수 일반동사 현재형의 의문문은 「Does + 주어 + 동사원형?」으로 쓴다.

6. ④ mind는 동명사를 목적어로 쓴다.

7. ④번은 주어가 3인칭 복수이므로 Do를, 나머지는 주어가 3인칭 단수이므로 Does[does]를 쓴다.

8. Be not late again. → Don't be late again.
   Washes your hands. → Wash your hands.
   Don't be lose your ticket. → Don't lose your ticket.

9. '어떻게' 가는지 물을 때는 의문사 How를 쓰며, 병원의 위치는 곧장 가서 오른쪽으로 꺾으면 우체국과 슈퍼마켓 사이에 있다.

10. A: 이 근처에 꽃가게가 있습니까?
    B: 네, 이 곳에는 하나도 없습니다.
    Yes를 No로 고쳐야 자연스럽다.

11. ① I bought a present for her.
    ② He made a nice desk for me.
    ④ Please show an interesting story to me.
    ⑤ Scott gives a special experience to you.

12. Don't sleep in class. = You should not sleep in class.

13. ① begin – began – begun

14. ⑤ It sounds wonderful tonight.

15. ③ You should not park here.

16. ① I have much homework to do.
    ② I need many glasses of water.
    ③ There are many books in the room
    ④ There is much water in the tank.

17. ③번의 must는 강한 추측을 나타내고 나머지 must는 의무를 나타낸다.